ROOTS OF THE RIGHT
READINGS IN FASCIST, RACIST AND ELITIST IDEOLOGY

General Editor: GEORGE STEINER
FELLOW OF CHURCHILL COLLEGE, CAMBRIDGE

THE FRENCH RIGHT

THE
FRENCH RIGHT
(FROM DE MAISTRE TO MAURRAS)

Edited and Introduced by

J. S. McCLELLAND

LECTURER IN POLITICS IN
THE UNIVERSITY OF NOTTINGHAM

Translation of Maurras by
JOHN FREARS

1817

HARPER & ROW, PUBLISHERS
New York and Evanston

GENERAL EDITOR'S PREFACE

Reliable estimates put at about seventy million the figure of those dead through war, revolution and famine in Europe and Russia between 1914 and 1945. To all but a few visionaries and pessimistic thinkers of the nineteenth century, the image of such an apocalypse, of a return to barbarism, torture and mass extermination in the heartlands of civilized life, would have seemed a macabre fantasy. Much of the crisis of identity and society that has overshadowed twentieth-century history comes from an impulse towards totalitarian politics. The theory of man as a rational animal, entitled to a wide exercise of political and economic decision, of man as a being equally endowed whatever his race, has been attacked at its religious, moral and philosophic roots. The most 'radical' attack – 'radical' in that it demands a total revaluation of man's place in society and of the status of different races in the general scheme of power and human dignity – has come from the Right.

Using the concept of the Fall of Man, of man as an instinctual savage requiring total leadership and repeated bloodletting, a number of elitist, racist and totalitarian dreamers and publicists have offered an alternative statement of the human condition. Fascism, Nazism, the programme of the Falange or the *Croix de Feu*, represent different variants of a related vision. Although this vision is often lunatic and nakedly barbaric, it can provide acute, tragic insights into the myths and taboos that underlie democracy.

Because the political and philosophical programme of the Right has come so near to destroying our civilization and is so alive still, it must be studied. Hence this series of source-readings in elitist, racist and fascist theory as it was articulated in France, Germany, Italy, Spain and other national communities between the 1860s and the Second World War. These 'black books' fill an almost complete gap in the source material available to any serious student of modern history, psychology, politics and sociology (most of the texts have never been available in English and several have all but disappeared in their original language). But these books also touch on the intractable puzzle of the co-existence in the same mind of profound inhumanity and obvious philosophic and literary importance.

GEORGE STEINER.

CONTENTS

ACKNOWLEDGMENTS

The editor and publishers gratefully acknowledge permission to reproduce extracts from the following published works: *The Works of Joseph de Maistre*, trs. by Jack Lively (Allen & Unwin Ltd, 1965, and the Macmillan Company, Free Press of Glencoe, 1965); *The Origins of Contemporary France*, by H. Taine, trs. by John Durand (Holt, Rinehart & Winston Inc., New York, 1876–91, and Peter Smith, Gloucester, Mass., 1931–62); *Reflections on Violence*, by Georges Sorel, edited by E. A. Shils, trs. by J. Roth and T. E. Hulme (the Macmillan Company Inc., Free Press of Glencoe, 1950) from *Réflexions sur la violence* (Librairie Marcel Rivière et Cie, Paris); *The Crowd: a Study of the Popular Mind*, by Gustave le Bon (Ernest Benn Ltd, 1920, and Presses Universitaires de France, 1938); *The Undying Spirit of France*, by Maurice Barrès, trs. by M. W. B. Corwin (Yale University Press, 1917, and Oxford University Press, London, 1917); *Scènes et Doctrines du Nationalisme*, by M. Barrès (Plon, Paris, 1925); *Poèmes et Paroles durant la Guerre de Trente Ans*, by Paul Claudel (Librairie Gallimard, Paris, 1945); and *Œuvres Capitales*, by Charles Maurras (Flammarion, Paris, 1954).

For P. and K.

INTRODUCTION

This collection of readings is not a documentary history of the French right. Nor is it an indictment of various writers on the grounds that they are fascist or proto-fascist; such a claim in the case of, say, Taine would amount to a serious distortion. In the case of de Maistre it would be merely absurd. Yet the fact remains that in the nineteenth century in France there took place an attack on the principles and practice of the French Revolution which was based on certain assumptions about the nature of man and political society which were close to, and in some cases identical to, the assumptions which were to underly much fascist thinking. Mussolini's testimony that fascism was against everything that the French Revolution was for cannot be ignored; equally, it does not follow that everybody who attacked the French Revolution was, in a crude sense, on Mussolini's side.

The selection of passages, some translated for the first time, is not based on any rigorous definition of what fascism *is*. Definitions of this kind are either misleading, or at best, inadequate. What we are concerned with here is the intellectual history and pre-history of the radical right in France – the progenitors of fascism, if one prefers – and no remotely satisfying definition of fascism is possible without an account of its sociology and of its immediate political causes. The sociology of fascism, the notion that, for instance, it is a stage in the late development of capitalism, can have no place in a collection of this kind.

If we begin from Mussolini's description of fascism as a

reaction to the French Revolution, it follows that French intellectual history is a fruitful locus of inquiry into the origins and nature of fascist thought. It also goes some way towards explaining the intellectual respectability of extreme right-wing thought in France at the end of the nineteenth and in the twentieth century. It could be argued that to set out to explain the intellectual attractiveness of a tradition of thought unbroken since the Revolution and which includes in our period writers of the standing of Péguy, Bernanos, de Montherlant, Bloy and Drieu la Rochelle is to beg a serious question. One finds it strange that so many first-rate writers supported extreme right-wing positions only because Vichy was such a squalid episode. What really has to be explained is why, unlike anywhere else in Europe, in France the radical right attracted writers of genius. Again, despite the tawdriness and self-deception of Vichy, the intellectual right in France is entirely characteristic if placed in the context of a particular view of French political and cultural history.

Paul Bourget once said that the Académie Française was one of the four great fortresses in Europe against the French Revolution, the others being the House of Lords, the Papacy and the Prussian General Staff. In the Dreyfus affair the Académie was anti-Dreyfusard almost to a man. In 1940, the Académie, with exceptions, went over to Vichy. The position of the Académie in French intellectual life represents, in palpable form, the complete integration of the intellectual and the political. Maurras and Pétain were both members. Both were removed after the liberation, but neither was replaced in his own lifetime, though Pétain lived till 1951 and Maurras till 1952. Pétain had learned his catechism from a chaplain who had been a veteran of the Grand Army. Maurras made his name dur-

ing the Dreyfus affair. Both shared a particular view of
French history which goes some way to explaining why
the institutions of aristocracy, army and Church found
defenders of such outstanding intellectual calibre. This
view rests on the assumption that the greatness of France
is patrician and Catholic greatness. The century of glory
is the seventeenth century, the most glorious period the
period of *le Roi Soleil*. His reign represented the fusion of
strong government and a healthy aristocratic patronage
of the arts and learning. There was no contradiction in
this; it was left to the eighteenth-century intellectuals to
desert the state.

It has been very well said that French intellectuals are
very intellectual. If books caused the revolution of 1789,
books can undo it. If, as the right argued, all France's
troubles can be attributed to the Revolution, then it
follows that to save the nation, the Revolution and its
mythology in the present must be destroyed. That this is
a matter of books follows from the original premise. If
this is coupled with the extraordinary respect that the
French have for intellectuals, it explains why both sides
of the Dreyfus affair were so proud of their intellectual
protagonists. It also explains, paradoxically, why after the
liberation the purge of collaborators seemed unduly
weighted against the pro-Vichy intellectuals. It seemed to
have been a greater crime to have written something
compromising than to have done something compromising.
Maurras met Pétain on only four occasions. He held no
official position in Vichy, yet he was a natural target for
the liberators as the ideologue of a right which had produced Vichy. This is, in itself, evidence of how literally in
France the written word can be taken. At the trial of
Maurras, his accuser felt obliged to say, after he had
accused Maurras of the crime of passing information to the

enemy, that he was, none the less a genius, as though this was in some sense a mitigating factor and that geniuses were not to be judged solely by the standards of ordinary men.

What will be argued in this introduction is that in France at least, thinkers like Maurice Barrès and Charles Maurras followed in the path of other thinkers of European status and pushed the ideas which they found in their predecessors just a little further to the right so that positions which were fascist or proto-fascist by any definition appeared to have the sanction of writers of universal and unblemished reputation.

The attack on the Revolution in the nineteenth century centred on the connection between eighteenth-century political thought and the Revolution itself. In Taine one sometimes gets the feeling that Rousseau caused the Revolution single-handed. As in most political arguments drawn from the supposed lessons of history, there was a tendency to falsify the record of the past in order to point a moral for the future. In particular, the nineteenth-century critics of the Enlightenment exaggerated the radicalism of the *philosophes*. Thus in de Maistre and Barrès, a degree of literalness is attributed to the idea of social contract and universal federation which might have surprised some of its eighteenth-century exponents; democratic and equalizing sentiments are attributed where they were never possessed. Yet despite the distortions and plain misunderstanding, the line of attack centred with a fair degree of accuracy on the principle of rationalism and the line of defence on the principle of nationalism. The edges of these two principles are blurred, but they have clearly recognizable centres.

The debate over the principle of rationality, and the attendant political implications, involved the kind of basic judgments about the nature of man which have now, fortunately, gone out of fashion. That men have access to something called reason nobody denied. Whether it was a faculty of the soul, as the Greeks maintained, or a principle inherent in nature, as the natural lawyers argued, or something different from both, the problem was how to define its place in human experience in general and political experience in particular. Locke and, following Locke, Condillac were the psychological mentors of the Enlightenment. Locke had argued that mind at birth was a *tabula rasa*, containing no innate ideas. It followed that men were not innately sinful, but became so through the impressions and ideas which they received from the outside world. Men achieved rationality through the development of the mental apparatus inherited at birth. The denial of original sin and the idea of the development of mind from a lower to a higher state of mental functioning formed the basis of progressive and rationalist political thought in the Enlightenment. If the conditions of society were changed, the impressions which the *tabula rasa* received would change. Men could be changed; history could be snatched from the pessimistic Augustinian time-scale. All men could become rational, all could make the transition, in the new favourable circumstances, to the higher plain of rationality. Reason would reign supreme and alone in the world.

Other political implications seemed to follow from these psychological premises. If it was possible to single out a basic composition for the human soul, and if it was asserted that all men were, at bottom, the same creatures, with a tendency to seek pleasure and avoid pain, and were born with the possibility of reaching a stage of development where rationality was possible, it followed that the same institutions could be applied to all men regardless of local difference. Hume, though a conservative, gave this idea its classic statement when he wrote:

> Mankind are so much the same, in all times and places, that history informs us of nothing new in this particular. Its chief use is only to discover the constant and uniform principles of human nature.

If mankind were the same at all times and places; if, as Cicero had proclaimed, there was not one law at Rome and another at Athens, then all that was required was an exact and reasoned account of those institutions which best conformed to the innate constitution of this universal man and to export them to the ends of the earth. It followed that the Revolutionary wars were not wars of conquest in the old sense, but on the contrary were the first of the great wars of liberation. It should be emphasized that there was nothing anti-empirical about this. The critics of the Enlightenment and the Revolution write as if thinkers like Rousseau in particular and the *philosophes* in general were totally unaware of the differences which separate men. This is clearly not the case. The eighteenth century saw a great vogue for travellers' tales whose fascination lay in exotic detail, and there are examples of manuscripts being returned to authors with instructions to emphasize the outlandishness of the detail and at the same time to make the work more 'philosophical'. The combination of the exotic and the philosophical is significant. The 'philosophy' required consists of drawing general conclusions about man from particular detail. In the *Encyclopaedia*, for instance, a wealth of anthropological data is sifted in such a way that the local difference is separated from the deep, underlying similarities which unite men in a uniform human nature. What separates is secondary; only the uniting factors are primary.

From the principles of rationality and universality some radical spirits deduced the principles of democracy and popular sovereignty. The critics of the Enlightenment write as if the *philosophes* were democrats red in tooth and claw, but this was far from being the case. The principles of rationality and universality did not necessarily imply democratic principles; Locke himself had been no friend of the people for all his Whiggish talk about consent, and there was no reason why rational political principles should not be realized through the good offices of an enlightened despot for which there was a powerful Platonic precedent. Where, then, did democracy and popular sovereignty enter in? The answer is deceptively simple – in the debate on the nature of community. If the old regime was to be destroyed in the Revolution, a new community was to take its place. How was such a community to be formed? By real consent and real will. Following the notions of social contract as interpreted by Rousseau, rational men were to make a real choice in coming into political community with their fellows for the first time, because the previous community which they lived in was no true community at all because it had involved no rational choice. Men were no longer born to their allegiance to kingdoms distributed by an inscrutable creator for some purpose at which men could, at best, only guess. Communities were now made and bestowed by man because that was the way they chose to organize their lives together. As Taine was to remark, echoing Burke, the new state was to be a state of men without history. In this specific sense, he was right. History was to be given a fresh start, as Barère proclaimed to the National Assembly.

The new dawn of reason broke first in Paris. It was clearly the duty of those who first received that light to bear witness to it in the rest of Europe and beyond.

Principles which were true at Paris were true in the Batavian Republic, in the Confederation of the Rhine, in Malta, in Egypt and in Syria. The declaration of war on error was the prelude to universal peace and federation. Under French direction, the old warring states would become a single family of nations under the same law. Such was the rationalist dream, interpreted by the ideologues of the Revolution and attempted by Napoleon.

This, crudely, was the vision of politics which the nineteenth-century critics of the Enlightenment and the Revolution set out to destroy. The difficulties involved in separating out from the general attack those aspects which may be specifically dubbed pre-fascist are obvious. For instance, Burke lurks effectively at the back of a good deal of this writing,[1] yet it would be absurd to call Burke a progenitor of fascism. The same must be said of de Tocqueville and Comte. De Tocqueville was one of the first critics of democracy who had first-hand knowledge of democratic political experience; he patronized Gobineau; his writings were influential on Taine. Comte attacked the notion that society could be remade on the basis of reason and choice, so that the father of sociology's argument constituted a powerful, positive attack on one of the fundamental implications of the principles of 1789. None the less, it must be said that such writings seemed to give weight to the extreme right-wing position.

The right in France attacked rationality, universality and democracy and in so doing worked out an opposing position of great coherence and force. Taine's position in this attack is central. As Dimier, the *Action Française* publicist remarked, it was Taine's attack on the Revolu-

---

[1] A French translation of the *Reflections* was in progress at least a week before the publication of the English edition. It was also pirated in France.

tion and the revolutionary tradition which turned the flank of the pro-revolutionary positions of Michelet and Lamartine, the high priests of Republican orthodoxy. The *Origins of Contemporary France* (1875–93) had the effect of elevating the preceding anti-revolutionary broadsides of de Maistre and Bonald; Taine supplied the hard basis of fact and scholarship for anti-revolutionary opinion. And Taine's own intellectual ancestry was impeccable. Burke, de Tocqueville, Hegel, Herder, Michelet, Guizot, Carlyle and J. S. Mill jostled easily against one another in Taine's generous eclecticism. This is the real point, intellectually, in the pre-history of fascism in France; Taine was the intellectual giant of his generation. Where Taine appeared to lead, who would not follow?

But where did Taine lead? This may best be answered by Taine's examination of the problem of the irony of revolution. What Taine wants to find out is how a revolution which began in an attempt to destroy a despotism itself ended in tyranny. The reason he gives is that the doctrine of the sovereignty of the people causes anarchy when used against an existing government and tyranny when used as the intellectual support of a popular regime. He accuses the Jacobins of an abuse of rationalism in the form of a doctrinaire blindness to political reality coupled, paradoxically, with a cynical manipulation of popular uproar in the direction of personal aggrandizement. It is this Jacobin obsession with *idées fixes* — the rights of man, popular sovereignty and the social contract — which is responsible for all the troubles which have assailed France since 1789, including the June days, the plebiscitary despotism of Napoleon III, the defeat at the hands of Prussia and the Commune. Since 1789 France had been rebuilt after a false principle, the *esprit classique*, the principle of reason which ignored history. Taine sets against these revolutionary ideas a theory of society and history which lays emphasis on those aspects of political and social development which are independent of the human will and reason. Societies are the product of their history; they are not things that we choose. If all men were the rational creatures which the *philosophes* and Rousseau said they were, then of course they would choose the form of social and political organization they wanted. Some men, a Gibbon, a Fontenelle or a Voltaire, might even be capable of doing so, but never the majority. Taine turns the eighteenth century back against itself. Condillac, following Locke, had argued that in the natural history of the soul we can trace a movement from the lower to the higher in mental life. Men progress to rationality. The notion is double-edged. Some men may progress, others may not. The elite may reach the higher stage of reason, the majority certainly do not. One has only to look at the scenes of mob violence during the Revolution, the June days or the Commune to realize that no matter how rational and appropriate the doctrine, in untutored minds the doctrine becomes a series of collective slogans which are used as an excuse to indulge in a temporary collective insanity. In short, Taine is at the beginning of a tradition of insight into collective psychopathology. Taine's message is, finally, that reason cannot be a political slogan of the left. Only the few reason; reason is on the right.

Taine is, therefore, against Rousseau and for Montesquieu. A nation is not something one chooses, it *is*. Despite his attack on the Enlightenment Taine's standards remain those of the Enlightenment. He argues that all that is good or humane in the world is the product of reason. As a positivist he had unbounded faith in the future of science. His elitism implies the existence of a rational elite making judgments for an irrational mass. For Taine, the intellectual position remains unassailable, though assailed by a culture-hostile mass.

Taine is on the edge. He is an irrationalist, but not an anti-rationalist. He recognizes the value of reason, but also sees its limitations. He is not against democracy, but recognizes there are certain things which the people cannot legislate for and it would be better if they did not try. With a sociologist's relativism well learned in Herder and Montesquieu, he recognizes that for some peoples certain things are appropriate and some things are not. But, again following Burke, he makes a fatal distinction between two kinds of reason, a *raison raisonnante*, which he thinks characterized the *esprit classique* of the Enlightenment, and a *raison qui s'ignore*. The distinction is crucial for the development of our theme. The *raison raisonnante* is the individual reason, such as a man will bring to the problems of man in society. It operates according to the rules of logic, and hopes to attain the certainty of geometry. The ideal is, as in geometry, a situation in which there are only true or false arguments, not strong or weak ones. Rigorous deduction from universally accepted premises characterizes this activity; it is what in normal language is meant by reasoning. The *raison qui s'ignore* is not reason at all in the first sense, at least not in Taine or Burke. It refers to wisdom, the accumulated wisdom of the ages which is slowly deposited in institutions. The philosopher has access to it, but the method of access differs from the method used in the first kind of reasoning in that it does not involve deduction from premises but an empathetic research into history, geography, literature and myth. The forces with which the philosopher may have to deal if he is to find out what it is may be unconscious, for the *raison qui s'ignore* is not itself the product of that self-conscious reason and clarity which, according to Taine, was characteristic of the eighteenth century and which threatens to ruin France.

In Taine's successors, this line of argument is pushed one stage further. The rejection of Taine in Barrès's novel *Les Déracinés* is a cultural moment in the intellectual history of the French right. It marks the end of the distinction which Taine drew between the two reasons. Barrès asserts that they are two ways of describing the same thing; they are organically connected. One must be subordinate to the other. What Barrès attacked was what he called the 'official philosophy' of the French educational system, an 'unhealthy Kantianism'. Bouteiller, in *Les Déracinés*, is the archtypical Kantian. He always acts in such a way that his action could serve as a general rule of conduct, irrespective of time and place. The individual reason, for Bouteiller, is a means of finding out this general moral precept. What is right is a universal moral standard, rationally determinable. Barrès sets his face against this. There is no 'right', only a relative 'right'. What I do is not subject to a self-consciously deduced system of moral precept. Such a conceit is not only erroneous but absurd. Thought is not free, but a result of a particular kind of determinism. This determinism is nationalism. Each nation has a particular past and a particular present. The nation is real, and is to be found in those provincial grave-yards which exerted such an unhealthy fascination on Barrès. Communion with your dead ancestors is as near to a feeling for the true France as you can possibly get. Judgment, moral or political, lies close to such a feeling. One does not ask whether a particular action, say the breaking of Dreyfus, is right. That for Barrès has literally no meaning. How can it have when there is no universal moral standard by which a proposition could be judged true or false? The question to be asked must be, 'In what

degree is such an action in accordance with the interests
and wishes of France?' This question is anti-rational.
That is not to say that anti-rationalists argue less than
rationalists; the point is that they argue in a different
way. Barrès is not smiling when he says that his dead
ancestors have more to tell him about the Dreyfus affair
than Zola.

Hence Barrès's attack on the intellectuals, who, educated
at the great lycées and at the universities, and infected
with Kantianism, are incapable of asking the right
questions. What they want to know is whether Dreyfus
actually did what his prosecutors accused him of. If he
did not, then an injustice has been committed. Their
error, according to Barrès, is that they expect something
from French institutions which they cannot in the nature
of things give. Absolute justice is beyond them. It may
exist, but only in heaven. What French courts can give is
French justice, a relative justice. It is the duty of each
Frenchman who has a care for the future of France to
subordinate any individual feeling that he has for the
absolute to the relative. Far from the courts being unfair
to Dreyfus, the Dreyfusard intellectuals are being unfair
to French justice through their inability to understand
it.

Stated baldly, Barrès's argument may seem crude. It
may be, but the journalistic genius of Barrès brings to it
a real force. The fundamental assumption is psychological.
What we are, what is most important in us is something
we cannot fully comprehend. It is subterranean, dark,
mysterious and terrifying. Moral and political precept
derive from this source. Creon knows because he has
learned, Antigone because she feels, because of what she is.
Knowing is not a function of the intelligence, but of the
unconscious: Barrès is not convinced by argument; he has

to be moved, to feel his whole race on the march, and then he knows. If the precepts of his unconscious are contradictory, he does not try to reconcile them, as a rationalist would. He affirms the contradiction. Hence the subtlety of much of Barrès's argument. He does not peddle the kind of crude biological racialism and anti-semitism that Drumont turned into an industry. Barrès has not the slightest interest in showing that Jews are racially degenerate, or even morally and intellectually inferior. The point is that they are different. If they were the highest aristocracy in the world, the case would not be altered. The Jew is a cosmopolite and dispersed; he does not call where he lives Fatherland; he is alien, other. Barrès may find himself compelled to condemn the good Jew. So be it.

The Jew was Dreyfus. To understand why the case of an obscure artillery captain became the case of the whole nation would require an account of the whole history of the Third Republic. However, certain things can be said which show the significance of the affair for our theme. If the condemnation of Dreyfus was the result of a witch-hunt – and all the evidence points in that direction – then it was one witch-hunt among many. The central theme of political writing and much of political life in the period up to 1914 was, as Barrès pointed out with his customary clarity, that France was in decline and somebody was to blame. Some, like Taine, blamed history; others, like Drumont, blamed the Jews. Le Bon blamed the masses, and so did Sorel, but with a fine impartiality included the bourgeoisie as well. The evidence of that decline lay ready to hand. The defeat of 1870 and the Commune were clearly someone's fault. But whose? The left suspected that the army had not tried very hard in 1870, preserving itself for the real enemy, the new revolution within. (Similar suspicions were to be voiced about 1940.) The

right argued that the Commune was but another example
of that revolutionary spirit which had been the cause of
all France's troubles since 1789. The failure of 1870, the
ignominious military defeat of a Bonaparte seemed, for
some, to indicate that something fundamental was wrong
with Bonapartism in general, though the alternative did
not emerge clearly. It could lie with a socialist republic,
or, as with Maurras, with a return to monarchy. Or it
could equally well be argued, as it was by the Boulangists,
that nothing was wrong with the principle of the Caesar,
but that Napoleon le Petit simply was not the right
man. General Boulanger might be. While the dispute
about fundamentals went on, the lost provinces, Alsace
and Lorraine, remained in German hands, and as
scandal after scandal weakened the already diminished
credit of the republic, their recovery seemed less and less
likely.

The scandals were spectacular; their frequency almost
made them a new political style. The first was the Wilson
scandal, which seemed to compromise the republic so
deeply that sane men went over to the Boulangist movement in the belief that a strong general was what was
required to cleanse the Augean stable. Daniel Wilson,
son-in-law of the President of the Republic (Grévy), and
owner of several newspapers, used his position to traffic
in honours. Wilson was gaoled for two years, and the effect
of the conviction of the President's secretary forced the
President's resignation. A successor was hard to find, and
all the time Boulanger was pressing at the gates. Eventually, the parties of the republic rallied to its support, and
Boulangism ended in farce, but the movement of Caesarism against the republic in the years 1887–9 had at the
time a frightening reality. The second great affair was the
Panama scandal. De Lesseps, a great national hero after

his exploits at Suez, began to build the Panama Canal in 1881. It was to be a venture of the whole nation, with money raised by small investors as well as great. Owing in part to de Lesseps's obstinacy in the matter of locks, and in part to natural difficulties, the work went badly. It became necessary to bribe large sections of the press in order to keep the difficulties quiet, and certain sections of the Assembly in order to get government backing to help the project out of its difficulties. In 1888 the Chamber authorized the issue of lottery bonds. All seemed well, with the well-known Jewish banker Reinach in control of finances. But the business did not end there. Not only was Drumont's paper, *Libre Parole*, accusing Reinach of bribing deputies, but Reinach was himself being black-mailed by a mysterious Jew, Cornelius Hertz, who had an entrée to the highest society, presidential circles not excluded. What Hertz's hold over Reinach was, is not known, but Reinach killed himself in 1892. To the anti-semites the affair was a god-send. One Jew blackmailing another (did this not show how treacherous they were?); the victim paying his tormentor out of public money (did this not show that the public purse was open to the Jews at will?); the final sufferers were, of course, the small bourgeois and peasant investors, who, the soul of France, had invested their savings in the Panama scheme at the outset. International, cosmopolitan financiers, Jews, were destroying the nation. And was not democracy foreign and Jewish too? And Marxism? And had the Jews not welcomed the attacks on the true, Catholic, religion in 1789? And had not Gambetta himself, the high priest of anti-clericalism, been a Jew?

These two scandals seemed to compromise the republic, the press, the Chamber and high finance. Only the army was left; only the army would preserve the purity of the

real France and reclaim the lost provinces in the war of
revanche against Germany. There at least lay a bed-rock
of certainty. Until the Dreyfus affair. The facts of the
case are deceptively simple. In 1894, it was discovered
that secret information was being passed to Germany.
Alfred Dreyfus was suspected and interrogated. The news
leaked out to Drumont and the anti-semitic press and there
was pressure for a trial. Dreyfus was arrested, tried by
secret court martial and condemned to Devils Island. Not
everyone believed in Dreyfus's guilt, and Colonel Piquart
found that one of the principal pieces of evidence had been
written by a poverty-stricken infantry officer, Esterhazy,
and that another had been forged by his successor (Piquart
had been posted abroad after his inquiries), Colonel
Henry. A small, but determined pro-Dreyfusard party
began to form, including Zola and Clemenceau, and they
managed to bring a charge against Esterhazy, who was
found not guilty in yet another secret court martial. The
Dreyfusards did not give up, and Zola wrote his famous
open letter, '*J'accuse*', to the President of the Republic,
Félix Faure, claiming, among other things, that Esterhazy
had been acquitted on instructions from above. In the
summer of 1898 Cavaignac was appointed Minister of
War. He wanted to prove that Dreyfus was guilty through
a public trial, but once the evidence against Dreyfus was
reviewed it was shown that Henry was a forger – he committed suicide – and Esterhazy a liar – he fled to England.
A grand retrial was now inevitable, and this was held at
Rennes in the Court of Appeal (*Cour de Cassation*) in 1899.
Dreyfus was found guilty, but with mitigating circumstances. It was an absurd verdict. Either Dreyfus had
betrayed France – in which case there were no possible
mitigating circumstances – or he had not. A court cannot
compromise. The President pardoned Dreyfus. In 1906 the

proceedings of the re-trial at Rennes were quashed, and Dreyfus was rehabilitated, promoted and awarded the Legion of Honour.

Instead of being a squalid episode, the Dreyfus affair put the whole nation on trial. It seemed to crystallize out all the inherent antagonisms of French politics. For the right, the defence of the army against the imputation of a plot to break Dreyfus was the defence of the nation in both a general and a specific sense. Not only was the army the only hope for the restoration of the territorial integrity of the country in the matter of Alsace and Lorraine, but also the scandals of the Third Republic had so compromised public life in France that only the army was left. By admitting that the army was corrupt, the right admitted that the nation herself was totally corrupted, and, as Déroulède pointed out, for the right the innocence of Dreyfus might be a matter of debate; what was certain was that France herself was innocent. Dreyfus's Jewishness was crucial. It would be wildly unhistorical to accuse the whole French right of anti-semitism of the kind preached with such effectiveness by Drumont; Drumont is a classic Jew-baiter, dealing in scandal and the direct lie. Yet his anti-semitism is perhaps more easily opposed than the kind of anti-Jewish sentiment found in Barrès and Maurras. For them, the Jew is not a specific person at whom specific charges are made. On the contrary, 'Jew' is for them an ideogram which serves as a shorthand for certain attitudes and doctrines of which they disapprove. Like the anti-semitic mayor of Vienna, Karl Lueger, they decide who is a Jew. Thus for Maurras ideas of liberty and democracy are 'Jewish'; corrupt finance is 'Jewish'; the rights of man are 'Jewish'. All that tends to break down national difference is 'Jewish'; all that threatens the France of his imagination is 'Jewish'. 'Jewish' means rotten, foreign, democratic, libertarian, anti-clerical, anti-militarist, Marxist. From being a specific description, the word becomes a general term of abuse. Maurras uses the term in the same way that Goebbels used it. When Maurras cried, 'It is Dreyfus's revenge', on being condemned as a collaborator after the end of Hitler's war, he was making a *doctrinal* statement.

In *Romanticism and Revolution* Maurras argues that the revolutionary impulse, far from being the product of the classical spirit as Taine had argued, stems from romanticism. Romanticism is itself the product of the Reformation and pietism, and more distantly, of Jerusalem. Montesquieu and Voltaire came into contact with this Jewish spirit in England; even Plato was tainted with it, but the chief culprit was Rousseau, who put a Jewish, morbidly nervous spirit of turmoil at the service of alien elements to destroy the old France. The old France was both Catholic and classical; indeed the two entail and imply each other, for the Roman Church is the carrier of Roman values to medieval and modern Europe. While Taine argued that the revolutionary spirit was classical and superficial because it failed to grasp the profound historical roots of established polities – classical for him meaning a faith in the efficacy of *a priori* reasoning, thus enabling him to make a genuine intellectual judgment on the grounds of inadequacy – Maurras opposes classicism and romanticism as two opposing profundities, and denies that for a true Frenchman there is any choice to be made. Romanticism is German and Jewish, anti-national and anti-Catholic, other. Classicism is in the bones of France, is France. Choice depends on what one is, not how one reasons. This assertion of the absence of choice is the cornerstone of Maurras's political thought, just as in Barrès it simply does not matter whether one regards the Jews as racial degenerates or the highest aristocracy in the world. What one is determines one's attitude from the beginning. The illusion of choice, of reason, can only lead to personal *déracinement* and political disaster.

For Maurras, this denial of choice is more 'natural' than the 'natural man' of Rousseau and the state of nature. He correctly sees that the rational, natural man who can rationally perceive the principles of the rights of man and citizen is an ethical ideal. He makes no judgment on this ideal. He regards it as superfluous, for there is a more immediate sense of the natural in the soil and in history. The royal line of France is truly natural in that it is rooted in nature, in the soil. They made France, the France of blood and soil, and the authority which comes from such a tradition outweighs the puny authority of an elected parliament or of a corrupt republic.

The final attack on reason lies in the direction of myth, and implies yet another of those general judgments on the human condition. If men are not rational in the sense of the Enlightenment, if they are not moved by the demonstration of the truth of a proposition, then they must be moved in a different way. The paradigm case of the new insight into human motivation is mythology. Sorel saw this more clearly than anyone else, so that despite his residual Marxism he is part of the tradition of the right. Like Barrès and Maurras, he is concerned with decadence. The cause, for Sorel, is parliamentary democracy. Like Spengler, he sees democracy as the paradise of which crooked financiers dream. This distrust of politics, of bargaining and manœuvre, leads Sorel to the belief that only in a noble myth of the proletarian general strike as Napoleonic battlefield will the proletariat find that Homeric moral grandeur which alone can save them from the morass of democratic politics. Marxism must be accepted not as a rational system of politics based on historical, economic and sociological argument, for in the examination of the argument revolutionary energy is dissipated. Marxism is not a series of empirically based propositions about the nature of capitalism, more or less true. It is a call to action, and in that action lies the clue to the solution of the problem of moral decadence. It is through the cleansing nature of proletarian violence, and a return to the master-race morality of Nietzsche that the proletariat will realize its moral destiny. The doctrine is nothing, the act everything. Mussolini found Sorel congenial. Sorel is specific in his advocacy of myth, but in Maurras and Barrès there is an implied use of myth. For Barrès, the real France of the provincial graveyards is a mythology; it may not have existed in the past, but it points the way to action in the present. The same is true of Maurras. His Romano-Catholic France of the Middle Ages may not have been like Maurras's vision of what it was, but this does not matter; again, it points to a line of action in the present. The effectiveness of myth in moving the masses is given a scientific basis by Le Bon in his study of mass psychology, *The Crowd*, which Mussolini, in his *Autobiography*, claims as the only work ever to have influenced him.

Sorel's advocacy of violence as morally cleansing again finds its equivalent in de Maistre and Barrès. For de Maistre, the horrors of war do not coarsen the moral nature of the warrior; amidst the slaughter of armies he would be sickened by what the cook does when he kills a bird for the pot. War is ennobling; the virtues of a soldier are incorruptible. Barrès shares the same feeling for war. War is a necessary part of human life. The socialist vision of a Europe perpetually at peace is a chimera. War is a religious duty; on the Western Front,

God will raise the dead to fight for France; the clash of armies is a mystical experience. Even the war of attrition on the Western Front could not cool Barrès's ardour. The cult of *La France et les Morts* was the mystique which enabled France to survive the holocaust of Verdun. There is a straight line from Barrès's mythologized version of war and the call to Pétain in 1940.

How far did Pétain's Vichy embody the ideology of the right? Did the France of Roncevalles, of La Vendée and of Joan of Arc live again? The answer is that it did, though only as a parody of itself. The republic destroyed itself on July 10th, 1940, when the Assembly, or what was left of it, voted away its powers to the Marshal. Maurras received his reward in the form of a copy of the Marshal's speeches inscribed by the author '*A Charles Maurras, le plus Français des Français*'. Under a slogan borrowed from Italian fascism as an antidote to Liberty, Equality and Fraternity, Vichy attempted a National Revolution in the name of Work, Family, Country. As Pétain claimed, in his appeal to the nation on the occasion of the armistice with Germany:

> A new order is about to begin ... I urge you in the first place to an intellectual and moral regeneration. Frenchmen, you will accomplish this and you will see, I promise you, a new France arise from your fervour.

The doctrine of the National Revolution, as set out in Pétain's *Words to the French People* was based on two principles, a return to a Catholic, nationalist and French civilization and a reaction to the republic which had just been abolished. The style is simple, paternal, presupposing a direct, filial relationship between the Marshal and his people far removed, as Robert Aron remarks, from Hitler's frenzy or Mussolini's emphasis:

You have suffered. You will have more to suffer yet.
Many among you will not recover your trade or your
house. Your life will be hard. I shall not endeavour
to soothe you with false words. I hate the lies which
have done you so much harm. But the earth does not
lie. It remains your recourse. It is the Fatherland
itself. A field lying fallow is a portion of France dying.
Fallow land that is sown again is a portion of France
reborn.

Life is not neutral; it consists in taking sides boldly.
No neutrality is possible between truth and falsehood,
good and evil, between health and sickness, between
order and disorder, between France and anti-France.

The primary object of the National Revolution was to
remake man in the image of a *homo nationalis* whose
intellectual level was accompanied by the highest moral
tone. This was to be inculcated in a remodelled education
system designed to teach the fledgling *homo nationalis* his
duty to the state, respect for the law and a national pride.
Ten hours a week in primary education and nine in
secondary education were to be devoted to physical
exercise and manual labour. His character was to be
further moulded in an eight-month session in a youth
camp. His working life would be protected by the state,
which would also keep him from the vice of alcoholism,
and his wife in the home. The girl who promised not to
take paid employment would receive a grant from the
state; women were rewarded after their third child and
their husbands were accorded special tax privileges and
the right to work overtime. Their home would be protected by stringent divorce laws. He would himself be
far removed from the making of these laws, for what need
was there of elections when France was ruled in her best

interest by those who held these interests close to their hearts? He was protected from 'the microbe which was producing in it [France] the fatal anaemia' by anti-semitic legislation.

This was a parodistic version of the *France sacrée* of which the *Action Française* publicists had dreamed. No doubt Vichy did some positive work of reconstruction in the restoration of the order which had totally broken down in 1940, but its discriminatory legislation blots its record, and it deceived itself in thinking it could ever have a free hand in the unoccupied zone. The exigencies of the war made it clearer and clearer that any attempt to build the 'real France' was illusory. No doubt the politicians of Vichy attempted to assert an independence, but the fundamental fact was that France had lost the war and would have to pay accordingly.

What unites the right ideologically in France is the fundamental attack on reason and the rights of man. Thomas Mann, writing in another context, furnished the epigraph to the progenitors of Vichy:

> … this insight into the feebleness of the reason and the intellect, their oft-proven incapacity to condition life, has not given rise to a wish to pity and protect their weakness. On the contrary, they are treated by this school of thought as though there were a danger that they might ever become too strong, that there could ever be too much of them on this earth; the weakness of mind is one reason more to hate it, to make a religion of decrying it as the grave-digger of life.

J. S. McClelland

JOSEPH DE MAISTRE
(1753–1821)

De Maistre was, with Bonald, the most passionate of the early critics of the Enlightenment and the Revolution. In his *Considérations sur la France* (1796) he denounced the double crime of the Revolution as the attack on king and Church. In exile after 1793, he became Sardinian ambassador to the imperial court at St Petersburg where he counted Tsar Alexander I among his friends. It was during the St Petersburg period (1802–17) that he wrote his great works, including the *St Petersburg Dialogues*, a section from which is reprinted here. Against the reason so dear to the ideologues of the eighteenth century he opposed the sense of community and of history, faith, intuition, providence and a narrow, totally committed Catholicism. De Maistre's attack on the Revolution is doubly based. Not only did Rousseau and Paine, with their ideas of the social contract and the rights of man, commit intellectual errors, and so can easily be disposed of, but they were responsible for moral crimes as well. The attempt to recreate a state after 1789 was fundamentally impious, a result of an overweening pride in reason which is man's basic weakness. The Revolution was a challenge to God, an attempt at God's work, creation, and as such it was bound to fail. It followed that strong and harsh authority was required to curb this pride of reason; also, war is to be seen as divine retribution for men's sinfulness. Finally, we can know only dimly the truths of the political order. They are part of the mind of God, and to try to know the mind of God too completely may in itself be blasphemous.

Reason can tell us little; only revelation contains those grains of truth which it has pleased God that we should know. This revelation is contained in prejudice, in the simple heart and in established institutions which have a relationship with God which reason cannot pretend to have.

De Maistre not only represents the early development of the anti-revolutionary and anti-rationalist theme, but is also, in a sense, in the middle of it because the complete works, including the publication for the first time of the important *Study of Sovereignty*, did not appear until 1884.

The selections from de Maistre are taken from Jack Lively's edition of *The Works of Joseph de Maistre* (London, 1965).

TWO EXTRACTS FROM THE
STUDY OF SOVEREIGNTY

It is one of man's curious idiosyncrasies to create difficulties for the pleasure of resolving them. The mysteries that surround him on all sides are not sufficient for him; he still rejects clear ideas and reduces everything to a problem by some inexplicable twist of pride, which makes him regard it as below him to believe what everyone believes. So, for example, there have long been disputes on the origin of society; and in place of the quite simple solutions that naturally present themselves to the mind, all sorts of metaphysical theories have been put forward to support airy hypotheses rejected by common sense and experience.

If the causes of the origins of society are posed as a problem, it is obviously assumed that there was a human era before society; but this is precisely what needs to be proved.

Doubtless it will not be denied that the earth as a whole is intended for man's habitation; now, as the multiplication of man is part of the Creator's intentions, it follows that the nature of man is to be united in great societies over the whole surface of the globe. For the nature of a being is to exist as the Creator has willed it. And this will is made perfectly plain by the facts.

The isolated man is therefore by no means the *man of nature*. When a handful of men were scattered over vast territories, humanity was not what it was to become. At that time, there were only families, and these scattered families, either *individually* or by their subsequent union, were nothing but embryonic peoples.

And so, long after the formation of the great societies,

some small desert tribes still show us the spectacle of humanity in its infancy. There are still infant nations that are not yet what they are to become.

What would one think of a naturalist who said that man is an animal thirty to thirty-five inches high, without strength or intelligence, and giving voice only to inarticulate cries? Yet this naturalist, in sketching man's physical and moral nature in terms of an infant's characteristics, would be no more ridiculous than the philosopher who seeks the political nature of this same being in the *rudiments* of society.

Every question about the *nature* of man must be resolved by history. The philosopher who wants to show us by *a priori* reasoning what man must be does not deserve an audience. He is substituting expediency for experience and his own decisions for the Creator's will.

Let me assume that someone manages to prove that an American savage is happier and less vicious than a civilized man. Could it be concluded from this that the latter is a degraded being or, if you like, further from *nature* than the former? Not at all. This is just like saying that the nature of the individual man is to remain a child because at that age he is free from the vices and misfortunes that will beset him in his maturity. History continually shows us men joined together in more or less numerous societies, ruled by different sovereignties. Once they have multiplied beyond a certain point, they cannot exist in any other fashion.

Thus, properly speaking, there has never been a time previous to society for *man*, because, before the formations of political societies, man was not a complete man, and because it is ridiculous to seek the characteristics of any being whatever in the embryo of that being.

Thus society is not the work of man, but the immediate

result of the will of the Creator who has willed that man should be what he has always and everywhere been.

Rousseau and all the thinkers of his stamp imagine or try to imagine a people *in the state of nature* (this is their expression), deliberating formally on the advantages and disadvantages of the social state and finally deciding to pass from one to the other. But there is not a grain of common sense in this idea. What were these men like before the *national convention* in which they finally decided to find themselves a sovereign? Apparently they lived without laws and government; but for how long?

It is a basic mistake to represent the social state as an optional state based on human consent, on deliberation and on an original contract, something which is an impossibility. To talk of a state of *nature* in opposition to the social state is to talk nonsense voluntarily. The word *nature* is one of those general terms which, like all abstract terms, are open to abuse. In its most extensive sense, this word really signifies only the totality of all the laws, power and springs of action that *make up* the world, and the *particular* nature of such and such a being is the totality of all the qualities which make it what it is and without which it would be some other thing and could no longer fulfil the intentions of its creator. Thus the combination of all the parts which make up a machine intended to tell the time forms the *nature* or the essence of a *watch*; and the *nature* or essence of the *balance wheel* is to have such and such a form, dimensions and position, otherwise it would no longer be a balance wheel and could not fulfil its functions. The *nature* of a viper is to crawl, to have a scaly skin, hollow and movable fangs which exude poisonous venom; and the *nature* of man is to be a cognitive, religious and sociable animal. All experience teaches us this; and, to my knowledge, nothing has contradicted this experience. If someone wants to prove that the nature of the viper is to have wings and a sweet voice, and that of a beaver is to live alone at the top of the highest mountains, it is up to him to prove it. In the meantime, we will believe that what is must be and has always been.

'The social order', says Rousseau, 'is a sacred right which is the basis of all others. Yet this right does not come from *nature*: it is therefore founded on convention.'

What is *nature*? What is a *right*? And how is an *order* a *right*? But let us leave these difficulties: such questions are endless with a man who misuses every term and defines none. One has the right at least to ask him to prove the big assertion that *the social order does not come from nature*. 'I must', he says himself, 'establish what I have just advanced.' This is indeed what should be done, but the way in which he goes about it is truly curious. He spends three chapters in proving that the social order does not derive from family society or from force or from slavery (chapters 2, 3, 4) and concludes (chapter 5) *that we must always go back to a first convention*. This method of proof is very useful: it lacked only the majestic formula of the geometers, '*Which was to be proved.*'

It is also curious that Rousseau has not even tried to prove the one thing that it was necessary to prove; for if the social order derives from nature, there is no social compact.

'Before examining', he says, 'the act by which a people choose a king, it would be as well to examine the act by which a people is a people: for this act, being necessarily previous to the other, is the true foundation of society' (chapter 5). This same Rousseau says elsewhere, 'It is the inveterate habit of philosophers to deny what is and to explain what is not.' Let us on our side add that it is the inveterate habit of Rousseau to mock the philosopher without suspecting that he also was a *philosopher* in all the force he gave to the word; so, for example, the *Social Contract* denies from beginning to end the nature of man, which *is*, in order to explain the social compact, which *does not exist.*

This is how one reasons when one separates man from the Divinity. Rather than tiring oneself out in the search of error, it would take little effort to turn one's eyes to the source of all creation; but so simple, sure and consoling a method of philosophizing is not to the taste of writers of this unhappy age whose true illness is an aversion to good sense.

Might it not be said that man, this property of the Divinity, was cast on this earth by a blind cause, that he could be either this or that, and that it is as a consequence of his choice that he is what he is? Surely God intended some sort of end in creating man: the question can thus be reduced to whether man has become a *political animal*, as Aristotle put it, *through* or *against* the divine will. Although this question stated explicitly is a real sign of folly, it is nevertheless put indirectly in a host of writings, and fairly often the authors even decide that the latter is the case. The word *nature* has given rise to a multitude of errors. Let me repeat that the nature of any being is the sum of the qualities attributed to it by the Creator. With immeasurable profundity, Burke said that art is man's nature. This is beyond doubt; man with all his affections, all his knowledge, all his arts is the true *natural man*, and the weaver's cloth is as *natural* as the web.

Man's *natural state* is therefore to be what he is today and what he has always been, that is to say, *sociable*. All human records attest to this truth ...

In his evil book on the rights of man, Paine said that a constitution is antecedent to government; that it is to government what laws are to the courts; that it is visible and material, article by article, or else it does not exist: so that the English people has no constitution, its government being the product of conquest and not of the will of the people.

It would be difficult to get more errors into fewer lines. Not only can a people not give itself a constitution, but no assembly, a small number of men in relation to the total population, can ever carry through such a task ...

There has never been, there will never be, there cannot be a nation constituted *a priori*. Reason and experience join to prove this great truth. What eye is capable of comprehending all the circumstances that must fit a nation to a particular constitution? How especially can a number of men be capable of this effort of intelligence? Unless they refuse to see the truth, they must agree that this is impossible; and history which should decide all these questions again supports theory. A small number of free nations have shone in history, but not one of them has been constituted in Paine's manner. Every particular form of government is a divine construction, just like sovereignty in general. A constitution in the philosophic sense is thus only the political way of life bestowed on each nation by a power above it; and, in an inferior sense, a constitution is only the assemblage of those more or less numerous laws which declare this way of life. It is not at all necessary for these laws to be written. On the contrary, it is particularly to constitutional laws that the maxim of Tacitus, *pessimae republicae plurimae leges*, can be applied. The wiser and more public-spirited a nation is, and the more excellent its constitution, the fewer written constitutional laws it has, for these laws are only props, and a building has no need of props except when it has slipped out of vertical or been violently shaken by some external force ...

What Paine and so many others regard as a fault is therefore a law of nature. The *natural* constitution of a nation is always anterior to its *written* constitution and can dispense with it. There has never been and can never be a written constitution made all at once, particularly by an assembly, and the very fact that it is written all at once proves it false and impractical. Every constitution is properly speaking a *creation* in the full meaning of the word, and all *creation* is beyond men's powers. A written law is only the declaration of an anterior and unwritten law. Man cannot bestow rights on himself; he can only defend those which have been granted to him by a superior power; and these rights are *good customs*, good because they are not written and because no beginning or author can be assigned to them ...

Human reason left to its own resources is completely incapable *not only of creating but also of conserving any religious or political association*, because it can only give rise to disputes and because, to conduct himself well, man needs beliefs, not problems. His cradle should be surrounded by dogmas; and, when his reason awakes, all his opinions should be given, at least all those relating to his conduct. Nothing is more vital to him than *prejudices*. Let us not take this word in bad part. It does not necessarily signify false ideas, but only, in the strict sense of the word, any opinions adopted without examination. Now, these kinds of opinion are essential to man; they are the real basis of his happiness and the palladium of empires. Without them, there can be neither religion, morality, nor government. There should be a state religion just as there is a state political system; or rather, religion and political dogmas, mingled and merged together, should together form a *general* or *national mind* sufficiently strong to repress the aberrations of the individual reason which is, of its nature, the mortal enemy of any association whatever because it gives birth only to divergent opinions.

All known nations have been happy and powerful to the degree that they have faithfully obeyed this national mind, which is nothing other than the destruction of individual dogmas and the absolute and general rule of national dogmas, that is to say, useful prejudices. Once let everyone rely on his individual reason in religion, and you will see immediately the rise of anarchy of belief or the annihilation of religious sovereignty. Likewise, if each man makes himself the judge of the principles of government you will see immediately the rise of civil anarchy or the annihilation of political sovereignty. Government is a true religion; it has its dogmas, its mysteries, its priests; to submit it to individual discussion is to destroy it; it has life only through the national mind, that is to say, political faith, which is a *creed*. Man's primary need is that his nascent reason should be curbed under a double yoke; it should be frustrated, and it should lose itself in the national mind, so that it changes its individual existence for another communal existence, just as a river which flows into the ocean still exists in the mass of water, but without name and distinct reality.

What is patriotism? It is this national mind of which I am speaking; it is individual *abnegation*. Faith and patriotism are the two great thaumaturges of the world. Both are divine. All their actions are miracles. Do not talk to them of scrutiny, choice, discussion, for they will say that you blaspheme. They know only two words, *submission* and *belief*; with these two levers, they raise the world. Their very errors are sublime. These two infants of Heaven prove their origin to all by creating and conserving; and if they unite, join their forces and together take possession of a nation, they exalt it, make it divine and increase its power a hundredfold ...

But can you, insignificant man, light this sacred fire that inflames nations? Can you give a common soul to several million men? Unite them under your laws? Range them closely around a common centre? Shape the mind of men yet unborn? Make future generations obey you and create those age-old customs, those conserving *prejudices*, which are the father of the laws and stronger than them? What nonsense! ...

EXTRACT FROM THE SEVENTH OF
THE *ST PETERSBURG DIALOGUES*

THE SENATOR. I would put several questions to you if I was not afraid of losing the thread of my ideas. I asked you then to look at a fact well worthy of your attention. It is that the profession of arms does not in the least tend to degrade or to make wild and hard at least those who follow it, as we might believe or fear if experience did not teach us: on the contrary, it tends to improve them. The most honest man is commonly the honest soldier, and, as I said not long ago, I have always for my own part had a particular respect for military good sense. I infinitely prefer it to the long circumlocutions of men of affairs. In ordinary human relationships, soldiers are often more pleasant, more relaxed and, it seems to me, often even more civil than other men. Amid political upheavals, they generally act as intrepid defenders of ancient beliefs, and the most dazzling sophistries are almost always wrecked on their uprightness. They willingly turn their attention to useful works and knowledge, political economy, for example. Perhaps the only work antiquity has left us on this subject is by a soldier, Xenophon, and the first recorded French work on the same subject is also by a soldier, Marshal de Vauban. In them religion combines with honour in a remarkable way; and even when religion reproaches them gravely for their conduct they will not refuse it their sword if it needs it. Much is said about the *licence of camps*; no doubt it is great, but usually the soldier does not find these vices in his camps; he carries them there. A moral and austere people always make excellent soldiers, fright-

ening only on the battlefield. Virtue, even piety, easily
allies itself with military courage, and, far from enfeebling
the warrior, it exalts him ... Not only does the profession
of arms generally ally itself very well with morality, but
what is quite extraordinary is that it does not at all
weaken those gentle virtues which seem the most opposed
to military attitudes. The gentlest of men love war, desire
war and go to war with passion. At the first call, this
likable young man here, brought up with a horror of
violence and blood, rushes from his father's house, his
weapons in his hand, to seek on the battlefield what he
calls *the enemy* without yet knowing what an *enemy* is.
Yesterday he would have fainted if he had accidentally
killed his sister's canary; tomorrow you will see him climb
a pile of corpses *in order to see further,* as Charron put it.
The blood flowing on all sides serves only to inspire him
to spill his own and that of others. He gradually inflames
himself until he reaches *an enthusiasm for carnage.*

THE KNIGHT. You do not exaggerate. Before I was twenty-
five, I had seen *the enthusiasm for carnage* three times. I have
experienced it myself and I especially remember a terrible
moment when I would have put an entire army to the
sword if I had been able.

THE SENATOR. But if, at this moment, someone asked you
to catch a white dove as cold-bloodedly as a cook, then —

THE KNIGHT. For shame, you make me sick at heart!

THE SENATOR. This is precisely what I was just talking
about. The terrifying sight of carnage does not harden the
warrior. Amid the blood he spills, he is humane, just as
the wife is chaste in the transports of love. Once he has put
back the sword into its scabbard, saintly humanity
regains its sway, and perhaps the highest and most generous feelings are found among soldiers ...

In short, gentlemen, the functions of the soldier are

terrible, but they must result from a great law of the
spiritual world, and no one should be astonished that every
nation in the world is united in seeing in this scourge
something still more peculiarly divine than in others. You
can well believe that there is a good and profound reason
for the title LORD OF HOSTS being found on every
page of the Holy Scriptures. Guilty, and unhappy because
we are guilty, we ourselves make necessary all physical
evils, but above all war. Usually and very naturally,
men lay the blame on their rulers: Horace wrote play-
fully, 'By the madness of kings nations are punished.'
But J.-J. Rousseau said more seriously and philosophically:

> The wrath of kings brings the earth to arms,
> The wrath of Heaven brings kings to arms.

Notice, moreover, that this law of war, terrible in itself, is yet
only a clause in the general law that hangs over the world.

In the immense sphere of living things, the obvious rule
is violence, a kind of inevitable frenzy which arms all
things *in mutua funera*. Once you leave the world of insensible substances, you find the decree of violent death
written on the very frontiers of life. Even in the vegetable
kingdom, this law can be perceived: from the huge catalpa
to the smallest of grasses, how many plants *die* and how
many are *killed*! But once you enter the animal kingdom,
the law suddenly becomes frighteningly obvious. A power
at once hidden and palpable appears constantly occupied
in bringing to light the principle of life by violent means.
In each great division of the animal world, it has chosen a
certain number of animals charged with devouring the
others; so there are insects of prey, reptiles of prey, birds
of prey, fish of prey and quadrupeds of prey. There is not
an instant of time when some living creature is not
devoured by another.

Above all these numerous animal species is placed man, whose destructive hand spares no living thing; he kills to eat, he kills for clothing, he kills for adornment, he kills to attack, he kills to defend himself, he kills for instruction, he kills for amusement, he kills for killing's sake: a proud and terrible king, he needs everything, and nothing can withstand him. He knows how many barrels of oil he can get from the head of a shark or a whale; in his museums, he mounts with his sharp pins elegant butterflies he has caught in flight on the top of Mont Blanc or Chimborazo; he stuffs the crocodile and embalms the hummingbird; on his command, the rattlesnake dies in preserving fluids to keep it intact for a long line of observers. The horse carrying its master to the tiger hunt struts about covered by the skin of this same animal. At one and the same time, man takes from the lamb its entrails for harp strings, from the whale its bones to stiffen the corsets of the young girl, from the wolf its most murderous tooth to polish frivolous manufactures, from the elephant its tusks to make a child's toy; his dining table is covered with corpses. The philosopher can even discern how this permanent carnage is provided for and ordained in the whole scheme of things. But without doubt this law will not stop at man. Yet what being is to destroy him who destroys all else? Man! It is man himself who is charged with butchering man.

But how is he to accomplish this law who is a moral and merciful being, who is born to love, who cries for others as for himself, who finds pleasure in weeping to the extent of creating fictions to make himself weep, to whom finally it has been said that *whoever sheds blood unjustly will redeem it with the last drop of his own*? It is war that accomplishes this decree. Do you not hear the earth itself demanding and crying out for blood? The blood of animals does not satisfy it, nor even that of criminals spilled by the sword of the law. If human justice struck them all, there would be no war; but it can catch up with only a small number of them, and often it even spares them without suspecting that this cruel humanity contributes to the necessity for war, especially if at the same time another no less stupid and dangerous blindness works to diminish atonement among men. The earth did not cry in vain: war breaks out. Man, seized suddenly by a divine fury foreign to both hatred and anger, goes to the battlefield without knowing what he intends or even what he is doing. How can this dreadful enigma be explained? Nothing could be more contrary to his nature, yet nothing is less repugnant to him: he undertakes with enthusiasm what he holds in horror. Have you never noticed that no one ever disobeys on the field of death? They might well slaughter a Nerva or a Henry IV, but they will never say, even to the most abominable tyrant or the most flagrant butcher of human flesh, *We no longer want to follow you.* A revolt on the battle-field, an agreement to unite to repudiate a tyrant is something I cannot remember. Nothing resists, nothing can resist the force that drags man into conflict; an innocent murderer, a passive instrument in a formidable hand, *he plunges unseeing into the abyss he himself has dug; he died without suspecting that it is he himself who has brought about his death.*

Thus is worked out, from maggots up to man, the universal law of the violent destruction of living beings. The whole earth, continually steeped in blood, is nothing but an immense altar on which every living thing must be sacrificed without end, without restraint, without re-spite until the consummation of the world, the extinction of evil, the death of death.

But the curse must be aimed most directly and obviously at man: the avenging angel circles like the sun around this unhappy globe and lets one nation breathe only to strike at others. But when crimes, especially those of a particular kind, accumulate to a certain point, the angel relentlessly quickens his tireless flight. Like a rapidly turned torch, his immense speed allows him to be present at all points on his huge orbit at the same time. He strikes every nation on earth at the same moment. At other times, minister of an unerring and infallible vengeance, he turns against particular nations and bathes them in blood. Do not expect them to make any effort to escape or abridge their sentence. It is as if these sinful nations, enlightened by conscience, were asking for punishment and accepting it in order to find expiation in it. So long as they have blood left, they will come forward to offer it, and soon *golden youth* will grow used to telling of devastating wars caused by their fathers' crimes.

War is thus divine in itself, since it is a law of the world.

War is divine through its consequences of a supernatural nature which are as much general as particular, consequences little known because they are little sought but which are none the less indisputable. Who would doubt the benefits that death in war brings? And who could believe that the victims of this dreadful judgment have shed their blood in vain? But this is not the time to insist on this kind of question; our age is not yet ready to concern itself with it. Let us leave it to its physics and for our own part keep our eyes fixed firmly to that invisible world which will explain everything.

War is divine in the mysterious glory that surrounds it and in the no less inexplicable attraction that draws us to it.

War is divine in the protection granted to the great leaders, even the most daring, who are rarely struck down in battle, and only when their renown can no longer be increased and when their mission is completed.

War is divine by the manner in which it breaks out. I

do not want to excuse anyone inopportunely, but how many of those who are regarded as the immediate authors of wars are themselves carried along by circumstances! At the exact moment brought about by men and prescribed by justice, God comes forward to exact vengeance for the iniquity committed by the inhabitants of this world against him ...

War is divine in its results which cannot be predicted by human reason, for they can be quite different for two different nations, although the war seems to have affected both equally. There are wars that degrade nations, and degrade them for centuries; others exalt them, improve them in all kinds of ways and, what is more extraordinary, very quickly replace momentary losses by a rapid increase in population. History often shows us the sight of a population growing in wealth and numbers during the most murderous conflicts; but there are vicious wars, accursed wars, more easily recognized by conscience than by reason: nations are mortally wounded by them, both in their power and in their character; then you can see the victor himself degraded, impoverished and miserable among his victory laurels, whereas you will find that in the vanquished land, in a very short time, there is not an unused workshop or plough.

War is divine through the indefinable power that determines success in it. Surely you were not thinking, my dear Knight, when you repeated the other day the well-known saying that *God is always on the side of the big battalions.* I will never believe that it was really said by the great man to whom it is attributed; perhaps he put forward this maxim as a jest, or seriously in a limited and very true sense, for God in his providential temporal government does not depart (except in the case of miracles) from the general laws he has laid down for all time. Thus, as two men are stronger than one, so a hundred thousand must be more powerful and effective than fifty thousand. When we ask God for victory, it would be foolish to be asking him to depart from the general laws of the world. but these laws combine in a thousand different ways and can bring victory in a manner which cannot be foreseen. Doubtless three men are stronger than one: the general proposition cannot be contested; but one clever man can profit from certain circumstances, and one Horatius will kill three Curiatii. *A body with the greater mass has the greater momentum*: this is true if speeds are equal, but three parts of mass and two of speed are equivalent to three of speed and two of mass. In the same way, an army of forty thousand men is physically inferior to another of sixty thousand, but, if the former has more courage, experience and discipline, it can beat the latter, for it is more effective with fewer numbers. This we can witness on every page of history. Wars, moreover, always suppose a certain equality, otherwise there would be no wars. I have never read of the republic of Ragusa declaring war on the sultans, nor that of Geneva on the kings of France. There is always a certain balance in the political world and (if certain rare, precise and limited cases are excepted) man cannot upset it at will. This is why coalitions are so difficult. If they were not, since politics is little governed by justice, there would be continual combinations to destroy a particular power; but such projects seldom succeed, and history shows even the weakest power escaping from them with an astonishing ease. When an overdominant power frightens the world, men are angry that no means have been found of checking it, and bitter reproaches are levelled against the selfishness and immorality of the rulers who are preventing an alliance to ward off the common danger. This was the cry heard at the height of Louis XIV's power. But at bottom these complaints are not valid. A coalition between several powers, based on a pure and disinterested morality, would be a miracle. God, who is not obliged to do miracles and never does one needlessly, uses two very simple means to restore the balance: sometimes the giant kills itself; sometimes a much weaker power throws in its path some small obstacle, which yet then grows in some unaccountable way and becomes insurmountable, just as a small branch, stuck in the current of a river, can in the end cause a blockage which diverts its course.

Starting, then, from this hypothesis of a balance, ever present at least in a rough form either because the belligerent powers are equal or because the weakest have allies, how many unforeseen circumstances can disrupt the balance and bring frustration or success to the greatest plans in spite of every prudential calculation! ... Moreover, if you take a more general look at the role played by moral power in war, you will agree that nowhere does the divine hand make itself felt more acutely to man. It might be said that this is a *department*, if you will allow me the phrase, whose direction Providence has reserved to itself and in which it has left to man the ability to act only in a well-nigh mechanical manner, since success here depends almost entirely on something he can at least control. At no time other than in war is he warned more often and more sharply of his own feebleness and of the inexorable power ruling all things. It is opinion that loses and wins battles. *The fearless Spartan used to sacrifice from fear* (Rousseau somewhere expresses astonishment at this, I do not know why); Alexander also sacrificed from fear before the Battle of Arbela. Certainly these people were quite right and, to correct this sensible devotion, it is enough *to pray to God that he deigns not to send fear to us*. Fear! Charles V made great fun of that epitaph he read in passing, *Here lies one who never felt fear.* And what man never has felt fear in his life? Who has never had occasion to realize, both in himself, in those around him and in history, the way in which men can be overcome by this passion, which often seems to have the more sway over us the fewer the reasonable causes for it. *Let us then pray, Knight, for it is to you that I should like to address this discourse,* since you have called up these reflections; let us pray to God that he keeps us and our friends from fear, which is within his power and which can ruin in an instant the most splendid military ventures.

And do not be frightened by this word *fear,* for if you take it in its strictest sense you can say that the experience it expresses is rare and that it is shameful to be afraid of it. There is a womanish fear reflected in panicky flight, and this it is proper, even necessary, to dismiss entirely, although it is not a completely unknown sight. But there is another very much more terrible fear that descends on the most masculine heart, freezes it and persuades it that it is beaten. This is the appalling scourge constantly hanging over armies. I put this question one day to a soldier of the highest rank whom you both know. *Tell me, General, what is a lost battle? I have never been able to understand this.* After a moment's silence, he answered, *I do not know.* After another pause he added, *It is a battle one thinks one has lost.* Nothing could be truer. One man fighting with another is beaten when he is killed or overthrown while the other is standing. It is not so with two armies; the one cannot be killed while the other remains on its feet. The balance of strength swings one way, then the other, as does the number of deaths, and, especially since the invention of gunpowder gave more equality in the means of destruction, a battle is no longer lost materially, that is to say, because there are more dead on one side than on the other. It was Frederick II, no mean thinker on this question, who said, *To win is to advance.* But who is the person who advances? It is he whose conscience and bearing make the other fall back. Do you recall, Count, that young soldier of your own acquaintance who one day portrayed to you in one of his letters *that solemn moment when, without knowing why, an army feels itself carried forward, as if it was sliding down an inclined plane.* I remember that you were struck by this phrase which indeed described exactly the crucial moment; but this moment is far from a matter of reflection. Notice particularly that it is by no means a question of numbers. Has the soldier *who slides forward* counted the dead? Opinion is so powerful in war that it can alter the nature of the same event; and give it two different names, for no reason other than its own whim. A general throws his men between two enemy armies and he writes to his king, *I have split him, he has lost.* His opponent writes to his king, *He has put himself between two fires, he is lost.* Which of the two is mistaken? Whoever is seized by *the cold goddess.* Assuming that all things, especially size, are at least approximately equal, the only difference between the two positions is a purely moral one ... It is imagination that loses battles.

It is not even by any means always on the day they are fought that it is known whether they have been lost or won; it is on the next day, even two or three days afterwards. Men talk a great deal about battles in ignorance of what they are. There is an especial tendency to consider them as happening on a particular spot, whereas they stretch over five or six miles. One is asked seriously, *How is it that you do not know what happened in this battle when you were there?* Whereas precisely the opposite could very often be said. Does the man on the right flank know what is happening on the left? Does he even know what is happening two paces from him?

I can very well imagine one of these frightful scenes. On a vast field covered with all the apparatus of carnage and seeming to shudder beneath the feet of men and horses, amid the fire and the whirling smoke, dazed and befuddled by the din of firearms and cannons, by voices that command, howl or die away, surrounded by dead, dying and mutilated corpses, possessed in turn by fear, hope, anger, by five or six different passions, what happens to a man? What does he see? What does he know after a few hours? What can he know about himself and others? Among this host of fighting men who have battled the whole day, there is often not a single one, not even the general, who knows who the victor is. I need only cite modern battles to you, famous battles whose memory will never fade, battles which have changed the face of Europe, and which have been lost only because such and such a man has believed they were lost; whereas, in the same circumstances and with the same losses, another general would have had the *Te Deum* sung in his country and forced history to say quite the opposite of what it will say. But, I ask you, what age has seen moral power play a more astonishing role in war than our own? Is not what we have seen for the last twenty years truly magical? Without doubt it behoves men of this epoch to cry out:

And what age has ever been more fertile in miracles? ...

HIPPOLYTE TAINE
(1828–93)

Taine's service to the French right was to present, in *The Origins of Contemporary France* (1875–93), an anti-Jacobin account of the Revolution and its causes which rested on a firm foundation of empirical research. He claimed to have shown Frenchmen what their grandfathers had been like; the Revolution had not been a pastoral idyll, but the institution of a bloody despotism accompanied by an outburst of primal barbarism. In this extract from John Durand's translation of the *Origins* (published in separate volumes from 1876) Taine places the responsibility for the statism and barbarism of the Revolution squarely on the shoulders of Rousseau. The idea that the state is something men choose can lead, paradoxically, only to despotism and anarchy. Like Barrès and Maurras whom he influenced, Taine regards the social contract as both a politically naive and a politically disastrous doctrine. Centralization reduces liberty, and the doctrine of popular sovereignty ignores the political fact that no assembly can abolish history by popular fiat. What is natural is what is historical; men do not have to meet together to make a social contract by common consent because the very fact that they are born into established polities presupposes a real, positive contract, an agreement of their ancestors about how the polity should be run. The preaching of such nonsensical ideas as popular sovereignty can lead only to the destruction of the real contract, which is not the work of a single man, or even of a generation of men, but of a whole race and a whole tradition. If there is to be democracy, let it be a democracy of the dead.

THE ORGANIZATION OF
SOCIETY IN THE FUTURE

Consider future society as it appears at this moment to our legislators of the closet and bear in mind that it will soon appear under the same aspect to the legislators of the Assembly. In their eyes the decisive moment has come. Henceforth two histories are to exist; one, that of the past, the other, that of the future, formerly a history of man still deprived of his reason, and at present the history of the rational man. At length the rule of right is to begin. Of all that the past has founded and transmitted nothing is legitimate. Overlaying the natural man it has created an artificial man, either ecclesiastic or laic, noble or plebeian, sovereign or subject, proprietor or proletary, ignorant or cultivated, peasant or citizen, slave or master, all being factitious qualities which we are not to heed, as their origin is tainted with violence and robbery. Strip off these superadded garments; let us take man in himself, the same under all conditions, in all situations, in all countries, in all ages, and strive to ascertain what sort of association is the best adapted to him. The problem thus stated the rest follows.

Conformably to the ways of the classic spirit, and to the precepts of the prevailing ideology, a political system is constructed after a mathematical model. A simple proposition is selected, and set apart, very general, familiar, readily apparent and easily understood by the most ignorant and inattentive schoolboy. Reject every difference which separates one man from other men; retain of him only the portion common to him and to others. This remainder constitutes man in general, or in other words, 'a sensitive and rational being who, thus endowed, avoids pain and seeks pleasure', and therefore aspiring to 'happiness, namely a stable condition in which one enjoys greater pleasure than pain', or, again, 'a sensitive being capable of forming rational opinions and of acquiring moral ideas'. The first-comer is cognizant of this notion in his own experience, and can verify it at the first glance. Such is the social unit; let several of these be combined, a thousand, a hundred thousand, a million, twenty-six millions, and you have the French people. Men born at twenty-one years of age, without relations, without a past, without traditions, without a country, are supposed to be assembled for the first time and, for the first time, to treat with each other. In this position, at the moment of contracting together, all are equal: for, as the definition states, the extrinsic and spurious qualities through which alone all differ have been rejected. All are free, for, according to the definition, the unjust thraldom imposed on all by brute force and by hereditary prejudice, has been suppressed. But, if all men are equal, no reason exists why, in this contract, any special advantage should be conceded to one more than to another. Accordingly all shall be equal before the law; no person, or family, or class, shall be allowed any privilege; no one shall claim a right of which another might be deprived; no one shall be subject to any duty of which another is exempted. On the other hand, all being free, each enters with a free will along with the group of wills constituting the new community; it is necessary that in the common resolutions, he should fully concur. Only on these conditions does he bind himself; he is bound to respect laws only because he has assisted in making them, and to obey magistrates only because he has aided in electing them. Underneath all legitimate authority his consent or his vote must be apparent, while, in the humblest citizen, the most exalted of public powers must recognize a member of their own sovereignty. No one may alienate or lose this portion of his sovereignty; it is inseparable from his person, and, on delegating it to another, he reserves to himself full possession of it. The liberty, equality and sovereignty of the people constitute the first articles of the social contract. These are rigorously deduced from a primary definition; other rights of the citizen are to be no less rigorously deduced from it, the main features of the constitution, the most important civil and political laws, in short, the order, the form and the spirit of the new state.

Hence, two consequences. In the first place, a society thus organized is the only just one; for, the reverse of all others, it is not the result of a blind subjection to traditions, but of a contract concluded among equals, examined in open daylight, and assented to in full freedom. The social contract, composed of demonstrated theorems, has the authority of geometry; hence an equal value at all times, in every place and for every people; it is accordingly rightfully established. Whatever interposes any obstacle thereto is inimical to the human race; whether a government, an aristocracy or a clergy, it must be overthrown. Revolt is simply just defence; in withdrawing ourselves from such hands we recover only what has been wrongfully retained and which legitimately belongs to us. In the second place, this social code, as just set forth, once promulgated, is applicable without misconception or resistance; for it is a species of moral geometry, simpler than any other, reduced to first principles, founded on the clearest and most popular notions, and, in four steps, leading to capital truths. The comprehension and application of these truths demand no preparatory study or profound reflection; good sense suffices, and even common sense. Prejudice and selfishness alone impair the testimony; but never will testimony be wanting in a sound brain and in an upright heart. Explain the rights of man to a labourer or to a peasant and at once he becomes an able politician; teach children the citizen's catechism and on leaving school they comprehend duties and rights as well as the four arithmetical principles. Thereupon hope spreads her wings to the fullest extent and all obstacles seem removed. It is admitted that of itself, and through its own force, the theory engenders its own application; it suffices for men to decree or accept the social compact to acquire, under this same act, at once a capacity for comprehending it and the disposition to carry it out.

Such trust, marvellous, and, at the first glance, inexplicable, supposes, in regard to man, an idea which we no longer possess. Man, indeed, was regarded as essentially good and reasonable. Reasonable, that is to say capable of assenting to a clearly defined principle, of following an ulterior chain of arguments, of understanding and accepting a final conclusion, of extracting for himself, on the occasion calling for it, the varied consequences to which it leads: such is the ordinary man in the eyes of the writers of the day; they judge him by themselves. To them the human intellect is their own, the classic intellect. For a hundred and fifty years it rules in literature, in philosophy, in science, in education, in conversation, by virtue of tradition, of usage and of good taste. No other is tolerated and no other is imagined, and if, within this closed circle, a stranger succeeds in introducing himself it is on condition of adopting the oratorical idiom which the *raison raisonnante* imposes on all its guests, on Greeks, Englishmen, barbarians, peasants and savages, however

different from each other and however different they may
be amongst themselves. In Buffon, the first man, on
narrating the first hours of his being, analyses his sensations, emotions and impulses, with as much subtlety as
Condillac himself. With Diderot, Otou the Otaheitian,
with Bernardin de St Pierre, a semi-savage Hindu and an
old colonist of the Île-de-France, with Rousseau a country
vicar, a gardener and a juggler are accomplished con-
versationists and moralists. In Marmontel and in Florian,
in all the literature of inferior rank preceding or accom-
panying the Revolution, also in the tragic or comic drama,
the chief talent of the personage, whoever he may be,
whether an uncultivated rustic, tattooed barbarian or
naked savage, consists in explaining himself, in arguing and
in following an abstract discourse with intelligence and
attention, in tracing for himself, or in the footsteps of a
guide, the rectilinear pathway of general ideas. Thus, to
observers in the eighteenth century, reason is everywhere and she stands alone in the world. A form of intellect
so universal necessarily strikes them as natural; they
resemble people who, speaking but one language, and one
they have always spoken with facility, cannot imagine
any other language being spoken or that they may be
surrounded by the deaf and the dumb. And so much the
more inasmuch as their theory authorizes this prejudice.
According to the new ideology all minds are within reach
of all truths. If the mind does not attain to them the fault
is ours in not being properly prepared; it will attain to
them if we take the trouble to guide it properly. For it
has senses the same as our own, and sensations, revived,
combined and noted by signs, suffice to form 'not only all
our conceptions but again all our faculties'. An exact and
constant filiation of ideas attaches our simplest percep-
tions to the most complex sciences and, from the lowest to

the highest degree, a scale is practicable; if the scholar stops on the way it is owing to our having left too great an interval between two degrees of the scale; let no intermediary degrees be omitted and he will mount to the top of it. To this exalted idea of the faculties of man is added a no less exalted idea of his heart. Rousseau having declared this to be naturally good, the refined class plunge into the belief with all the exaggerations of fashion and all the sentimentality of the drawing-room. The conviction is widespread that man, and especially the man of the people, is sensitive and affectionate by nature, that he is immediately impressed by benefactions and disposed to be grateful for them, that he softens at the slightest sign of interest in him, and that he is capable of every refinement. A series of engravings represents two children in a dilapidated cottage, one five and the other three years of age, by the side of an infirm grandmother, one supporting her head and the other giving her drink; the father and mother enter and, on seeing this touching incident, 'these good people find themselves so happy in possessing such children they forget they are poor'. 'Oh, my father,' cries a shepherd youth of the Pyrenees, 'accept this faithful dog, so true to me for seven years; in future let him follow and defend you, for never will he have served me so usefully.' It would require too much space to follow in the literature of the end of the century, from Marmontel to Bernardin de Saint-Pierre, and from Florian to Berquin and Bitaubé, the interminable repetition of these sweet insipidities. The illusion even reaches statesmen. 'Sire,' says Turgot, on presenting the king with a plan of political education, 'I venture to assert that in ten years your nation will no longer be recognizable, and through enlightenment and good morals, in intelligent zeal for your service and for the country, it will rise above all other nations. Children who are now ten years of age will then be men prepared for the state, loving their country, submissive to authority, not through fear but through reason, aiding their fellow citizens, and accustomed to recognizing and respecting justice.' In the month of January 1789, Necker, to whom M. de Bouillé pointed out the imminent danger arising from the inevitable usurpation of the Third Estate, 'coldly replied, turning his eyes upward, "Reliance must be placed on the moral virtues of man."' In the main, on the imagination forming any conception of human society, this consists of a vague, semi-bucolic, semi-theatric scene, somewhat resembling those displayed on the frontispieces of the illustrated works on morals and politics. Half-naked men, with others clothed in skins, assemble together under a large oak tree; in the centre of the group a venerable old man arises and makes an address, using 'the language of nature and reason', proposing that all should be united, and explaining how men are bound together by mutual obligations; he shows them the harmony of private and of public interests, and ends by making them sensible of the beauties of virtue. All utter shouts of joy, embrace each other, gather round the speaker and elect him chief magistrate; dancing is going on under the branches in the background and henceforth happiness on earth is fully established. This is no exaggeration. The National Assembly addresses the nation in harangues of this style. For many years the government speaks to the people as it would to one of Gessner's shepherds. The peasants are entreated not to burn castles because it is painful for their good king to see such sights. They are exhorted 'to surprise him with their virtues in order that he may be the sooner rewarded for his own'. At the height of the Jacquerie tumults the sages of the day seem to think they are living in a state of pastoral simplicity and that with an air on the flute they may restore to its fold the howling pack of bestial animosities and unchained appetites.

It is a sad thing to fall asleep in a sheepcot and, on awakening, to find the sheep transformed into wolves. And yet, in case of a revolution, this is what we may expect. What we call reason in man is not an innate endowment, primitive and enduring, but a tardy acquisition and a fragile composition. The slightest physiological knowledge suffices to show that it is a state of unstable equilibrium, dependent on the no less greater instability of the brain, nerves, circulation and digestion. Take women that are hungry and men that have been drinking; place a thousand of these together, and let them excite each other with their exclamations, their anxieties and the contagious reaction of their ever increasing emotions; it will not be long before you find them a crowd of dangerous maniacs. This is evident in 1789 and more besides. Now, interrogate psychology. The simplest mental operation, a sensuous perception, an act of memory, the appliance of a name, an ordinary act of judgment is the play of complicated mechanism, the joint and final result of several millions of wheels which, like those of a clock, turn and propel blindly, each for itself, each through its own force, and each kept in place and in functional activity by a system of balance and compensation. If the hands mark the hour with any degree of accuracy it is due to a wonderful if not miraculous conjunction, while hallucination, delirium and monomania, ever at the door, are always ready to enter it. Properly speaking man is imbecile, as the body is morbid, by nature; the health of our minds, like the health of our organs, is simply a repeated achievement and a happy accident. If such happens to be the case with the coarse woof and canvas, with the large and approxi-matively strong threads of our intellect, what risks are imminent for the ulterior and superadded embroidery, the subtle and complicated netting forming reason properly so called and which is composed of general ideas? Formed by a slow and delicate process of weaving, through a long system of signs, amidst the agitations of pride, of enthusi-asm and of dogmatic obstinacy, how many chances there are, even in the most perfect brain, of these ideas inade-quately corresponding with outward things! All that we require in this connection is to witness the operation of the idyll in vogue with the philosophers and politicians. These being the superior minds, what can be said of the masses of the people, of the uncultivated or semi-cultivated brains? Not only is reason crippled in man, but it is rare in humanity. General ideas and accurate reasoning are found only in a select few. The comprehension of abstract terms and the habit of making accurate deductions require previous and special preparation, a prolonged mental exercise and steady practice, and besides this, where political matters are concerned, a degree of composure which, affording every facility for reflection, enables a man to detach himself for a moment from himself for the consideration of his interests as a disinterested observer. If one of these conditions is wanting, reason, especially in relation to politics, is absent. In a peasant or a villager, in any man brought up from infancy to manual labour, not only is the network of superior conceptions defective, but again the internal machinery by which they are woven is not perfected. Accustomed to the open air, to the exercise of his limbs, his attention flags if he stands inactive for a quarter of an hour; generalized expressions find their way into his mind only as sound; the mental com-bination they ought to excite cannot be produced. He becomes drowsy unless a powerful vibrating voice contagiously arouses in him the instincts of flesh and blood, the personal cravings, the secret enmities which, restrained by outward discipline, are always ready to be set free. In the half-cultivated mind, even with the man who thinks himself cultivated and who reads the newspapers, principles are generally disproportionate guests; they are above his comprehension; he does not measure their bearings, he does not appreciate their limitations, he is insensible to their restrictions and he falsifies their application. They are like those preparations of the laboratory which, harmless in the chemist's hands, become destructive in the street under the feet of passing people. Too soon will this be apparent when, in the name of popular sovereignty, each commune, each mob, shall regard itself as the nation and act accordingly; when reason, in the hands of its new interpreters, shall inaugurate riots in the streets and peasant insurrections in the fields.

This is owing to the philosophers of the age having been mistaken in two ways. Not only is reason not natural to man nor universal in humanity, but again, in the conduct of man and of humanity, its influence is small. Except with a few cool and clear intellects, a Fontenelle, a Hume, a Gibbon, with whom it may prevail because it encounters no rivals, it is very far from playing the leading part; it belongs to other forces born within us, and which, by virtue of being the first-comers, remain in possession of the field. The place obtained by reason is always restricted; the office it fulfils is generally secondary. Openly or secretly, it is only a convenient subaltern, a domestic advocate unceasingly suborned, employed by the proprietors to plead in their behalf; if they yield it precedence in public it is only through decorum. Vainly do they proclaim it the recognized sovereign; they grant

it only a passing authority, and, under its nominal
control, they remain the inward masters. These masters
of man consist of physical temperament, bodily needs,
animal instinct, hereditary prejudice, imagination, generally the dominant passion, and more particularly personal
or family interest, also that of caste or party. We should
labour under serious error were we to suppose ourselves
naturally good, generous, sympathetic or, even at the
least, gentle, pliable and ready to sacrifice ourselves to
social interests or to those of others. There are several of
them, and of the most powerful kind, and which, if left to
themselves, would make only havoc. In the first place, if
there is no certainty of man being a remote blood cousin
of the monkey, it is at least certain that, in his structure,
he is an animal closely related to the monkey, provided
with canine teeth, carnivorous, formerly cannibal and,
therefore, a hunter and bellicose. Hence there is in him a
steady substratum of brutality and ferocity, and of violent
and destructive instincts, to which must be added, if he is
French, gaiety, laughter and a strange propensity to
gambol and act insanely in the havoc he makes; — we
shall see him at work. In the second place, at the outset, his
condition casts him naked and destitute on an ungrateful
soil on which subsistence is difficult, where, at the risk of
death, he is obliged to save and to economize. Hence a
constant preoccupation and the rooted idea of acquiring,
accumulating and possessing, rapacity and avarice, more
particularly in the class which, tied to the glebe, fasts for
sixty generations in order to support other classes and
whose crooked fingers are always outstretched to clutch
the soil whose fruits they cause to grow; — we shall see
this class at work. Finally, his more delicate mental organization makes of him from the earliest days an imaginative
being in which swarming fancies develop themselves into

monstrous chimeras to expand his hopes, fears and desires
beyond all bounds. Hence an excess of sensibility, sudden
outbursts of emotion, contagious transports, irresistible
currents of passion, epidemics of credulity and suspicion,
in short, enthusiasm and panic, especially if he is French,
that is to say, excitable and communicative, easily thrown
off his balance and prompt to accept foreign impulsion,
deprived of the natural ballast which a phlegmatic temperament and the concentration of lonely meditations
secure to his German or Latin neighbours; — and all this
we shall see at work. These constitute some of the brute
forces that control human life. In ordinary times we pay
no attention to them; being subordinated they do not
seem to us formidable. We take it for granted that they
are allayed and pacified; we flatter ourselves that the
discipline imposed on them has made them natural, and
that by dint of flowing between dykes they are settled
down into their accustomed beds. The truth is that, like
all brute forces, like a stream or a torrent, they remain in
these only under constraint; it is the dyke which, through
its resistance, produces this moderation. Another force
equal to their force had to be installed against their
outbreaks and devastations, graduated according to their
scale, all the firmer as they are more menacing, despotic
if need be against their despotism, in any event constrain-
ing and repressive, at the outset a feudal chief, later an
army general, all modes consisting in an elective or hereditary gendarme, possessing vigilant eyes and vigorous arms,
and who, with blows, excites fear and, through fear,
maintains order. In the regulation and limitation of his
blows divers instrumentalities are employed, a pre-
established constitution, a division of powers, a code of
laws, tribunals and legal formalities. At the bottom of
all these wheels ever appears the principal lever, the

efficacious instrument, namely, the gendarme armed against the savage, brigand and madman each of us harbours, in repose or manacled, but always living, in the recesses of his own breast.

On the contrary, in the new theory, every principle promulged, every precaution taken, every suspicion awakened is aimed at the gendarme. In the name of the sovereignty of the people all authority is withdrawn from the government, every prerogative, every initiative, its continuance and its force. The people being sovereign the government is simply its clerk, and less than its clerk, merely its domestic. Between them 'no contract' indefinite or at least enduring, 'and which may be cancelled only by mutual consent or the unfaithfulness of one of the two parties'. 'It is against the nature of a political body for the sovereign to impose a law on himself which he cannot set aside.' There is no sacred and inviolable charter 'binding a people to the forms of an established constitution'. 'The right to change these is the first guarantee of all rights.' 'There is not, and can never be, any fundamental, obligatory law for the entire body of a people, not even the social contract.' It is through usurpation and deception that a prince, an assembly and a body of magistrates declare themselves representatives of the people. 'Sovereignty is not to be represented for the same reason that it is not to be alienated ... The moment a people gives itself representatives it is no longer free, it exists no more ... The English people think themselves free but they deceive themselves; they are free only during an election of members of parliament; on the election of these they become slaves and are null ... The deputies of the people are not, nor can they be, its representatives; they are simply its commissioners and can establish no final compact. Every law not ratified by the people themselves is null and is no law.' 'A body of laws sanctioned by an assembly of the people through a fixed constitution of the state, does not suffice; other fixed and periodical assemblies are necessary which cannot be abolished or prorogued, or arranged that on a given day the people may be legitimately convoked by the law, no other formal convocation being requisite ... The moment the people are thus assembled the jurisdiction of the government is to cease and the executive power is to be suspended', society commencing anew, while citizens, restored to their primitive independence, may reconstitute at will, for any period they determine, the provisional contract to which they have assented only for a determined time. 'The opening of these assemblies, whose sole object is to maintain the social compact, should always take place with two propositions, never suppressed and which are to be passed on separately; the first one, *whether the sovereign is willing to maintain the actual form of the government*; and the second, *whether the people are willing to leave its administration in the hands of those actually performing its duties*.' This, 'the act by which a people is subject to its chiefs is absolutely only a commission, a service in which, as simple officers of their sovereign, they exercise in his name the power of which he has made them depositaries and which he may modify, limit and resume at pleasure'. Not only does it always reserve to itself 'the legislative power which belongs to it and which can belong only to it', but again, it delegates and withdraws the executive power according to its fancy. Those who exercise it are its employees. 'It may establish and depose them when it pleases.' In relation to it they have no rights. 'It is not a matter of contract with them but one of obedience'; they have 'no conditions' to prescribe; they cannot demand of it the fulfilment of any engagement. It is useless to raise the objection that, according to this, every man of spirit or of culture will decline our offices and that our chiefs will bear the character of lackeys. We will not leave them the freedom of accepting or declining office; we impose it on them authoritatively. 'In every true democracy the magistrature is not an advantage but an onerous burden, not to be assigned to one more than to another.' We can lay hands on our magistrates, take them by the collar and seat them on their benches in their own despite. By fair means or foul they are the working subjects (*corvéables*) of the state, in a lower condition than a valet or a mechanic, since the mechanic does his work according to acceptable conditions and the discharged valet can claim his eight days' notice to quit. When government throws off this humble attitude it usurps, while constitutions are to proclaim that, in such an event, insurrection is not only the most sacred right but the most imperative duty.

Practice, accordingly, accompanies the theory, and the dogma of the sovereignty of the people, interpreted by the mass, is to produce a perfect anarchy, up to the moment when, interpreted by its chiefs, it produces a perfect despotism.

For there are two sides to this theory; whilst one side leads to the perpetual demolition of government, the other terminates in the illimitable dictation of the state. The new contract is not a historical fact like the English Declaration of Rights in 1688 or the Dutch federation in 1579, entered into by actual and living individuals, admitting acquired situations, groups already formed, established positions, and drawn up to recognize, define, guarantee and complete an anterior right. Antecedent to the social contract no veritable right exists; for veritable rights are born solely out of the social contract, the only valid one, since it is the only one agreed upon between beings perfectly equal and perfectly free, so many abstract creatures, so many species of mathematical units, all of the same value, all playing the same part and whose inequality or constraint never disturbs the common understanding. Hence, at the moment of its completion, all other pacts are nullified. Property, family, Church, no ancient institution may invoke any right against the new state. The area on which it is built up must be considered vacant; if old structures are partly allowed to remain it is only in its name and for its benefit, to be enclosed within its barriers and appropriated to its use; the entire soil of humanity is its property. On the other hand it is not, according to the American doctrine, an association for mutual protection, a society like other societies, circumscribed in its purpose, restricted to its office, limited in its powers, and by which individuals, reserving to themselves the better portion of their property and persons, assess each other for the maintenance of an army, a policy, tribunals, highways, schools, in short, the major instrumentalities of public safety and utility, at the same time withholding the remainder of local, general, spiritual and material services in favour of private initiative and of spontaneous associations that may arise as occasion or necessity calls for them. Our state is not to be a simple utilitarian machine, a convenient, handy implement, of which the workman avails himself without abandoning the free use of his hand, or the simultaneous use of other implements. Being elder born, the only son and sole representative of reason, it must, to ensure its sway, leave nothing beyond its grasp. In this respect the old regime paves the way for the new one, while the established system inclines minds beforehand to the budding theory. Through administrative centralization the state already, for a long time, has its hands everywhere. 'You must know', says Law to the Marquis d'Argenson, 'that the kingdom of France is governed by thirty intendants. You have neither parliaments, assemblies or governors, simply thirty masters of requests, provincial clerks, on whom depends the happiness or misery, the fruitfulness or sterility of these provinces.' The king, in fact, sovereign, father and universal guardian, manages local affairs through his delegates and intervenes in private affairs through his pardons or *lettres de cachet*. Such an example and such a course followed for fifty years excites the imagination. No other instrumentality is better calculated to effect reforms on a large scale and at one stroke. Hence, far from restricting the central power the economists are desirous of extending its action. Instead of setting up new dykes against it they interest themselves only in destroying what is left of the old dykes still interfering with it. 'The system of counter-forces in a government', say Quesnay and his disciples, 'is a fatal idea ... The speculations on which the system of counterbalance is founded are chimerical ... Let the government have a full comprehension of its duties and be left free ... The state must govern according to the essential laws of order and in this case unlimited power is requisite.' On the approach of the Revolution the same doctrine reappears except in the substitution of one term for another term. In the place of the sovereignty of the king the *Contrat social* substitutes the sovereignty of the people. The latter, however, is much more absolute than the former, and, in the democratic convent which Rousseau constructs, on the Spartan and Roman model, the individual is nothing and the state everything.

In effect, 'the clauses of the social contract reduce themselves to one, namely, the total transfer of each associate with all his rights to the community.' Everyone surrenders himself entirely, 'just as he stands, he and all his forces and of which his property forms a portion'. There is no exception nor reservation; whatever he may have been previously and whatever may have belonged to him is no longer his own. Henceforth whatever he becomes or whatever he may possess devolves on him only through the delegation of the social body, the universal proprietor and absolute master. All rights must be vested in the state and none in the individual; otherwise there would be litigation between them, and, 'as there is no common superior to decide between them', their litigation would never end. On the contrary, through the complete donation which each one makes of himself, 'the unity is as perfect as possible'; having renounced all and renounced himself, 'he has no further claim to make'.

This being admitted, let us trace the consequences. In the first place, I enjoy my property only through tolerance and at second-hand; for, according to the social contract, I have surrendered it; 'it now forms a portion of the national estate'; if I retain the use of it for the time being it is through a concession of the state which makes me a 'depositary' of it. And this favour must not be considered as a restitution. 'Far from accepting the property of individuals, society despoils them of it, simply converting the usurpation into a veritable right, the enjoyment of it into proprietorship.' Previous to the social contract I was possessor not by right in fact, and even unjustly if I had large possessions; for, 'every man has naturally a right to whatever he needs', and I was robbing other men of all that I possessed beyond my subsistence. Hence, so far from the state being under obligation to me, I am under obligation to it, the property which it returns to me not being mine but that with which the state favours me. It follows, accordingly, that the state may impose conditions on its gift, limit the use I may make of it according to its fancy, restrict and regulate my disposition of it, my right to bequeath it. 'According to nature, the right of property does not extend beyond the life of its owner; the moment he dies his possessions are no longer his own. Thus, to prescribe the conditions on which he may dispose of it is really less to change his right in appearance than to extend it in effect.' In any event as my title is an effect of the social contract it is precarious like the contract itself; a new stipulation suffices to limit it or to destroy it. 'The sovereign may legitimately appropriate to himself all property as was done in Sparta in the time of Lycurgus.' In our laical convent whatever each monk possesses is only a revocable gift by the convent.

In the second place, this convent is a seminary. I have no right to bring up my children in my own house and in my own way. 'As the reason of each man must not be the sole arbiter of his rights so much less should the education of children, which is of more consequence to the state than to fathers, be left to the intelligence and prejudices of their fathers.' 'If public authority, taking the place of fathers in assuming this important function, acquires their rights in fulfilling their duties, they have so much the less reason to complain inasmuch as they merely undergo a change of name, and, under the title of citizens, exercise in common the same authority over their children that they have separately exercised under the title of fathers.' In other words you cease to be a father, but, in exchange, become a school inspector; one is as good as the other and what complaint have you to make? Such was the case in that perpetual army called Sparta; there, the children, genuine regimental children, equally obeyed all properly formed men. Thus, 'public education, within laws prescribed by the government and under magistrates appointed by sovereign will, is one of the fundamental maxims of popular or legitimate government'. Through this the citizen is formed in advance. 'It gives the national form to souls. Nations, in the long run, are what the government makes them — soldiers, citizens, men when so disposed, a populace, *canaille* if it pleases,' being fashioned by their education. 'Would you obtain an idea of public education? Read Plato's *Republic* ... The best social institutions are those the best qualified to change man's nature, to destroy his absolute being, to give him a relative being, and to convert *self* into the common unity, so that each individual may not regard himself as one by himself, but a part of the unity and no longer sensitive but through the whole. An infant, on opening its eyes, must behold the common patrimony and, to the day of its death, behold that only ... He should be disciplined so as never to contemplate the individual except in his relations with the body of the state.' Such was the practice of Sparta, and the sole aim of the 'great Lycurgus'. 'All being equal through the law, they must be brought up together and in the same manner.' 'The law must regulate the subjects, the order and the form of their studies.' They must, at the very least, take part in public exercises, in horse-races, in the games of strength and of agility instituted 'to accustom them to law, equality, fraternity and competition'; to teach them how 'to live under the eyes of their fellow citizens and to crave public applause'. Through these games they become democrats from their early youth, since, the prizes being awarded, not through the arbitrament of masters, but through the cheers of spectators, they accustom themselves to recognizing as sovereign the legitimate sovereignty, consisting of the verdict of the assembled people. The important interest of the state is, always, to form the wills of those by which it lasts, to prepare the votes that are to maintain it, to uproot passions in the soul that might be opposed to it, to implant passions that will prove favourable to it, to fix firmly within the breasts of its future citizens the sentiments and prejudices it will at some time need. If it does not secure the children it will not possess the adults. Novices in a convent must be educated as monks, otherwise, when they grow up, the convent will no longer exist.

Finally, our lay convent has its own religion, a lay religion. If I possess any other it is through its condescension and under restrictions. It is, by nature, hostile to other associations than its own; they are rivals, they annoy it, they absorb the will and pervert the votes of its members. 'To ensure a full declaration of the general will it is an important matter not to allow any special society in the state, and that each citizen should determine for himself alone.' 'Whatever breaks up social unity is worthless', and it would be better for the state if there were no Church. Not only is every Church suspicious, but, if I am a Christian, my belief is regarded unfavourably. According to this new legislator, 'nothing is more opposed to the social spirit than Christianity ... A society of true Christians would no longer form a society of men.' For, 'the Christian patrimony is not of this world'. It cannot zealously serve the state, being bound by its conscience to support tyrants. Its law 'preaches only servitude and dependence ... it is made for a slave', and never will a citizen be made out of a slave. '*Christian republic*, each of these two words excludes the other.' Therefore, if the future republic allows me to remain a Christian, it must be on the understood condition that my doctrine shall be shut up in my mind, without even affecting my heart. If I am a Catholic (and twenty-five out of twenty-six million

Frenchmen are like me), my condition is worse. For the social pact does not tolerate an intolerant religion; any sect that condemns other sects is a public enemy; 'whoever presumes to say that *there is no salvation out of the Church* must be driven out of the state.' Should I be, finally, a free-thinker, a positivist or sceptic, my situation is little better. 'There is a civil religion', a catechism, 'a profession of faith, of which the sovereign has the right to dictate the articles, not exactly as religious dogmas but as sentiments of social import without which we cannot be a good citizen or a loyal subject'. These articles embrace 'the existence of a powerful, intelligent, beneficent, foreseeing and provident divinity, the future life, the happiness of the good, the punishment of the wicked, the sacredness of the social contract and of the laws. Without forcing anyone to believe in this creed, whoever does not believe in it must be expelled from the state; it is necessary to banish such persons not on account of impiety, but as unsociable beings, incapable of sincerely loving law and justice and, if need be, of giving up life for duty.' Take heed that this profession of faith be not a vain one, for a new inquisition is to test its sincerity. 'Should any person, after having publicly assented to these dogmas, act as an unbeliever let him be punished with death. He has committed the greatest of crimes: he has lied before the law.' Truly, as I said above, we belong to a convent.

EDOUARD DRUMONT
(1844–1917)

A journalist of peasant origin who devoted his life to the fight against the money power which he thought rested with the Jews. In 1886 he published *La France Juive* in two volumes, a massive indictment of the Jewish takeover in France and the rest of Europe. A popular edition followed. The work made him famous and he founded the *Libre Parole*, a newspaper of nationalist and anti-semitic sentiment where he exposed the Panama scandal in 1892. Drumont's anti-semitism was coarse and plebian, so that coupled with the civilized, literary and aristocratic anti-semitism of Barrès, the anti-semites covered the whole market, by catering for all possible tastes. The very crudity of Drumont's anti-semitism was an advantage. Drumont had already attacked Ferdinand Dreyfus in the *Libre Parole* before the Dreyfus affair broke. No one seemed to notice that Alfred was no relation, and Drumont was not the one to point this out. The name Dreyfus was as common as Lévy or Mayer, and could stand as a general symbol for the Jews. The Jewish conquest was not confined to France. Unlike many of his allies on the right, notably Déroulède, Drumont was not concerned with *revanche*; for him 1870 was not a just defeat for France. That was the simpleton's view. On the contrary, both Aryan peoples had been the victims of a quarrel engendered by Jewish high finance which needed a war to enable Rothschild and Bleichroeder to combine to plunder France. A new war would be a repetition of a faked Jews' quarrel. Drumont was deputy for Algiers 1898–1902, but gradually lost influence as the *Action Française* gained it.

The following extract, translated by R. H. L. Phillipson, is taken from the first volume of *La France Juive*.

From the outset of this study, we must try to analyse this singular, vivacious and unique individual, the Jew. At first glance, the task seems to be easy. No other human type has such a strikingly distinctive physiognomy, or retained the characteristics of his first incarnation with greater authenticity. The difficulty is that our own preconceptions prevent us from understanding and describing the Jew truthfully; our own point of view is totally different from his.

The common man says the Jew is cowardly, but the lesson of eighteen centuries of persecution borne with incredible powers of endurance is that even if the Jew does not have the spirit of a fighter, the way he resists is courage indeed. And when certain rich men, who used to be held in high esteem, can be seen to work for a government which goes against all their beliefs, can we seriously consider as cowardly a people who have been prepared to suffer every indignity rather than renounce their faith?

'The Jew makes a cult of money.' This is an assertion of an obvious fact, but for most people expressing this feeling it is bombast.

There are great lords and pious women, and people who frequent Sainte-Astilde and Saint-Thomas d'Aquin who after church exchange profuse salaams with one of the Rothschilds who considers the Christ they adore as the basest of impostors. Who obliges them to go there? Has the Amphitryon which attracts them an outstanding mind? Is he a brilliant conversationalist? Has he rendered services to France? In no way. He is a foreigner, a reticent, capricious German who is often rude to the aristocratic guests that he is vain enough to invite to his house.

What brings these representatives of the nobility under this roof? Respect for money. How are they occupied there? They kneel before the golden calf.

The remark made about the Duke of La Rochefoucauld-Bisaccia is also true of the Duke of Aumale. When he arrives, looking humble, to pay his respects to Rothschild, who calls him 'the old sergeant-major', one cannot avoid the conclusion that by not staying at home in comfort to re-read the glorious history of his race, the descendant of the Condé is admitting that earning a lot of money by more or less honest speculation is equivalent to winning the battle of Rocroi; after all, one only visits one's equals, and he calls on these people.

At heart, all those people who despise money are quite happy when people who have plenty are prepared to share the fruits of it with them. After their fall from grace, they are the first to poke a little fun at themselves.

'Do you want to see how blood speaks?' a French duke once asked his friends. He had married a Rothschild from Frankfurt in spite of his mother's tears. He called his little son, pulled a golden louis from his pocket and showed it to him. The child's eyes lit up. 'You see,' continued the duke, 'the semitic instinct reveals itself straight away.'

Let us now leave aside these commonplaces. Let us see how a more attentive and serious examination will reveal the essential features distinguishing Jews from other men, and let us begin by an ethnographical, physiological and psychological comparison of the Semite and the Aryan. They represent two distinct races which are irremediably hostile to each other, whose antagonism has filled the world in the past and will disturb it even more in the future.

The generic term Aryan comes from a Sanskrit word meaning noble, illustrious and high-minded, and is commonly applied to the superior branch of the white race, the Indo-European family which had its cradle in the vast plains of Iran. The Aryan race spread out across the world in successive waves of migration ... [the Greeks and Romans] had as their frontier the shores of the Hellespont and the Mediterranean but the Celts, the Ario-Slavs and the Ario-Germans headed west, went round the Caspian Sea and crossed the Danube.

To quote from Littré:

All the evidence points to the fact that the Romans were Aryans. The Latin they spoke is clear proof of this. It was a complete surprise when Latin and Greek were authoritatively shown to be related and were classed with Persian and Sanskrit as members of one and the same family.

The Christians of Western Europe are the direct descendants of the Romans, and by virtue of this, they are seized of all the rights of their progenitors. But that is not all: when their credentials are examined in the light of linguistic science, then Christians are seen to be Aryans in their own right. The Italians are Latins, and as such are obviously Aryans. So too are the Celts of Gaul and Albion: Celtic is a dialect of a language spoken by many tribes, some of which dispersed to the far ends of the West. It was from one of these emigrant tribes that Germany took its language, and hence can be called Aryan like the others. The only doubtful case is that of Spain. Its people are Iberians who are not indebted to the Aryans either for their language or their race. However the government of Rome, by dint of long occupation and their superior civilization, obliged them to speak Latin, and, in spite of early divergencies, it is no longer possible to separate Iberians from the Gauls and the Italians, who are all brothers by education.[1]

It can be seen thus that all the nations of Europe are very closely linked to the Aryan race, from which have sprung all the great civilizations.

The Semitic race consists of diverse purities, the Aramaic, the Hebrews and the Arab, which seem to have come originally from the plains of Mesopotamia.

Doubtless Tyre, Sidon and Carthage did for a time achieve a high degree of commercial prosperity. Later on, the Arab Empire knew a fleeting glory, but nothing about those ephemeral states was comparable to the fertile, durable civilizations of Greece and Rome, and the admirable Christian society of the Middle Ages.

The Aryan or Indo-European race is the only one to uphold the principles of justice, to experience freedom and to value beauty.

M. Gellion-Danglar states in *The Semites and Semitism*:

The Semitic civilizations, however brilliant they might appear, are only vain images, more or less coarse parodies, painted cardboard pictures which some people are gullible enough to take as works of marble and bronze. In these artificial societies, whims and pleasure are everything; the word 'justice' had been prostituted as a cover for them, and means nothing. The bizarre and the monstrous are what they consider beautiful and superabundance has banished taste and decency from their art. The Semite is not suitable for

[1] Emile Littré (1801–81), positivist, politician and erudite; founder of the *Revue de philosophie positive*.

civilization and the sedentary life. In his tent in the desert he has his beauty, and his own grandeur. He leads his own life. He is in harmony with the rest of humanity. Elsewhere he is out of place: all his qualities disappear, his vices show their face. The Semite, a man of prey in the Arabian sands, not without a certain heroism, becomes in society a man of vile intrigues.

Ever since the dawn of history the Aryan has been at odds with the Semite. Ilion was a completely Semitic town, and the Trojan war was particularly momentous because it was a duel between two races. This conflict has continued over the ages, and it was almost invariably the Semite who sparked off a clash, only to be repulsed.

In fact the Semite has dreamt constantly, obsessively of reducing the Aryan into a state of slavery, and tying him to the land. He tried to achieve this through war. Littré, with his customary clarity, has revealed the true nature of the great invasions which almost gave the Semite world hegemony. Hannibal was very near to it when he camped outside the walls of Rome. Abd ar-Rahman[1] conquered Spain, went as far north as Poitiers, with some grounds for hoping Europe would be his. The ruins of Carthage, and the bones of Saracens which the plough sometimes throws up in the fields of Charles Martel's triumph, are testimony to the lesson such presumption had to learn.

Today the Semites believe their victory is certain. It is no longer the Carthaginian or the Saracen, who is in the vanguard, it is the Jew — he has replaced violence with

[1] The first Emir of Cordoba, whose intention of further European conquest was frustrated by Charlemagne; the battle of Roncevalles took place during his emirate (778).

cunning. Dangerous invasion has given way to silent, progressive and slow encroachment. The noisy armed hordes have been replaced by single individuals, gradually forming little groups, advancing sporadically, unobtrusively occupying all the jobs, from the lowest of all to the highest in the land. Instead of making a frontal assault, the Semites have attacked Europe from behind. They have outflanked it. In the country round Vilna, the *Vagina Judaeorum*, a succession of exoduses were organized: Germany was occupied, the Vosges Mountains were crossed and France conquered.

No violence has been used, and I dwell on this point, but there has been a sort of gentle takeover, an insinuating process of hunting the indigenous people from their houses and jobs, of gently stripping them first of their property, then of their traditions and customs, and finally of their religion. I believe this last element will prove to be a stumbling-block.

The two races are doomed to come into conflict, because of both their qualities and their shortcomings. The Semite is mercantile, covetous, scheming, subtle and cunning. The Aryan is enthusiastic, heroic, chivalrous, disinterested, frank and trusting to the point of naïvety. The Semite is earth-bound with scarcely any concern for the life hereafter; the Aryan is a child of heaven who is constantly preoccupied by higher aspirations. One lives in the world of reality, the other in the world of the ideal.

The Semite is a businessman by instinct; he is a born trader, dealing in everything imaginable, seizing every opportunity to get the better of the next man. The Aryan on the other hand is a peasant, a poet, a monk and, above all, a soldier. On the battlefield he is really in his element, he happily affronts danger and braves death.

The Semite has no creative ability, whereas the Aryan

is an inventor. Not a single invention has been the work
of a Semite. He exploits, organizes and produces whatever
the creative Aryan has invented, and, needless to say,
retains the profits for himself.

The Aryan is an adventurer, and discovered America.
The Semite then had an admirable opportunity to leave
Europe behind and escape persecution, and, in so doing,
to show he was capable of doing something on his own, but
he waited until all the pioneer exploration had been
accomplished, until the land was under cultivation, before
going off to get rich at the expense of others.

To sum up, anything which takes man on to unfamiliar
paths, anything which involves an effort to extend man's
knowledge of this earthly sphere, is quite beyond the
Semite, and above all, the Jew. He can live only at the
common expense, within a society which he did not help
to build. What is unfortunate for the Semite – and this
crucial observation should be remembered in my memory
– is that he always goes just a little bit too far for the
Aryan.

The Aryan is a good-natured giant. He is happy whenever the needs of his romantic imagination are satisfied
by a recital of one of the old legends. He is not amused
by such stories as the Semitic *Thousand and One Nights*,
in which singers find hoards of treasure, or fishermen
throw their nets into the sea and draw them in full of
diamonds. For him to be moved, he needs to be able to
see a noble figure standing out from the backcloth of
fantasy, like Parsifal meeting a thousand dangers in his
conquest of the Holy Grail, his cup filled with the blood
of God.

The Aryan has remained as ingenuous as he was in the
Middle Ages, swooning over the *chansons de geste*, or the
adventures of Garin le Lorrain, Olivier de Béthune or

Gilbert de Roussillon,[1] who, after refusing to marry the daughter of a sultan, ran through five thousand infidels with a single blow from his lance. The legend of 1789 is listened to attentively, as though it was the account of a cycle from the days of chivalry. The editors of the *République française*[2] might almost make him believe that the members of the Government of National Defence, mounted on fiery steeds like knights of old, had braved the most terrible dangers in order to win the battle for a Morgan loan.[3] And while the Aryan takes a naive interest in such acts of valour, nothing is easier than to deprive him of his purse or even to remove his books, on the pretext that they might impede his advance on the path of progress.

The Aryan, I repeat, will allow anything to be done to him; only he must not be unduly provoked. He can be stripped of all his possessions, and then suddenly fly into a rage over a cherished trifle, such as a rose. Then he jerks out of his stupor, understands the situation at once, seizes the sword which was collecting dust in a corner, lashes out and inflicts a terrible vengeance on the Semite, who was exploiting, pillaging and tricking him, but who will bear the marks of this punishment for three centuries.

Moreover this in no way surprises the Semite. He is by nature an oppressor and is familiar with punishment. There is almost a certain satisfaction in things returning

[1] Legendary heroes of the *chansons de geste*. Garin le Lorrain is the hero and name of one of the series of *chansons de geste*, *La Geste des Lorrains*, dealing with the warfare of two rival families of Lorraine. Olivier de Béthune is one of the heroes of the *Geste du roi* (Charlemagne) and of the *Geste de Garin de Monglane*.

[2] The newspaper founded, *inter alia*, by Gambetta to assure the victory of republican ideas. Stopped publication in 1914.

[3] A scathing reference to the American financier J. Pierpoint Morgan (1837–1913); the implication is that, for Gambetta the Jew, persuading Morgan to lend money is the equivalent of the deeds of the legendary heroes.

to normal. He disappears, fades into the mist, digs his heels in somewhere, and plots how to start all over again in a few centuries' time. By contrast, when he is at peace and happy, he experiences what a witty member of the Académie called '*la nostalgie du san-benito*'.

The Semite, though shrewd and nimble-witted, is in fact of limited intelligence. He has no foresight, he cannot see beyond the end of his hooked nose, and is unable to grasp any of the subtleties which give life its meaning.

It is the Semite's faults which are responsible for the natural antipathy between him and the Aryan continuing over the centuries. If you want to understand the Middle Ages, take a look at what is happening in our own country at the present day.

France, thanks to the principles of 1789 which the Jews had cleverly exploited, was disintegrating. Jews had taken control of the public purse, and invaded all sectors except the army. The representatives of the old families of the aristocracy and the bourgeoisie were split into two classes: one led a life of pleasure, had Jewish mistresses who corrupted or ruined them, and Jewish horse merchants and usurers, who were in league with the girls; the other was drawn by the attraction the Aryan race feels for the Hindu nirvana, the paradise of Odin; they took little interest in contemporary developments, were lost in ecstasy; they barely had a foothold in real life.

If the Jews had been patient for a little longer, they would have been near their aim. One of the few really wise men of their race, Jules Simon,[1] a disciple of Philo, a

[1] Jules Simon (1814–96), professor of philosophy at the Sorbonne, politician of the left centre and Minister of Education in Gambetta's Government of National Defence; anti-Boulangist, publishing in 1889 *Souviens-toi du Deux-Decembre*, 'Remember the Second of December', a reference to the *coup d'état* of Napoleon III on December 2nd, 1851.

representative of the Jewish school of Alexandria, was to give them good advice: occupy the earth quietly and leave the Aryans to emigrate to heaven.

However, the Jews never wanted to listen to such counsel. They preferred the Semite Gambetta[1] to the Semite Simon. Under the pretence that this charlatan had made the French swallow the most incredible humbug, they supported, financed and upheld him. They believed he was going to rid them of the Christ they hated as much as on the day of his crucifixion. The Freemasons contributed, the Jewish newspapers inflamed general opinion, gold was squandered, and large sums were paid to police commissioners, who right until the last moment had refused to cooperate in any crime.

What did happen? Exactly what was described earlier. The Aryan, provoked, worried, his innate feelings of nobility and honour wounded, felt the blood rush to his head when he saw helpless old men being dragged from their rooms by thugs. He needed a little time for reflection to gather his thoughts and collect himself.

'But what is the guiding principle behind these acts?' he asked. 'The principle of liberty,' the newspapers of Porgès, Reinach, Dreyfus, Eugène Mayer, Camille Sée and Naquet answered in chorus.

'What does this principle consist of?'

'Of this: a Jew leaves Hamburg, Frankfurt or Vilna, or anywhere else for that matter, amasses a few million at the expense of the *goym* and then he is universally accepted, and his house inviolable, because he would naturally never be called upon to explain his actions in a court of

---

[1] Leon Gambetta (1838–82), organizer of the resistance to Prussia after the military defeat in 1870, and a leader of the republican left in the Third Republic. Famous for the remark: 'Clericalism, there is the enemy.'

law. A native-born Frenchman, on the other hand, or, to use Saint-Simon's term, a natural Frenchman, divests himself of all his possessions, to give to the poor; he walks barefoot, and lives in a cramped, whitewashed room which Rothschild's servant's servant would object to; he is outside the law and can be thrown into the street like a dog.'

Once the Aryan had woken from his slumber, he judged, not incorrectly, that since his tolerance, of which so much had been made over the past century, had been interpreted in this way, it would be preferable to start giving blows rather than just receiving them; he felt it was high time to wrest the country from such testy masters. 'Since your rough monk's habit gets in the way of your frock-coat, we will replace them with yellow rags, old Semite.' This was the conclusion his meditations led him to. The first anti-semitic, or, to be more precise, anti-Jewish committee, was set up at this period.

The French experience is similar to what has taken place in Germany. The Jews helped the *Kulturkampf*[1] as much as they could, and strove with all their energy to harass the Catholics. The *Kulturkampf* is over and the anti-semitic war is just beginning.

A perusal of the entire book would reveal that the same thing has happened in almost identical circumstances in all ages and in all countries.

It appears that the Jew is in reality obeying an irresistible impulse. The idea of conforming to other people's habits, traditions and religions never occurs to him. You are the ones who have to submit to the Jew, adapt to his customs, and suppress everything he dislikes. None the less, they are quite happy to accept anything from this society of

[1] The attack by Bismarck and the German Empire on Roman Catholic influence on German life and politics.

the past which flatters their vanity. They are grotesquely hasty in seeking for the military titles 'baron' and 'count', which are about as suitable for these manipulators of money as a woman's hat is for a monkey. Even the most abject speculator or nut and bolt merchant with close or distant ties with Israel is at least a knight of the *Légion d'honneur*. But there his condescension is at an end: any of our customs which shocks him must go.

The Jew's right to oppress other people is rooted in his religion; for him it is an article of faith; it is proclaimed in every line of the Bible and the Talmud.

The Psalms of David (Psalm 2): 'I shall give thee the heathen for thine inheritance, and the uttermost parts of the earth for thy possession. Thou shalt break them with a rod of iron; thou shalt dash them in pieces like a potter's vessel.'

Deuteronomy vii: 'And the Lord thy God will put out those nations before thee little by little: thou mayest not consume them at once, lest the beasts of the field increase upon thee. And he shall deliver their kings into thine hand, and thou shalt destroy their name from under heaven: there shall no man be able to stand before thee, until thou have destroyed them.'

Against the Christian, the Gentile, the *goy* (singular *goy*, plural *goym*), all means are good. In their connection the Talmud contains some assertions which our deputies, who are so touchy on theological matters, would do well not to bring up in parliament; otherwise they might be refused service in the Jewish banks where they draw their salaries.

One can and one must kill the best of the *goym*.

The money of the *goym* devolves from the Jew. Thus it is permitted to rob them and deceive them.

The social evolution itself of the Jew is totally different from ours. The typical Aryan family lives in civilization and the Romans *gens* which became the feudal family. For many generations the life force, the genius, lies dormant, and then the tree whose roots sink into the earth brings to the summit an illustrious man who seems to represent all the qualities of his fellow men. This predestined being sometimes takes a century to develop, but from the most humble origins springs forth a figure who is complete, charming and valiant, a hero and a scholar; in the pages of our history many such men can be found.

With the Semitic race, matters are different. In the orient, a camel-driver, a water-carrier or a barber is singled out by his sovereign. He suddenly becomes a pasha, a vizier, the prince's right-hand man, like, for instance, Mustapha-ben-Ismaïl who found his way into the Bardo by selling cakes and who, to borrow M. Dauphin the Attorney General's ribald comment, 'was of service to his master day and night'. As a result our government, dishonest as we know it to be, rewarded him with the cross of grand officer of the *Légion d'honneur*.

It is the same with the Jew. Apart from the priestly class, which constitutes a real aristocracy, there is no nobility. There are no illustrious families; some transmit credit from father to son, there is never a legacy of glory.

In less than twenty years, if he strikes lucky, the Jew achieves his full development. He is born at the bottom of a ghetto, his first venture brings him in a few sous, he sets up in Paris, obtains a decoration thanks to the mediation of some Dreyfus or other, buys a baronetcy, introduces himself boldly to a wide circle, and acts as though he has always been rich. His transformation is more or less instantaneous; this does not surprise him in the least, and he has absolutely no timidity.

Take a Russian Jew, with his filthy thouloupe, and his corkscrew curls and carriage, and after a month's bathing, he will take his seat in a box at the opera with the aplomb of a Stern or a Gunzburg.

By contrast take a good French building contractor, who has amassed his wealth honourably. He will always have a slightly unnatural, awkward air about him, and will shun the more elegant circles. His son, born in better circumstances and initiated into the refinements of life, will be quite different. The grandson, if the family continues to rise and remain honest and Christian, will be a true gentleman: he will possess a subtlety of thought and a nobility of feeling which the yid will never have.

On the other hand, though the Jew may achieve aplomb straight away, he never achieves distinction. With the exception of a few Portuguese Jews who, when young, have beautiful eyes, and when old, a certain oriental majesty, you will never find in them the kind of calm, leisured, courteous dignity which makes it easy to recognize an authentic French lord, a pure-bred Frenchman, wherever he may be and even though his coat may be frayed. The Jew is insolent and never proud. He can never rise above the basic level of life, which admittedly he achieves very easily. The Rothschilds, in spite of their billions, look like hawkers of second-hand clothes; their wives, with all the diamonds of Golconda, will always look like haberdashers, dressed up not for Sunday, but for the Sabbath.

Vis-à-vis the Christian, the Jew will always lack the chief attraction of social relations, equality. The Jew – and pay close attention to this observation – will never be the equal of a man of the Christian race. He either grovels at your feet, or crushes you under his heel; he is either on top or beneath, never beside.

There is a further reason for Jews not being suited for intercourse where gain is not the sole motive, and that is their uniformity; there is a total absence of the refined culture and free-ranging intellect which are essential as the spice of all conversation. One seldom hears from them the brilliant, imaginative theories, the sharp insights or the amusing paradoxes with which some talkers sprinkle their discourse. If such ideas did ever occur to the Jew he would take good care not to waste them on his friends, he would try to make money out of them. But the reality is otherwise: he lives off other people. He plays a single tune, and the most lengthy conversation never presents any surprises.

Whereas the Aryan race counts an infinite variety of organizations and temperaments, a Jew always resembles any other Jew; he does not have a variety of gifts, but one single aptitude, which is used for everything: this is the Thebouna, the practical subtlety so highly praised in the *Moschlim*, the marvellous, unanalysable gift which is the same for the politician as for the courtier and which serves him admirably in life.

The truth is that the Jew is incapable of rising above a certain level. The Semites have no man of genius of the stature of Dante, Shakespeare, Bossuet, Victor Hugo, Raphael, Michelangelo or Newton, and it is difficult to imagine how they could. The genius is almost always unrecognized and persecuted, a superior being who gives something to humanity; now the very essence of the Jew is that he does not give anything. It is not surprising that what they cherish is a talent for which there is a ready market. Their Corneille is Adolphe d'Ennery,[1] their Raphael Worms.

In art they have created no original, powerful or touching statues, no masterpieces. The criterion is whether the

[1] Adolphe d'Ennery (1811–99), playwright with a remarkable facility for the dramatic portrayal of intrigue, and who is widely believed to have plagiarized many of his plots.

work will sell; the sublime is commissioned to order, a false sublime of course. They prefer to concentrate on the real, as it enables them both to get rich by flattering the coarse appetites of the masses, and to serve their cause by making a mockery of the enthusiasm, the pious memories and the august traditions of the people who are the source of their wealth.

The Jesuit is the exact opposite of the Jew. Ignatius Loyola is a pure Aryan. The hero of the siege of Pamplona, knight of the Holy Virgin, is the last of the Paladins. There is something of the Don Quixote about this saint, a very modern one, of course, who went to Paris late in life, to sit on the benches of the university, and though he was the personification of the movement which was spreading across the world, when henceforth the pen would play the role played in the past by the sword.

It is certain that Disraeli knew the Jews better than the Jesuits, and the English statesman is worth consulting. In *Endymion* Disraeli considers the occult diplomacy which, over the previous century, had turned the world upside down.

Nowadays the Semites exercise a vast influence over the world of business through their smallest but most original wing, the Jews. There is no other race which is blest with such tenacity and organizing ability. With these gifts they have acquired an unprecedented empire of property and unlimited credit. As you advance through life and become experienced, Jews will block your path everywhere. They infiltrated our secret diplomacy a long time ago, and almost control it; within a quarter of a century, they will claim their share of government openly. Now there are races whose men and corporations, each man in their own particular way, must enter into the calculations of statesmen.

It is easy to appreciate that Jews who are not distinguished by their costume are all the more effective because they are less visible. In the civil service, in diplomacy, in the offices of conservative newspapers, even in the priest's cassock, they live unsuspected.

The Jewish army thus disposes of three regiments: firstly, the true Jews, the notorious Jews as they are called in the Archives, who officially venerate Abraham and Jacob, and are satisfied with claiming the chance to make their fortune while remaining faithful to their God. Secondly, the Jews disguised as free-thinkers (like Gambetta, Dreyfus and Raynal) who conceal the fact that they are Jews, and persecute Christians in the name of the glorious principles of tolerance and the sacred rights of liberty. Thirdly, the conservative Jews who pretend to be Christians but whom the closest links unite with the first two classes, and who pass to their friends any secrets which might be useful. In these circumstances the incredible success of the Jew, however improbable it may appear, and the unheard-of way he multiplies, are easily comprehensible.

The strength of the Jews lies in their solidarity. They all feel a common bond with one another, as is proclaimed in the *Alliance Israélite* whose emblem is two hands clasped together beneath a halo. This principle is strictly observed from one end of the universe to the other in a truly touching manner.

It is obvious what advantages, from the human point of view, this principle of solidarity gives the Jew over the Christian, who esteems charity and to whom any feeling of solidarity is foreign. Believe me, no one could admire more than I do the sublime flower which Christianity has set in the human heart, indefatigable, inexhaustible, ardent charity, which always gives, gives unceasingly, which gives not money alone, but the heart itself, time and understanding. What I would like to indicate in this work, which is one of rigorous analysis, is the difference between the solidarity of the Jew and the charity of the Christian.

Christians welcome every disaster with open arms; they answer every appeal, but they do not club together. As they are accustomed to feeling at home, which is most natural in a country belonging to them, they never even consider the idea of forming serried ranks in order to resist the Jews.

It is thus only to be expected that the Jew strikes in one place at a time. One day it is a merchant whose capital is coveted by the Jew: Israeli traders agree quietly to reduce him to bankruptcy. The next day it is an irritating writer whom the Jews reduce to despair and push into drunkenness or madness. Another time it is a noble lord, with a beautiful name, who treated a baron of doubtful origins somewhat brusquely at the races: it is arranged for the unfortunate man to acquire a Jewish mistress, a broker affiliated to the band recommends an advantageous investment, sometimes the victim is led on by an initial gain, but in the end he finds himself both misused and shamed.

If the merchant, the writer and the lord had pooled their interests and united, they would have escaped, they would have joined in each other's defence. They would all have brought mutual help, but, and I repeat it, they succumb without seeing one another, without even suspecting who their real enemy was.

Thanks to their solidarity, everything which happens to

a Jew, even in the most remote corner of the desert, takes on the dimensions of an event. The Jew has indeed an incomparable way of squeaking; as they were told, 'Croak and multiply, sons of Abraham without number.'

The term mother country, as we use it, has no meaning for the Jew. The Jew – and here I am borrowing the forceful expression of the *Alliance Israélite* – is an inexorable universalist.

I do not see how the Jews can be reproached for thinking in these terms. What does 'country' mean? Land of one's fathers. The feeling of the mother country is engraved in the heart as names carved on a tree, which each passing year hollows and deepens into the bark as the tree grows older, so that the tree and the name become one. Patriots cannot be improvised; it is in the blood and the bones. The Semite is perpetually nomadic; can he experience such durable impressions?

It is certainly possible to change country, as some Italians did when Catherine de Medici arrived in France, and as the French Protestants did at the time of the revocation of the Edict of Nantes. But for these trans- plantations to succeed the moral soil must be more or less the same in the new country as in the old, and beneath the surface humus there must be a Christian foundation.

Moreover the first condition of adopting a new country is to give up the old. Now the Jew has a home which he will never renounce, Jerusalem, the holy, mysterious city. Jerusalem, triumphant or persecuted, joyful or sad, is a bond uniting all its children, who say each year at Roch Haschana, 'Next year in Jerusalem.'

Outside Jerusalem, any country, whether it is France, Germany or England, is simply a dwelling-place, much like anywhere else, a social agglomeration in which he can live well; it may even be profitable for him to serve the interests of that country for a while, but he participates only as a free associate, a temporary member.

Here I must examine a point which I have already raised and which I shall have to revert to later, and this is the incontestable degeneration of the French spirit, a partial softening which can be seen in a vague sympathy resulting in people liking everyone, and at the same time in an envious note which makes us detest our fellows. This is the case of a number of insane people who disinherit their children and shower civilities on foreigners.

If our fellow citizens' brains were functioning in their regular, normal manner, as in their fathers' time, they would quickly appreciate that the Jew can have no possible motive for being a patriot. Reflect for a moment and ask yourself why a Raynal, a Bischoffsheim or a Leven should be attached to the France of the crusades, of Bouvines, Marignano, Fontenoy, St Louis, Henry IV and Louis XIV. By virtue of its traditions, beliefs and memories, this France is an absolute negation of the Jewish character itself. This France, when it was not actually burning Jews, stubbornly closed its gate to them, covered them with scorn, and used their name as the cruellest of insults.

I am aware that the Jews believe a new France was born in the September massacres, that its old glories were purified by the blood flowing from the heads of old men and women, that the Revolution was, to adopt the Jew Salvador's expression, 'a new Sinai'. These words are sonorous but quite meaningless. A country remains as it was when it was born, just as a growing child retains its early nature. France, Germany and England will never be mother countries for the Jews, who are quite right in my opinion not to feel at home anywhere and to follow a distinct, characteristic policy in every latitude, namely the Jewish policy.

Our ancestors, who were sensible people, knew this perfectly well, and defended themselves. Let us do the same, if there is still time, and not be surprised by anything; Victor Hugo, who had to entrust his grandchildren to the care of a Jew, should be the only one to indulge in the indignant tirades against Deutz.

Again, Jews must not be judged by our standards. It is indisputable that every Jew betrays his employer. Cavour said of his secretary, the Jew Artom: 'This man is invaluable to us in publicizing what I have to say: I don't know how he goes about it, but after I have uttered only a word he has twisted it before he has even left my office.' And Prince Bismarck is quoted as saying, 'Why else should God have created the Jew, if they were not to be spies?'

From these facts, which it would be simple to multiply an infinite number of times, it is apparent that what we are dealing with is not an isolated case which would prove nothing against a community, but with the special calling of a particular race, the vocation of Abraham. Do such acts constitute spying or treachery for the Jew? Not in the least. It is not their mother country that they are betraying; they are merely making capital out of diplomacy and politics. The real traitors to their country are the native-born people who allow foreigners to interfere with matters that are not their business. Not content with making Oppert de Blowitz, a German by birth and a second-hand Englishman, an officer of the *Légion d'honneur*, the republican ministers take him into their confidence and hand over military secrets; this is despicable. But what right would you have to prevent a Jew who was vacillating between two countries from passing their information to whichever country paid better?

It is thus extremely difficult to study the criminality of the Jew. As the excellent Crémieux says, the intention is paramount. The evil which Jews perpetrate, terrible, unfathomable, unknown evil, falls into the category of crimes committed for reasons of state. To assassinate, ruin and despoil Christians counts as a crime which is pleasing to God. As Eisenmenger explains in his *Judaïsme dévoilé* ('Jewry Unmasked'), that is what they call a *Korban*.

It is a fact, the Jew smells bad. Even the smartest of them give off an odour, *fetor judaïca*, or as Zola would say, a whiff, which reveals the race and helps them to recognize one another. The most charming woman, because of the very perfumes she covers herself with, justifies what Martial said: '*Qui bene olet male olet.*'

This fact has been noted a hundred times. 'The Jews all stink,' said Victor Hugo, and he died surrounded by Jews. He recounted that in 1266 a memorable encounter took place before the King and Queen of Aragon between the learned Rabbi Zeckhiel and a very erudite Dominican father, Paul Cyriagne. After the Jewish doctor had quoted the Toldus Jechut, the Targum, the Archives of Sanhedrin, the Nissachon and the Talmud, the Queen was prompted to ask him why the Jews stank.

The question of understanding why the Jews stink has long preoccupied a number of well-intentioned people. In the Middle Ages it was felt that they could be purified of this odour by baptizing them. Bail claims that this feature is due to natural causes, and that there are still black men in Guinea who emit an unbearable odour. Banazzini, in his *Traité des Artisans*, attributes the evil smell of Jews to their lack of hygiene and their immoderate taste for goat's meat and geese.

The disease which implacably attacks Jews is neurosis. This people was for a long time persecuted, always living in an atmosphere of constant fear and ceaseless plotting; later they were shaken by the fever of speculation. In addition their work was almost invariably of a cerebral kind, and their nervous system has finally been affected.

In Prussia, the proportion of lunatics is much higher among Israelites than among Christians. Whereas there are 24·1 per 10,000 Protestants, and 23·7 for the same number of Catholics, per 10,000 Jews there are 38·9. In Italy the ratio is one lunatic per 384 Jews and one per 778 Catholics.

Dr Charcot made the most bizarre revelations about Russian Jews, and these are the only ones that can be discussed, because the others take great care to conceal their diseases behind their palace doors.

The *Archives Israélites*, while taking note of this terrible state of affairs, state that there is no need to comment upon it, and that it increases, if that were possible, the pity people feel for the unfortunate Israelites of Russia. Yes, indeed, let us hope all the Jews who are mentally sick will be treated. But why should they inflict the troubles of their own mind on peoples who were living quietly and happily so long as the Jewish race was not actively interfering with their way of life. With Hertzen in Russia, Karl Marx and Lassalle in Germany, everywhere one looks, there is, as in France, a Jew preaching communism or socialism, and demanding that the wealth of the old inhabitants be shared, while their co-religionists arrive barefoot, make their fortune, and do not show the least inclination to share anything.

The Jews are always well-informed about what is going on, in the world of facts, and in the world of ideas. They are therefore very concerned about the anti-semitic movement which has been spreading over the whole of

Europe. Their fury was unimaginable when *L'Anti-Sémitique*, a gallant little newspaper, very modern and well versed in financial jobbery, was launched in Paris. Whenever people think it has vanished, it reappears on the stalls.

To put it bluntly, the Jews have a vague premonition of what is coming to them. They went through a period of delirious pride between 1870 and 1879. The Jew Wolff used to write in the *National-Zeitung*, 'What joy to be born in such an age!', '*Es ist eine Lust zu leben!*', while on the banks of the Spree the Laskers, Bleichroeders and Hansemanns were skinning the Prussians, who were intoxicated by the laurels they had won, of their millions. 'What joy indeed!' the cosmopolitan band in France echoed, when they saw that the squares, money, hotels, carriages of the nobility, hunts, boxes at the opera, everything was theirs, and the good people's reaction was merely sincere comments on the 'new classes'.

They have moderated their tone a little now, and they recognize that concerted action is being taken by Christians everywhere, and that this could be stronger than the universal Israelite alliance.

The Jew is essentially a sad man. If he becomes rich, he is insolent but remains lugubrious; he is morosely arrogant, with the *tristis arrogantia* of Pallus in Tacitus.

Hypochondria, only one of the manifestations of neurosis, is the only present they have made to France, which was formerly cheerful and blithe, blooming with robust, healthy gaiety.

'The Jew is sombre,' said Shaftesbury in his *Characteristics*. It is a strong adjective, and his comment is deeper than would first appear. It is a mistake to believe the Jew enjoys himself with his fellows, even a mistake to believe that he loves them. Christians do not concert their activities, but they love one another, and enjoy being in company. Jews, on the other hand, support each other till their dying day, but they do not feel for their fellows, in fact they detest them, and when business does not bring them together, they avoid each other like the plague. They are scarcely more content in the company of Christians: if someone praises Christ, they at once feel sick; a little joke about Judas produces a sickly laugh, but quite puts them out. Fundamentally, the inscription which one can read on the walls of Italian ghettos is still applicable: *Ne populo regni coelestis hoeredi usus cum exhoerede sit.* May the people which inherits the kingdom of heaven have nothing to do with those who are excluded.

There is occasionally a sly smile to be detected when they think of how they have tricked the Christians. Indeed the allegorical representation of the Jew is the fox: the *Meschabot Schualim* ('Tales of the Fox') is the first book the young Hebrew child meets. As an adult, he is happy to underline how he has got the better of the Aryan. For example, Bleichroeder organized the Tunisian campaign, which cost France a number of lives and a lot of money, and resulted in the rupture of the Italian alliance, and then he goes on to ridicule his victim by getting an ignominious minister to appoint him commander of the *Légion d'honneur*.

These moods of evil joy can sometimes give way to more naïve pleasures. But, you will retort, how on earth can a Jew be naïve? Well, he does have a childish side to him. This representation of civilization in its most advanced, refined and morbid form, has the wiliness, and at the same time the naïve vanity, of the savage. When his success brings him a little cheap publicity, his mouth gapes open with pleasure, just as an African's eyes and teeth light up when he has a trinket or a shred of gaudy material in his hands.

When Louis Blanc was buried, I was watching the deputations line up in the rue de Rivoli and it made an incredible impression on me to see how all those people with yellowish, dirty beards swaggered past wearing the blue sash of a Freemason. These mean-looking people were experiencing a puerile pleasure in being there, opposite the Tuileries, respectfully treated by the policemen, in having a certain importance, a role to play in a semi-official ceremony, and in wearing something which distinguished them from other people. The Jew is more often like this than is commonly believed. When he tells you that he has been awarded some sort of a distinction, or that he has won a chocolate medal at an exhibition, he looks at you closely to make sure you are not laughing at him (which is his constant fear); reassured, his pale, bloodless face lights up with happiness, just like a child's.

There is one feeling which these corrupt, puffed up people still possess, and that is hatred, of the Church, of priests and above all of monks. On reflection, this hatred appears quite natural. If a man is born intelligent and rich, with a name that rings differently from all the noble Gerolsteins, and renounces everything in order to become just like the poor, does not such an act deny and suppress everything the Jew stands for, namely money? Is not the monk's vow of poverty a permanent mockery of the Jew's vow of wealth?

The woman who prefers a frieze garment, who does not want servants dressed in silk and lace, is not she, in spite of the gentleness of her angelic physiognomy, a living and perpetual insult to the Jew, who is quite incapable, with all his money, of buying what this indigent possesses, faith, hope and charity? She is quite indifferent to death, and a coffin, even one in whitewood, does not frighten her.

Simon Lockroy insults the monks and says they should be chased out of their cells. Dreyfus suggests that our honest republicans should deprive the Sisters of Charity of the bread which keeps starvation at bay. Nevertheless they will never be stripped of the crucifix they wear round their necks; it is in copper, and the Jewish barons like only whatever bears the stamp of the mint.

The very fact that such sublime virtues, such indifference to everything material, and such proud self-denial can exist reacts on the Jew like a thorn in a crude sybarite's bed; he thinks he is master over all things, yet he cannot influence these souls.

Another useful source when considering the mentality of the Jew is Renan. This portrait of the modern Jew in *L'Ecclésiaste* is priceless. In his work one can detect that the artist has a mysterious sympathy for Judas: when the truth is a little stark, he softens the blow; a comment which would wound is followed by a complimentary adjective. He admires this parasite, 'who quickly left dynastic prejudice behind him, knows how to get the best out of a world he did not make, and to harvest the fruits of a field he did not plough, to replace the idler by whom he is persecuted and to make himself indispensable to the foolish man who scorns him'.

You would think that it was for him that Clovis and his Franks struck such mighty blows with their swords, that the race of the Capets shaped policy over a thousand years, and that Philip Augustus was victorious at Bouvines and Condé at Rocroi. Vanity of vanities! The best way to obtain the joys of this earth is to proclaim that they are vain. We have all known these worldly-wise men, who are not distracted by any supernatural chimeras, who would surrender every dream of another world for a single hour of the realities of this one. He is strongly opposed to

injustice, but is as undemocratic as possible. He is both
flexible and proud in wielding his power. His delicate skin,
his nervous sensitivity and the impression he gives of
being someone who does not indulge in tiring work make
him an aristocrat; his low opinion of the bravery of the
warrior and an age-old feeling of being an underdog,
which his distinction cannot eradicate, make him a
bourgeois. His faith in the kingdom of God shook the
world, but now he believes only in wealth. This is because
wealth is indeed his true reward. He knows how to work
and to enjoy. Nothing in the annals of chivalry would make
him prefer hard-won glory to his luxurious home; no
stoic asceticism will induce him to abandon his prey for
obscurity. To his mind, everything life has to offer is
terrestrial. He has come to the perfect truth: to enjoy the
fruits of his labour in peace, surrounded by works of a
delicate art and the images of a pleasure which has been
exhausted.

This is a surprising confirmation of the philosophy of
vanity. Go and trouble the world, put God to death on the
cross, endure every torture, burn your country three or
four times, insult all the tyrants, smash all the idols, and
end up dying of a disease of the spinal cord in a comfortable
hotel off the Champs-Élysées, regretting that life was so
short and pleasure so elusive. Vanity of vanities!

No, dilettante, it was not so that a Jew should die of a
spinal disease in a hotel off the Champs-Élysées that
Clovis fought at Tolbiac and Philip Augustus at Bouvines.
If our fathers were courageous, if they fell on the battlefield, it was so that there should be a France just as there
is an England and a Germany, so that our children should
pray as their fathers prayed, with their faith as a staff in
life.

The Semites, those restless people, were happy to destroy

the foundation of the old society, and to use the money they extorted from it to found a new one. They have created a social problem, and it will be solved at their expense. The property which they have wrongfully acquired will be distributed to all those who take part in the great struggle which is getting under way, just as, in days gone by, land and fiefs were distributed to the most valiant.

In Germany, in Russia, in Austria-Hungary, in Rumania, and in France itself where the movement is still dormant, the nobility, the middle classes, and intelligent workers, in a word everyone with a Christian background — often without being practising Christians — are in agreement on this point: the Universal Anti-Semitic Alliance has been created, and the Universal Israelite Alliance will not prevail against it.

The committees may be more active in some countries than others, propaganda may be more or less protracted, but before the end of this century there will be yet another repetition of the following sequence of events: the Jew takes advantage of the divisions he has created, and his cunning makes him master of the whole country; he attempts to transform the ideas, the customs and traditional beliefs of the country, and, as a result of his provocation and insolence, people who hated one another are reconciled overnight and set upon the Jew with prodigious determination.

My own role is merely to announce modestly the curious events which will shortly take place. It is possible that I may die, insulted, defamed and misunderstood, without witnessing the things which I have predicted so confidently, but I do not think so. It is really of small importance, because I shall have done my duty and accomplished my task. Everything in the future will confirm my forecasts.

Bossuet wrote, 'Events are prepared, fostered and realized by different causes. The true science of history lies in observing what were the hidden factors which paved the way for great changes, and the important circumstances which brought them about.'

GEORGES SOREL
(1847-1922)

Sorel is the point where left and right meet in the attack on the institutions and *esprit* of the Third Republic. His Marxism leads him to see the only hope for Western civilization in the proletariat; his conviction that liberal democracy in its prevailing historical form (Sorel wrote the *Reflections on Violence* as a series of articles in 1906 and they appeared in book form in 1908) was decadent in the sense that Spengler and Maurras understood the term put him on the right. Sorel had admirers in both camps. Not only was his work much discussed in Russia before 1917 and caused Lenin some sleepless nights before he decided Sorel was a muddle-head, but also Mussolini claimed: 'I owe most to Georges Sorel.' (Elsewhere, he said exactly the same thing about Gustave Le Bon.) There is even some evidence to suggest that Sorel might at one time have flirted with monarchism. George Valois, Sorel's associate in revolutionary syndicalism, went over to the *Action Française* and Sorel himself was co-editor of *L'Indépendence* when Paul Bourget and Maurice Barrès were on the editorial council.

Sorel's solution to the problems posed by the political experience of the Third Republic lay in a return to heroic, pre-logical Homeric warrior values. Sorel is above all else a moralist; Marxism is for him 'social poetry', to be accepted as a 'mythology' which may not be true in a rationalist sense, but which has a value in that it can move men in the present. In this he points the way forward to a cult of violence which has affected left and right alike.

Sorel's glorification of violence is re-echoed both in Mussolini's fasces and in Fanon's notion that it is in violence that the new man can be made. Violence is creative in its own right. It is not, as in classic Marxism, the means by which socialism effects the transition from the old to the new, a temporary phase soon to be superseded by the serious business of the building of socialism. For much of the New Left, it is the violence itself which creates the new, socialist man.

These two extracts are taken from E. A. Shils's edition of J. Roth's and T. E. Hulme's translation of the *Reflections on Violence* (New York, 1961).

... My view, on the contrary, is that the *best way of understanding any group of ideas in the history of thought is to bring all the contradictions into sharp relief*. I shall adopt this method and take for a starting-point the celebrated opposition which Nietzsche has established between two groups of moral values, an opposition about which much has been written, but which has never been properly studied.

A. We know with what force Nietzsche praised the values constructed by the *masters*, by a superior class of warriors who, in their expeditions, enjoying to the full freedom from all social constraint, return to the simplicity of mind of a wild beast, become once more triumphant monsters who continually bring to mind 'the superb blond beast, prowling in search of prey and bloodshed', in whom 'a basis of hidden bestiality needs from time to time a purgative'. To understand this thesis properly, we must not attach too much importance to formulas which have at times been intentionally exaggerated, but should examine the historical facts; the author tells us that he has in mind 'the aristocracy of Rome, Arabia, Germany and Japan, the Homeric heroes, the Scandinavian vikings'.

It is chiefly the Homeric heroes that we must bear in mind in order to understand what Nietzsche wished to make clear to his contemporaries. We must remember that he has been professor of Greek at the University of Basel, and that his reputation began with a book devoted to the glorification of the Hellenic genius (*The Origin of*

Tragedy). He notices that, even at the period of their highest culture, the Greeks still preserved a memory of their former character of masters. 'Our daring', said Pericles, 'has traced a path over earth and sea, raising everywhere imperishable monuments both of good and evil.' It was of the heroes of Greek legend and history that he was thinking when he speaks of 'that audacity of noble races, that mad, absurd and spontaneous audacity, their influence and contempt for all security of the body, for life, for comfort'. Does not 'the terrible gaiety and the profound joy which the heroes tasted in destruction, in all the pleasures of victory and of cruelty', apply particularly to Achilles?

It was certainly to the type of classic Greek that Nietzsche alluded when he wrote: 'the moral judgments of the warrior aristocracy are founded on a powerful bodily constitution, a flourishing health without forgetfulness of what was necessary to the maintenance of that overflowing vigour – war, adventure, hunting, dancing, games and physical exercises, in short, everything implied by a robust, free and joyful activity.'

That very ancient type, the Achaean type celebrated by Homer, is not simply a memory; it has several times reappeared in the world. 'During the Renaissance there was a superb reawakening of the classic idea of the aristocratic valuation of all things; and after the Revolution the most prodigious and unexpected event came to pass, the antique ideal stood in person with unwonted splendour before the eyes of consciousness of humanity ... [Then] appeared Napoleon, isolated and belated example though he was.'

I believe that if the professor of philology had not been continually cropping up in Nietzsche he would have perceived that the master type still exists under our own eyes, and that it is this type which, at the present time, has created the extraordinary greatness of the United States. He would have been struck by the singing analogies which exist between the Yankee, ready for any kind of enterprise, and the ancient Greek sailor, sometimes a pirate, sometimes a colonist or merchant; above all, he would have established a parallel between the ancient heroes and the man who sets out on the conquest of the Far West. P. de Rousiers has described the *master* type admirably: 'To become and to remain an American, one must look upon life as *a struggle and not as a pleasure*, and seek in it, victorious effort, energetic and efficacious action, rather than pleasure, leisure embellished by the cultivation of the arts, the refinements proper to other societies. Everywhere — we have seen that what makes the American succeed, what constitutes his type — is character, personal energy, energy in action, creative energy.' The profound contempt which the Greek had for the barbarian is matched by that of the Yankee for the foreign worker who makes no effort to become truly American. 'Many of these people would be better if we took them in hand,' an old colonel of the War of Secession said to a French traveller, 'but we are a proud race'; a shopkeeper of Pottsville spoke of the Pennsylvania miners as 'the senseless populace'. J. Bourdeau has drawn attention to the strange likeness which exists between the ideas of A. Carnegie and Roosevelt, and those of Nietzsche, the first deploring the waste of money involved in maintaining incapables, the second urging the Americans to become conquerors, a race of prey.

I am not among those who consider Homer's Achaean type, the indomitable hero confident in his strength and putting himself above rules, as necessarily disappearing in the future. If it has often been believed that the type was bound to disappear, that was because the Homeric values were imagined to be irreconcilable with the other values which spring from an entirely different principle; Nietzsche committed this error, which all those who believe in the necessity of unity in thought are bound to make. It is quite evident that liberty would be seriously compromised if men came to regard the Homeric values (which are approximately the same as the Cornelian values) as suitable only to barbaric peoples. Many moral evils would for ever remain unremedied if some hero of revolt did not force the people to become aware of their own state of mind on the subject. And art, which is after all of some value, would lose the finest jewel in its crown.

The philosophers are little disposed to admit the right of art to support the cult of the 'will to power'; it seems to them that they ought to give lessons to artists, instead of receiving lessons from them; they think that only those sentiments which have received the stamp of the universities have the right to manifest themselves in poetry. Like industry, art has never adapted itself to the demands of theorists; it always upsets their plans of social harmony, and humanity has found the freedom of art far too satisfactory ever to think of allowing it to be controlled by the creators of dull systems of sociology. The Marxists are accustomed to seeing the ideologists look at things the wrong way round, and so, in contrast to their enemies, they should look upon art as a reality which begets ideas and not as an application of ideas.

B. To the values created by the *master* type, Nietzsche opposed the system constructed by sacerdotal castes – the ascetic ideal against which he has piled up so much invective. The history of these values is much more obscure and complicated than that of the preceding ones. Nietzsche tries to connect the origin of asceticism with psychological

reasons which I will not examine here. He certainly
makes a mistake in attributing a preponderating part to
the Jews. It is not at all evident that antique Judaism had
an ascetic character; doubtless, like the other Semitic
religions, it attached importance to pilgrimages, fasts and
prayers recited in ragged clothes. The Hebrew poets sang
the hope of revenge which existed in the heart of the
persecuted, but, until the second century of our era, the
Jews looked to be revenged by arms: on the other hand,
family life, with them, was too strong for the monkish ideal
ever to become important.

Imbued with Christianity as our civilization may be, it
is none the less evident that, even in the Middle Ages, it
submitted to influences foreign to the Church, with the
result that the old ascetic values were gradually transformed. The values to which the contemporary world
clings most closely, and which it considers the true *ethical
values*, are not realized in convents, but in the family;
respect for the human person, sexual fidelity and devotion
to the weak constitute the elements of morality of which
all high-minded men are proud; morality, even, is very
often made to consist of these alone.

When we examine in a critical spirit the numerous
writings which treat, today, of marriage, we see that the
reformers who are in earnest propose to improve family
relations in such a way as to assure the better realization
of these ethical values; thus, they demand that the scandals
of conjugal life shall not be exposed in the law courts,
that unions shall not be maintained when fidelity no
longer exists, and that the authority of the head of the
family shall not be diverted from its moral purpose to
become mere exploitation, etc.

On the other hand, it is curious to observe to what
extent the modern Church misunderstands the values that

classico-Christian civilization has produced. It sees in marriage, above all, a contract directed by financial and worldly interests; it is unwilling to allow of the union being dissolved when the household is a hell, and takes no account of the duty of devotion. The priests are wonderfully skilful in procuring rich dowries for impoverished nobles, so much so, indeed, that the Church has been accused of considering marriage as a mating of noblemen living as 'bullies' with middle-class women reduced to the role of the women who support such men. When it is heavily recompensed, the Church finds unexpected reasons for divorce, and finds means of annulling inconvenient unions for ridiculous motives. Proudhon asks ironically: 'Is it possible for a responsible man of a serious turn of mind and a true Christian to care for the love of his wife? ... If the husband seeking divorce, or the wife seeking separation, alleges the refusal of the conjugal right, then, of course, there is a legitimate reason for a rupture, for the service for which marriage is granted has not been carried out.'

Our civilization having come to consider nearly all morality as consisting of values derived from those observed in the normally constituted family, two serious consequences have been produced: (1) it has been asked if, instead of considering the family as an application of moral theories, it would not be more exact to say that it is the base of these theories; (2) it seems that the Church, having become incompetent on matters connected with sexual union, must also be incompetent as regards morality. These are precisely the conclusions to which Proudhon came. 'Sexual duality was created by nature to be the instrument of justice ... To produce justice is the highest aim of the bisexual division; generation, and what follows from it, only figure here as accessory.' 'Marriage, both in principle and in purpose, being the *instrument of human right*, and the living negation of the divine right, is thus in formal contradiction with theology and the Church.'

Love, by the enthusiasm it begets, can produce that sublimity without which there would be no effective morality. At the end of his book on justice, Proudhon has written pages, which will never be surpassed, on the role of women.

C. Finally we have to examine the values which escape Nietzsche's classification and which treat of *civil relations*. Originally magic was much mixed up in the evaluation of these values; among the Jews, until recent times, one finds a mixture of hygienic principles, rules about sexual relationships, precepts about honesty, benevolence and national solidarity, the whole wrapped up in magical superstitions; this mixture, which seems strange to the philosopher, had the happiest influence on their morality so long as they maintained their traditional mode of living, and one notices among them even now a particular exactitude in the carrying out of contracts.

The ideas held by modern ethical writers are drawn mainly from those of Greece in its time of decadence; Aristotle, living in a period of transition, combined ancient values with values that, as time went on, were to prevail; war and production had ceased to occupy the attention of the most distinguished men of the towns, who sought, on the contrary, to secure an easy existence for themselves; the most important thing was the establishment of friendly relations between the better educated men of the community, and the fundamental maxim was that of the golden mean. The new morality was to be acquired principally by means of the habits which the young Greek would pick up in mixing with cultivated people.

It may be said that here we are on the level of an ethic adapted to consumers; it is not astonishing then that Catholic theologians still find Aristotle's ethics an excellent one, for they themselves take the consumer's point of view.

In the civilization of antiquity, the ethics of producers could hardly be any other than that of slave owners, and it did not seem worth developing at length, at the time when philosophy made an inventory of Greek customs. Aristotle said that no far-reaching science was needed to employ slaves: 'For the master *need only know how to order what the slaves must know how to execute*. So, as soon as a man can save himself this trouble, he leaves it in the charge of a steward, so as to be himself free for a political or philosophical life.' A little farther on he wrote: 'It is manifest, then, that the master ought to be the source of excellence in the slave; but not merely because he possesses the art which trains him in his duties.' This clearly expresses the point of view of the urban consumer, who finds it very tiresome to be obliged to pay any attention whatever to the conditions of production.

As to the slave, he needs very limited virtues. 'He only needs enough to prevent him neglecting his work through intemperance or idleness.' He should be treated with 'more indulgence even than children', although certain people consider that slaves are deprived of reason and are fit only to receive orders.

It is quite easy to see that during a considerable period the moderns also did not think that there was anything more to be said about workers than Aristotle had said; they must be given orders, corrected with gentleness, like children, and treated as passive instruments who do not need to think. Revolutionary syndicalism would be impossible if the world of the workers were under the influence of such a *morality of the weak*. State socialism, on the contrary, could accommodate itself to this morality perfectly well, since the latter is based on the idea of a society divided into a class of producers and a class of thinkers applying the results of scientific investigation to the work of production.

... The attempt to construct hypotheses about the nature of the struggles of the future and the means of suppressing capitalism, on the model furnished by history, is a return to the old methods of the Utopists. There is no process by which the future can be predicted scientifically, nor even one which enables us to discuss whether one hypothesis about it is better than another; it has been proved by too many memorable examples that the greatest men have committed prodigious errors in thus desiring to make predictions about even the least distant future.

And yet without leaving the present, without reasoning about this future, which seems for ever condemned to escape our reason, we should be unable to act at all. Experience shows that the *framing of a future, in some indeterminate time*, may, when it is done in a certain way, be very effective, and have very few inconveniences; this happens when the anticipations of the future take the form of those myths, which enclose with them all the strongest inclinations of a people, of a party or of a class, inclinations which recur to the mind with the insistence of instincts in all the circumstances of life; and which give an aspect of complete reality to the hopes of immediate action by which, more easily than by any other method, men can reform their desires, passions and mental activity. We know, moreover, that these social myths in no way prevent a man profiting by the observations which he makes in the course of his life, and form no obstacle to the pursuit of his normal occupations.

The truth of this may be shown by numerous examples.

The first Christians expected the return of Christ and the total ruin of the pagan world, with the inauguration of the kingdom of the saints, at the end of the first generation. The catastrophe did not come to pass, but Christian thought profited so greatly from the apocalyptic myth that certain contemporary scholars maintain that the whole preaching of Christ referred solely to this one point. The hopes which Luther and Calvin had formed of the religious exaltation of Europe were by no means realized; these fathers of the Reformation very soon seemed men of a past era; for present-day Protestants they belong rather to the Middle Ages than to modern times, and the problems which troubled them most occupy very little place in contemporary Protestantism. Must we for that reason deny the immense result which came from their dreams of Christian renovation? It must be admitted that the real developments of the Revolution did not in any way resemble the enchanting pictures which created the enthusiasm of its first adepts; but without those pictures would the Revolution have been victorious? Many Utopias were mixed up with the revolutionary myth, because it had been formed by a society passionately fond of imaginative literature, full of confidence in the 'science', and very little acquainted with the economic history of the past. These Utopias came to nothing; but it may be asked whether the Revolution was not a much more profound transformation than those dreamed of by the people who in the eighteenth century had invented social Utopias. In our own times Mazzini pursued what the wiseacres of his time called a mad chimera; but it can no longer be denied that, without Mazzini, Italy would never have become a great power, and that he did more for Italian unity than Cavour and all the politicians of his school.

A knowledge of what the myths contain in the way of details which will actually form part of the history of the future is then of small importance; they are not astrological almanacs; it is even possible that nothing which they contain will ever come to pass – as was the case with the catastrophe expected by the first Christians. In our own daily life, are we not familiar with the fact that what actually happens is very different from our preconceived notion of it? And that does not prevent us from continuing to make resolutions. Psychologists say that there is heterogeneity between the ends in view and the ends actually realized: the slightest experience of life reveals this law to us, which Spencer transferred into nature, to extract therefrom his theory of the multiplication of effects.

The myth must be judged as a means of acting on the present; any attempt to discuss how far it can be taken literally as future history is devoid of sense. *It is the myth in its entirety which is alone important*: its parts are only of interest in so far as they bring out the main idea. No useful purpose is served, therefore, in arguing about the incidents which may occur in the course of a social war, and about the decisive conflicts which may give victory to the proletariat; even supposing the revolutionaries to have been wholly and entirely deluded in setting up this imaginary picture of the general strike, this picture may yet have been, in the course of the preparation for the Revolution, a great element of strength, if it has embraced all the aspirations of socialism, and if it has given to the whole body of revolutionary thought a precision and a rigidity which no other method of thought could have given.

To estimate, then, the significance of the idea of the

general strike, all the methods of discussions which are current among politicians, sociologists, or people with pretensions to political science, must be abandoned. Everything which its opponents endeavour to establish may be conceded to them, without reducing in any way the value of the theory which they think they have refuted. The question whether the general strike is a partial reality, or only a product of popular imagination, is of little importance. All that it is necessary to know is, whether the general strike contains everything that the socialist doctrine expects of the revolutionary proletariat.

To solve this question we are no longer compelled to argue learnedly about the future; we are not obliged to indulge in lofty reflections about philosophy, history or economics; we are not on the plane of theories, and we can remain on the level of observable facts. We have to question men who take a very active part in the real revolutionary movement amidst the proletariat, men who do not aspire to climb into the middle class and whose mind is not dominated by corporative prejudices. These men may be deceived about an infinite number of political, economical or moral questions; but their testimony is decisive, sovereign and irrefutable when it is a question of knowing what are the ideas which most powerfully move them and their comrades, which most appeal to them as being identical with their socialistic conceptions, and thanks to which their reason, their hopes and their way of looking at particular facts seem to make but one indivisible unity.

Thanks to these men, we know that the general strike is indeed what I have said: the *myth* in which socialism is wholly comprised, i.e. a body of images capable of evoking instinctively all the sentiments which correspond to the different manifestations of the war undertaken by socialism against modern society. Strikes have engendered in the proletariat the noblest, deepest and most moving sentiments that they possess; the general strike groups them all in a coordinated picture, and, by bringing them together, gives to each one of them its maximum of intensity; appealing to their painful memories of particular conflicts, it colours with an intense life all the details of the composition presented to consciousness. We thus obtain that intuition of socialism which language cannot give us with perfect clearness – and we obtain it as a whole, perceived instantaneously.

GUSTAVE LE BON
(1841–1931)

The political rationalism of the Enlightenment was a *political* theory, but it had in Locke and Condillac an underpinning in psychological theory. The anti-rationalism of the prophets of Vichy was a political attack, but it had psychological implications. These implications were given a scientific gloss by Gustave Le Bon. His psychology is the psychology of Boulangism and Caesarism. Arguing that the modern era is the era of the crowd (in French *foule*, in German *Masse*, both renderings which have political associations which the neutral 'crowd' lacks), he goes on to assert that the only way in which the crowd can be kept under control is through the agency of the strong man who can dominate the mass as the hypnotizer dominates the hypnotized, or the seducer the seduced.

Le Bon's theory is the psychological corollary of Barrès's notion of the *déraciné*. What is required, if the state is to survive, is a means of uniting the separate, anomic wills of the *déracinés* into a single will. Only the Caesar-Boulanger-Pétain is capable of doing this because he alone can make the separate single. Le Bon anticipates the classic sociological theory of totalitarianism as the mobilization of the uncommitted who are searching for a leader and a goal, and thus deserves this small emergence from his customary obscurity.

The selections from Le Bon are taken from the English translation of his *Psychologie des Foules* (Paris, 1895), published as *The Crowd, a Study of the Popular Mind* (London, 1896).

The age we are about to enter will in truth be the ERA OF CROWDS.

Scarcely a century ago the traditional policy of European states and the rivalries of sovereigns were the principal factors that shaped events. The opinion of the masses scarcely counted, and most frequently indeed did not count at all. Today it is the traditions which used to obtain in politics, and the individual tendencies and rivalries of rulers which do not count; while on the contrary, the voice of the masses has become preponderant. It is this voice that dictates their conduct to kings, whose endeavour is to take note of its utterances. The destinies of nations are elaborated at present in the heart of the masses, and no longer in the councils of princes.

The entry of the popular classes into political life – that is to say, in reality, their progressive transformation into governing classes – is one of the most striking characteristics of our epoch of transition. The introduction of universal suffrage, which exercised for a long time but little influence, is not, as might be thought, the distinguishing feature of this transference of political power. The progressive growth of the power of the masses took place at first by the propagation of certain ideas, which have slowly implanted themselves in men's minds, and afterwards by the gradual association of individuals bent on bringing about the realization of theoretical conceptions. It is by association that crowds have come to procure ideas with respect to their interests which are very clearly defined if not particularly just, and have arrived at a consciousness of their strength. The masses are founding syndicates before which the authorities capitulate one after the other; they are also founding labour unions, which in spite of all economic laws tend to regulate the conditions of labour and wages. They return to assemblies, in which the government is vested, representatives utterly lacking initiative and independence, and reduced most often to nothing else than the spokesmen of the committees that have chosen them.

Today the claims of the masses are becoming more and more sharply defined, and amount to nothing less than a determination to utterly destroy society as it now exists, with a view to making it hark back to that primitive communism which was the normal condition of all human groups before the dawn of civilization. Limitations of the hours of labour, the nationalization of mines, railways, factories and the soil, the equal distribution of all products, the elimination of all the upper classes for the benefit of the popular classes, etc.: such are these claims.

Little adapted to reasoning, crowds on the contrary are quick to act. As the result of their present organization their strength has become immense. The dogmas whose birth we are witnessing will soon have the forces of the old dogmas; of being above discussion. The divine right of the masses is about to replace the divine right of kings.

The writers who enjoy the favour of our middle classes, those who best represent their rather narrow ideas, their somewhat prescribed views, their rather superficial scepticism, and their at times somewhat excessive egoism, display profound alarm at this new power which they see growing; and to combat the disorder in men's minds they are addressing despairing appeals to those moral forces of the Church for which they formerly professed so much disdain. They talk to us of the bankruptcy of science, go back in penitence to Rome, and remind us of the teachings of revealed truth. These new converts forget that it is too late. Had they been really touched by grace, a like operation could not have the same influence on minds less concerned with the preoccupations which beset these recent adherents to religion. The masses repudiate today the gods which their admonishers repudiated yesterday and helped to destroy. There is no power, divine or human, that can oblige a stream to flow back to its source.

There has been no bankruptcy of science, and science has had no share in the present intellectual anarchy, nor in the making of the new power which is springing up in the midst of this anarchy. Science promised us truth, or at least a knowledge of such relations as our intelligence can seize: it never promised us peace or happiness. Sovereignly indifferent to our feelings, it is deaf to our lamentations. It is for us to endeavour to live with science, since nothing can bring back the illusions it has destroyed.

Universal symptoms, visible in all nations, show us the rapid growth of the power of crowds, and do not admit of our supposing that it is destined to cease growing at an early date. Whatever fate it may reserve for us, we shall have to submit to it. All reasoning against it is a mere vain war of words. Certainly it is possible that the advent to power of the masses marks one of the last stages of Western civilization, a complete return to those periods of confused anarchy which seem always destined to precede the birth of every new society. But may this result be prevented? Up to now these thoroughgoing destructions of a worn-out civilization have constituted the most obvious task of the masses. It is not indeed today merely that this can be traced. History tells us that from the moment when the moral forces on which a civilization rested have lost their strength, its final dissolution is brought about by those unconscious and brutal crowds known, justifiably enough, as barbarians. Civilizations as yet have been created and directed only by a small intellectual aristocracy, never by crowds. Crowds are powerful only for destruction. Their rule is always tantamount to a barbarian phase. A civilization involves fixed rules, discipline, a passing from the instinctive to the rational state, forethought for the future, an elevated degree of culture – all of them conditions that crowds, left to themselves, have invariably shown themselves incapable of realizing. In consequence of the purely destructive nature of their power, crowds act like those microbes which hasten the dissolution of enfeebled or dead bodies. When the structure of a civilization is rotten, it is always the masses that bring about its downfall. It is at such a juncture that their chief mission is plainly visible, and that for a while the philosophy of number seems the only philosophy of history.

Is the same fate in store for our civilization? There is ground to fear that this is the case, but we are not as yet in a position to be certain of it.

However this may be, we are bound to resign ourselves to the reign of the masses, since want of foresight has in succession overthrown all the barriers that might have kept the crowd in check.

We have a very slight knowledge of these crowds which are beginning to be the object of so much discussion. Professional students of psychology, having lived far from them, have always ignored them, and when, as of late, they have turned their attention in this direction, it has been only to consider the crimes crowds are capable of committing. Without a doubt criminal crowds exist, but virtuous and heroic crowds, and crowds of many other kinds, are also to be met with. The crimes of crowds constitute only a particular phase of their psychology. The mental constitution of crowds is not to be learnt merely by a study of their crimes, any more than that of an individual by a mere description of his vices.

However, in point of fact, all the world's masters, all the founders of religion or empires, the apostles of all beliefs, eminent statesmen, and, in a more modest sphere, the mere chiefs of small groups of men, have always been unconscious psychologists, possessed of an instinctive and often very sure knowledge of the character of crowds, and it is their accurate knowledge of this character that has enabled them to so easily establish their mastery. Napoleon had a marvellous insight into the psychology of the masses of the country over which he reigned, but he, at times, completely misunderstood the psychology of crowds belonging to other races; and it is because he thus misunderstood that he engaged in Spain, and notably in Russia, in conflicts in which his power received blows which were destined within a brief space of time to ruin it. A knowledge of the psychology of crowds is today the last resource of the statesman who wishes not to govern them – that is becoming a very difficult matter – but at any rate not to be too much governed by them.

It is only by obtaining some sort of insight into the psychology of crowds that it can be understood how slight is the action upon them of laws and institutions, how powerless they are to hold any opinions other than those which are imposed upon them, and that it is not with rules based on theories of pure equity that they are to be led, but by seeking what produces an impression on them, and what seduces them ...

As soon as a certain number of living beings are gathered together, whether they be animals or men, they place themselves instinctively under the authority of a chief.

In the case of human crowds the chief is often nothing more than a ringleader or agitator, but as such he plays a considerable part. His will is the nucleus around which the opinions of the crowd are grouped and attain to identity. He constitutes the first element towards the organization of heterogeneous crowds, and paves the way for their organization in sects; in the meantime he directs them. A crowd is a servile flock that is incapable of ever doing without a master.

The leader has most often started as one of the led. He has himself been hypnotized by the idea, whose apostle he has since become. It has taken possession of him to such a degree that everything outside it vanishes, and that every contrary opinion appears to him an error or superstition. An example in point is Robespierre, hypnotized by the philosophical ideas of Rousseau, and employing the methods of the Inquisition to propagate them.

The leaders we speak of are more frequently men of action than thinkers. They are not gifted with keen foresight, nor could they be, as this quality generally conduces to doubt and inactivity. They are especially recruited from the ranks of those morbidly nervous, excitable, half-deranged persons who are bordering on madness. However absurd may be the idea they uphold or the goal they pursue, their convictions are so strong that all reasoning is lost upon them. Contempt and persecution do not affect them, or only serve to excite them the more. They sacrifice their personal interest, their family – everything. The very instinct of self-preservation is entirely obliterated in them, and so much so that often the only recompense they solicit is that of martyrdom. The intensity of their faith gives great power of suggestion to their words. The multitude is always ready to listen to the strong-willed man, who knows how to impose himself upon it. Men gathered in a crowd lose all force of will, and turn instinctively to the person who possesses the quality they lack.

Nations have never lacked leaders, but all of the latter have by no means been animated by those strong convictions proper to apostles. These leaders are often subtle rhetoricians, seeking only their own personal interest, and endeavouring to persuade by flattering base instincts. The influence they can assert in this manner may be very great, but it is always ephemeral. The men of ardent convictions who have stirred the soul of crowds, the Peter the Hermits, the Luthers, the Savonarolas, the men of the French Revolution, have exercised their fascination only after having been themselves fascinated first of all by a creed. They are then able to call up in the souls of their fellows that formidable force known as faith, which renders a man the absolute slave of his dream.

The arousing of faith — whether religious, political or social, whether faith in a work, in a person or an idea — has always been the function of the great leaders of crowds, and it is on this account that their influence is always very great. Of all the forces at the disposal of humanity, faith has always been one of the most tremendous, and the gospel rightly attributes to it the power of moving mountains. To endow a man with faith is to multiply his strength tenfold. The great events of history have been brought about by obscure believers, who have had little beyond their faith in their favour. It is not by the aid of the learned or of philosophers, and still less of sceptics, that have been built up the great religions which have swayed the world, or the vast empires which have spread from one hemisphere to the other.

In the cases just cited, however, we are dealing with great leaders, and they are so few in number that history can easily reckon them up. They form the summit of a continuous series, which extends from these powerful masters of men down to the workman who, in the smoky atmosphere of an inn, slowly fascinates his comrades by ceaselessly drumming into their ears a few set phrases, whose purport he scarcely comprehends, but the application of which, according to him, must surely bring about the realization of all dreams and of every hope.

In every social sphere, from the highest to the lowest, as soon as a man ceases to be isolated he speedily falls under the influence of a leader. The majority of men, especially among the masses, do not possess clear and reasoned ideas on any subject whatever outside their own speciality. The leader serves them as guide. It is just possible that he may be replaced, though very inefficiently, by the periodical publications which manufacture opinions for their readers and supply them with ready-made phrases which absolve them of the trouble of reasoning.

The leaders of crowds wield a very despotic authority, and this despotism indeed is a condition of their obtaining a following. It has often been remarked how easily they extort obedience, although without any means of backing up their authority ...

Whether they be intelligent or narrow-minded is of no importance; the world belongs to them. The persistent will-force they possess is an immensely rare and immensely powerful faculty to which everything yields. What a strong and continuous will is capable of is not always properly appreciated. Nothing resists it; neither nature, gods, nor man.

MAURICE BARRÈS
(1862–1923)

If Maurras repelled even his supporters, Barrès charmed even his opponents. An anti-semite who could always count Jews among his admirers, the high priest of nationalism who came to admire Clemenceau, the hater of socialism who could write condolingly to Jaurès's daughter after his assassination could not but be an attractive figure. Some doubted his sincerity and others his wisdom, but all seemed to agree that the man who could become a member of the Académie Française at the age of forty-five must be something special, perhaps the new Alcibiades. Barrès died too early to be given the chance of going over to Sparta.

Barrès made his intellectual reputation with the idea of the *déraciné* – the rootless, cosmopolitan metic – and harnessed it to a mystical nationalism. Beyond this, his interest in political matters was limited, despite a political career in the Chamber which spanned over thirty years and several political labels. Nor is it perhaps altogether correct to put Barrès on the right – the same problems arise in classifying his political position as with Sorel. Barrès did not object to socialism as such. For him, the important thing was that if a man was to be a socialist, he ought to be a French socialist if he is French, a national socialist in a specific sense. What attracts Barrès in Proudhon is not that Proudhon is on the left, but that he is a Burgundian, French, and therefore within the pale. Barrès's work is full of his feeling for Lorraine, yet one wonders what Lorraine really meant for him. The Lorraine he writes of is not the Lorraine of reality. As the critic Berl wrote: 'Who would realize on reading this citizen of Lorraine that he is describing a metallurgical country? He has seen the *mirabelliers* and neglected the blast-furnaces.' Perhaps Michael Curtis is correct in describing Barrès's relationship with Lorraine as a marriage of convenience, in which Barrès left his faithful wife behind in order to lead that gilded Parisian life which in his writing is seen to be inferior to the life of Lorraine.

Yet the mystique of Lorraine was, and remains, a powerful symbol in French political life. Barrès began it; Claudel eulogized it in his poem *La Croix de Lorraine* with the line '*In hoc signo vinces*'; de Gaulle, with deep sagacity, exploited it as Barrès did.

The extracts from Barrès are translated from a collection of political writings, *Scènes et Doctrines du Nationalisme* (2 vols, Plon, Paris, 1925), with the exception of the piece 'The Undying Spirit of France'. The section 'From Hegel to the Workmen's Canteens of the North' is translated by the editor. Other translations are by Eric Harber.

FROM HEGEL TO THE WORKMEN'S CANTEENS OF THE NORTH

1. *The Philosophy outlives the Philosopher*

Heine describes to us the mechanically regulated life of Kant, always dressed in his grey suit, getting up in the morning, having breakfast, writing, giving his lectures, having dinner, going out for a walk, all at a set time for thirty years. Then Heine suddenly interrupts: 'Indeed, if the good citizens of Koenigsberg had been able to foresee the destructive power of Kant's thought, they would have shuddered much more violently at the sight of him than at the sight of the hangman who at least only kills men.'

But it is not just a man's fellow citizens who fail to see the seeds of revolution buried in his mind. I admit that Kant himself failed to grasp the consequences of what was taking shape in his own mind. He could not have directed or annulled the conclusions of the arguments which he invented. A principle is often destined for a mysterious future.

He who creates a principle is no longer a master of it. Almost before it is formulated, it becomes a force which strives to expand, to give life to everything in it which has the power to move men, even the contradictions. Even the most acute philosopher's vision is too restricted for him to be able to follow very far the shock-waves which emanate from him. He cannot even guess at the direction his ideas will follow, let alone calculate their effects. What arc will it describe in the world? Where will it insinuate itself? With what will it combine?

If it is put into action, what will it destroy? Perhaps the

145

idols dear to the heart of the thinker himself. One has seen ideas turned against those who conceived them.

Ah! Do not talk to me of love, of romantic journeys, or of conquest. Nothing really has the power to move us so much as this drama of ideas, this mystery in the impalpable.

About the year 1800, a young German tutor in a Frankfurt family caught a glimpse of the secret of the process by which the universe becomes conscious of itself. It was Hegel at the age of thirty. At Jena, Hegel was allowed to give his own course. Four students came. People were put off by his awkward delivery and by the range and subtlety of his argument.

Besides, Napoleon was diverting people's attention elsewhere in Germany.

And yet the ideas of the penniless professor quietly gained ground. Speaking about Hegel's first book, his disciple Strauss cried, very justly: 'There goes the master on a tour of the world on the ship he built with his own hands.'

Round the world, indeed! Sometimes, at Roubaix and Vierzon, at Carmaux, at Rive-de-Gier, in the poorest working men's canteens at Le Borinage, when listening in the evenings to some socialist evangelist, we can recognize in the phraseology or the historical method of the orator some fragment of the dialectic of the professor from Jena.

What an extraordinary migration, that after so many years and in very different classes, the mysterious doctrines of the professor of Jena should reappear. But, and this is even more extraordinary, those same ideas that the Prussian conservatives seized on with passion as a means of self-justification, have become the most dangerous weapons of revolution of uneducated workers! It is a fine example of the powerlessness of the most powerful thinkers. A principle grows across the world, with single-mindedly force. Nothing can stop it, and often the results of that development are so unforeseeable that they surpass the cruellest irony.

Hegel proudly thought that he had said all that needed to be said, but as soon as his system spread into the world it had to separate itself from its creator in order to survive. This always happens. A system runs amok in the universe, and has an influence not only on those who consciously accept it, but has an even greater influence on those who reject it; it even influences those who have never heard its name. Hegelianism has had an adventurous life.

For some fifty years, the French Revolution has been an event of total importance. Yes, it was that, but is no longer. In this year 1894, the Revolution, with Mirabeau and Danton, Robespierre and perhaps even Bonaparte, hardly counts at all. For a great man does not always remain a great man, nor does a great event always remain a great event. I am astounded how quickly the elegant society of the Second Empire reduced the glories of the First Empire to a curiosity or a knick-knack. A certain day arrives when the influence that a man or an event has on our imagination — and through it on our very existence — is exhausted to the extent that its domination and prestige cease to exist.

The French Revolution is like those old Polish heroes who, after they had astounded the Slav world, became, with a change of scene, mere waiters at table in cheap restaurants; the Revolution ought to be satisfied with its place of honour in the speeches at little rural banquets. Let us be more precise and say this: the tradition of 1789, which was for so long the really revolutionary element in our century, has now become a conservative force.

Rousseau, at least, has preserved his virtue intact. For a

hundred years he has continued to awaken individual consciousness and to fill the lovers of justice with generous emotion as he did in the last century. Remember that it is not necessary to know a doctrine in order to be influenced by it; it is enough to breathe it in. Rousseau hangs heavy in the air of France. It is in just such an atmosphere that the Hegelian idea crystallizes out.

Our different forms of socialism are a combination of the political sensibilities of Rousseau structured by Hegel's dialectic. The tribunes of social change would not say, if they plucked up the courage to speak honestly, 'We are the grandchildren of the Revolution.' That relationship is only valid for Bonapartists, Orleanists or the parliamentary republicans – that is to say, for those who wish to preserve the existing political and economic structure. But a truly revolutionary Frenchman, collectivist, federalist or anarchist, looks to Rousseau for his political sensibilities and to Hegel for his dialectic.

Proudhon, like Marx and Bakunin, is a son of Hegel. A formidable lineage! The honest bourgeois whose children were taught by Hegel at the same time as Hegel was working out his system, would have fainted with horror if he had the remotest idea of what was being conceived under his own roof. But Hegel himself had not the faintest notion of what the consequences of his ideas would be. Although the spiritual father of so many revolutionaries, he had no love for revolutions, and both the Prussian state and the Restoration looked to him for firm support.

This is a fine example of that delicious irony which we refer to: Hegel's system, blessing or plague, has swept the world, life-destroying and life-giving, without its author having the slightest idea of consequences which he could not predict and which, for all his genius, he would have been powerless to alter.

We are going to examine in the next two sections a principle which exhausts all the possibilities inherent in its inner logic. And what an intoxicating spectacle for the intellect!

2. *The Genealogy of an Idea*

At first, Hegel's system developed along two different lines, collectivism and anarchism, which, though contradictory, were equally logical deductions from his basic principles.

Logical consequences, though Hegel would have rejected both because he saw his philosophy as the realization of the Absolute. It seemed to him that he had found the key to the mysteries of the universe. All that remained was to apply it.

In fact, Hegel seriously contradicted the dialectic in believing that the world could stand still. His disciples believed in the method rather than the master. Using the dialectic, they rebelled against Hegel.

Forgive me for not trying to describe in more detail what Hegel's philosophy is, but that would overload this little study which can achieve clarity only by leaving certain things out ...

It is well known that according to Hegel's admirable dialectic, the Idea cannot be manifested in a particular fact or individual. The Idea is immanent only in a succession of phenomena moving towards the infinite. In other words, truth is partly manifest in being, but is completely manifest only in becoming. Again, every stage in the development of history into eternity contains a partial manifestation of the truth, without ever reaching the complete truth. Thus all innovations and all contradictions are in some sense justified. We now know how to follow the historical development of the nations; we now understand what has gone before; and more, we respect that development, for Hegel teaches us that the real is the rational, and that the rational is real, and that the truth of a thing consists in its place in the total scheme of things.

The Hegelians frenziedly invaded the whole realm of knowledge. One can see them as a conquering army distributing the kingdoms of the intellectual universe among themselves.

No doubt it is true that Hegel's system was quickly abandoned, but his method, after the progress of the experimental sciences, is still accepted today by historians, theologians and economists, and it produces startling results everywhere.

Hegelianism has produced some strange compounds which vary according to the temperament, and even more to the nationality of those whom it captivates.

It is that same Hegelian method which has kept alive collectivism and Karl Marx in Germany, Proudhon in France, and Bakunin and anarchist terrorism in Russia.

Powerful combinations indeed! Could there be a richer genealogy for those whose joy it is to trace the development of an idea?

Let us try to draw it in outline.

Strauss,[1] in 1835, and Feuerbach[2] in 1841, had revolu-

---

[1] David Friedrich Strauss (1808–74), disciple of Hegel and Schleiermacher, whose *Life of Jesus* (1835) argued that the existence of Christ was a myth, and the whole biblical account of the life of Christ could be investigated with the same intellectual equipment as other systems of mythology; the work caused a scandal and left him destitute.

[2] Ludwig Feuerbach (1804–72), disciple of Hegel who, breaking with the master, argued in *Essence of Christianity* (1841) that God was a projection of man and had no objective existence. Feuerbach influenced Marx in his attack on Hegel's idealism.

tionized politics and theology by the use of Hegelian ideas. Since 1844, Marx and Engels have been using the master's dialectic in the study of political economy. They put Hegelianism at the service of materialism, a considerable intellectual achievement which Engels himself has described in his study of Feuerbach ...

I do not deny that socialism existed before Hegel's dialectic, if by socialism we mean a feeling for a more perfect society. But Hegel's philosophy of history has taught us that nothing in this world stands still, that everything praiseworthy or sacred is but a single moment in the development of humanity and that it must make way for other institutions no less praiseworthy or sacred. Thus disorder is itself worthy of respect, because disorder is a series of convulsions in which a new order strives to replace the old. And further, truth as we understand it today is in part error. It is this double view of the universe which, in our opinion, makes a socialist, that is, a man who has a taste for social change.

It is not a question of being a prophet, but of committing oneself to a necessary evolution. Constructing a Utopia in the study and then attempting to impose it on humanity is the product of a superficial imagination! It is, however, an error into which Marx fell. Marxism began as a philosophy and ended up as a political programme.

Marx's disciples are trapped in that programme, that is, in that error. Marxists are not content with a forceful analysis of the successive forms of property: they take it upon themselves to reduce the future to a single formula, and to bend us in that direction. Just as Hegel thought he had arrived at a definitive analysis of the universe, so Marx in his turn thinks he can organize it for ever. Both misunderstood their dialectic; both attempt to fix human happiness in a given context instead of realizing that each stage of an infinite series of developments contains a part of that happiness.

Bakunin is surely right when, against the Marxists who run the risk of bringing history to a stop, he moves from destruction to destruction, heroically pursuing the infinite series of the moments of human truth.

It is said that Bakunin's anarchism owes a great deal to Stirner,[1] who set out the sacred law of egoism. I do not know enough about Stirner to discuss him properly, but at least I can see how in Bakunin's mind Hegelianism justifies anarchism.

If the anarchists understand the unity of destruction and creation, it is through Hegel's perceptive views on the importance of evil. Hegel wrote: 'It is considered a fine sentiment when it is said: "Man is good by nature"; what is forgotten is that to say "Man is naturally evil" displays an acuter insight. Evil and rebellion, the blows aimed at something sacred, are essential preconditions of human development; it is the evil passions which keep things on the move in humanity and in the universe ... '

Though we are treading on dangerous ground, it is perhaps fair to say that Bakunin thinks he is obliged to collaborate too actively and completely with the forces of negation and destruction which are, in effect, only one condition necessary for the development of the universe. Montaigne observed, 'One sets too high a price on conjectures which send men to the stake.'

In other words, Bakunin, obsessed with the importance of negation in the development of the universe, has failed to grasp the importance of conservation. He has failed to

[1] Max Stirner (1806–56), wrote *The Ego and His Own* (1845), an anarchist attack aimed at all authority, including his erstwhile master, Hegel. Was later attacked himself by Marx.

use that other Hegelian axiom: 'True reason gives a man patience.'

After all, assassination, incendiarism, dynamite, however terrible they may be in the normal order of things, are affirmations of the ill-considered desire for destruction on the part of a negative character. Terrorism is all too often the expedient of an overexcited brain. It is the last resource of races which see themselves falling behind, or of degenerates who feel that they are regarded as outcasts.

Thus collectivism and anarchist terrorism, both logical deductions from Hegel's system despite being in contradiction with each other, are 'objectionable' in terms of their own origin. I take them to be antitheses which can only resolve their dialectical origin in a new synthesis. What we must now do is to work out the details of this reconciliation.

3. *Federation gives every man a Fatherland*

Anarchism and collectivism, the twin deductions from Hegel's system made by Bakunin and Marx, are clearly contradictory. Bakunin sacrifices everything to negation; he invites the individual to a merciless criticism of society. Marx, on the contrary, gave forceful support to the element of conservation: he refounded an absolute, collective authority.

It might seem impossible to reconcile views which are so contradictory, but it is the singular merit of Hegelianism to enable us to realize the validity of contradiction, and to reconcile contradictions in a higher principle.

It is our belief that this higher principle is to be found in Proudhon.

Like Marx and Bakunin, Proudhon's thought is dependent on the Hegelian dialectic. He has put forward a single, great truth – which might well serve as an epigraph to the present work – that every economist, even those whose only concern is the laws of labour and exchange, is really a metaphysician. One of the most important parts of Proudhon's work is still his having pointed out the antinomies, the contradictions in society, just as the German philosopher worked out the system of contradictions in dialectic. 'Although it is unnecessary', he wrote to a friend, 'to follow Hegel in his fruitless attempt to construct the world of reality by so-called *a priori* reasoning, one can still maintain strongly that his logic is a magnificent tool.' And does Proudhon not still use a Hegelian formula when he says: 'Certain processes, like certain ideas, destroy themselves in the course of their natural development. Society is developing into a new form directly opposed to its present state, and it so develops according to the same principles which directed it to its present conditions'?

We are not trying to cast doubts on Proudhon's originality, or on his own self-generating qualities. It is said, for instance, that Marxism borrowed from him the theory of the accumulation of capital by robbing the labourer of his surplus value. In any case, what lies at the heart of Proudhonism is its native French quality, the heritage of the Rousseaus, the Saint-Simons, the Fouriers.

Proudhon's socialism, founded as it is on a combination of our native sensibilities and Hegelianism, satisfies and inspires Frenchmen who could never accept German collectivism or Russian anarchism, because these latter ideas are so obviously the signs of a different racial consciousness.

Does this mean that Proudhon presents us with the whole truth, the absolute? He would be a very poor Hegelian to claim that. We have traced the whole development of the Hegelian tradition of social inquiry;

we have seen the genius of Hegel divide into collectivism and anarchism; now we intend to reconcile the two, though not in Proudhon's formula, but rather in the direction that Proudhon has opened up for us. Proudhon himself, with his solid, Burgundian good sense, simply said: 'I have only begun to give the outlines of that new form of social organization, the final laws of which can be known only when new processes have come to light. Without these I can carry the investigation no further.'

To return to Proudhon's most simple proposition: the problem is to find the middle way between two elusive elements, collectivism and anarchy, authority and liberty, social cohesion and individualism. And now, what advice did the Hegelian dialectic give to Proudhon, that seems to us superior to the separate principles of authority and liberty, and which becomes, by their mutual reconciliation, a superior principle?

Federation and contract.

Federation and contract indeed! The way to reconcile individual freedom with social cohesion is through a federation of natural groupings – geographical regions possessing their own character, professional and other associations – which order their internal affairs on the basis of individual contract analogous to free enterprise and which are affiliated to the federation only as corporations. Thus unity is achieved without undue constraint.

This Proudhonian programme will always be attractive to the philosopher who shuns the role of prophet, preferring the outlook of sober inquiry to that of the single moment of inspiration.

This system of contract and federation makes it possible, at the same time, for the various minorities to procure a social system for themselves appropriate to their spirit and their customs. This freedom of action we take to be the most important political safeguard. The speculative intelligence can envisage a situation of such a hatred of the capitalist system that, on the day after the revolution, some kind of standardized collectivism, based on the model appropriate to the most powerful region, would be forced on the whole of France, not to mention the whole of Europe. But soon the varied influences of race, custom and climate would come again into their own, and real differences would reassert themselves. It is essential that these aspects of human development should be given free reign, so that humanity can affirm the life-giving nature of diversity, of variety, of difference. No single one contains the truth. Only the total diversity approaches that truth.

So, sons of Hegel, do not forget too quickly the fine laws of your old father ...

Remember, from beyond Hegel, the sublime incantation of the old Goethe (for he, the greatest poet, is also the best source of all thought): 'Nature for ever creates new forms. What is, has never existed before; what was will never be again; everything is new, everything old ... Life is her finest work, and death the means by which she creates new life ... '

One thing is well known to everybody, to anarchists, collectivists and thinkers generally: that capitalism and the present system of distribution are not forms of economic life that will last for ever. But what the collectivists do not give enough attention to is the fact that collectivism will itself be superseded. In this they show themselves for what they are: religious fanatics when their philosophy-cum-catechism is called into question. And it is not even enough for them to arrest the progress of human evolution at the stage of collectivization. They intend to go further, and to impose uniformity and inertness on the universe.

Uniformity – what a pathetic stupidity! I imagine that

it is obvious by now that Hegel has taught us that no fact or process is isolated, inward-looking, but contains infinite possibility; that nothing is complete in itself but is part of a greater whole; that everything under the sun is at the same time limited and unlimited. Nothing is false; nothing completely true. Can it follow that a single system of ideas can fit with any exactness the infinite variety of reality? Can one solution satisfy every need?

Merely by putting this question to anyone who has read Hegel, or indeed anyone whose intellectual outlook has been formed by the nineteenth century, one must receive an answer in the negative.

The desire to impose uniformity and immobility on the world, when everything is relative, when everything passes away, must be the result of a pathological egoism.

But hardly less surprising is the idea of individualism spread abroad by the anarchist terrorists. It is not enough for them to protect their own individuality, to assure its independence and its opportunity for free development; they refuse to respect the individuality of others and would intervene to remake the universe and the whole of humanity in the image of their own prejudices!

It is obvious that unless one accepts the idea of federation and contract, one has completely misunderstood both the law of evolution and the law of contradiction.

It is in federation that the moral and physical diversity of the universe is best respected. It is contract that allows each individual ego to work out for itself a tolerable relationship with other egos.

According to the circumstances of its development, the Hegelian system has resolved itself into two opposing formulae, collectivism and anarchism, but it will outgrow these two stages of its development. True to the original spirit of the dialectic, in our opinion it will reconcile these two opposites and, through a higher evolution, will bloom into federalism, a flower infinitely fertile in diversity.

This is our conclusion: if the revolutionary impetus of the Hegelian system, concentrated as it is in the working classes as we saw in those workers' canteens in the north, is to transform the world; if an old civilization must crumble away, then at least let a federation replace it, so that we can repeat the desperate words of that wise Venetian on the last day of that republic's existence: 'An honourable man always finds a Fatherland.'

Le Journal, November 30th, December
7th and 14th, 1894

SCÈNES ET DOCTRINES
DU NATIONALISME

Nationalism and Determinism

A Lorrainer remarked some time in the eighteenth century: 'I know that it has the virtue of being natural, but
I do not know if its nature is virtuous.'

The kind of reader who can use this little story as an
argument against us had better read quickly on into this
work, because he will find, in thousands of different ways,
that the problem for the individual and the nation is not
to make themselves into what they want to be (an impossible task!) but to preserve in themselves what the centuries have predestined for them ...

Nationalism is the acceptance of a particular kind of
determinism ...

Catholics see patriotism as an extension of morality.
Their commitment to the Fatherland finds its strength
in the precepts of the Church. But what if I am not a
believer?

For some people, the supernatural is dead. Their piety
is not directed towards some object in the heavens. I
have redirected my piety from the heavens to the earth,
the earth that contains my dead.

My *intelligence* is tempted on all sides; everything
interests me, stimulates me and amuses me. But there is,
at the very bottom of our souls, a fixed point, a delicate
nerve; if it is probed the result is a total reaction which I
cannot mistrust, a movement of my whole being. It is not
the awakening of the sensibilities of a mere individual;
what frightens me is the awakening of my whole race.

159

... Sweet Antigone, a maid of twenty, you wanted to hide, to survive and to marry. But the Antigone who was as old as the illustrious race of the Labdaciades had to make her stand.

Creon was both master and stranger. He said: 'I know the laws of this country and I will apply them.' He judges with his intelligence; the intelligence, that insignificant thing which is only the surface of ourselves!

How different he is from Antigone, who brings the depths of her heredity to the same question, whose inspiration comes from those regions of the unconscious where respect, love and fear unite in a single, magnificent drive towards veneration.

She can do no other, and it is through the affirmation of that drive towards veneration that the city is shaken to the roots and is reconciled to itself through Antigone.

And so Creon himself, moved more by sorrow than by reason, falls to his knees.

So *the best line of argument* and the most complete demonstrations are not enough to convince me. My heart has to be filled spontaneously with a great respect and a great love. It is in these moments of total emotion that my heart tells me which things I must put beyond the test of reason.

After the long, hard work of foraging, after a subtle and profound search, I found the gushing source in my little garden. It comes from the vast ice-sheet which supplies all the fountains in my city.

How do those who never gain access to those subterranean reservoirs, who never know themselves with respect, with love and with fear as the continuation of their ancestors, ever find their way in life?

It is my sense of descent which provides me with the axis around which my total, self-contained idea of life revolves.

As long as I stay there, neither my descendants nor my benefactors will crumble into dust. And I am sure that I will be sheltered myself by some of those whom I awaken when I can no longer look after myself.

Thus I have my fixed points, my own landmarks both in the past and in posterity. If I read them again, I become conscious of one of the great traditions of French classicism. How could I not be prepared to make all the sacrifices necessary for the protection of that classicism which is my backbone.

When I say *backbone*, it is not a metaphor but the most powerful analogy. A long series of intellectual exercises multiplied over the preceding centuries has educated our reflexes.

Even thought is not free. I can live only in relation to my dead. They, and the earth of my country, command me to a particular way of life.

Terrified of my dependence, powerless to make myself what I want myself to be, I still want to see the powers that govern me face to face. I want to live with these my masters, to share fully in their strength by working out a self-conscious cult for them.

Others lose their sense of the unity of things when they analyse them; it is through analysis that I regain my sense of unity and reach what for me is the truth.

What is truth? Truth is not something to be known intellectually. Truth is finding a particular point, the only point, that one and no other, from which everything appears to us in its proper perspective.

Let us be more precise. How I like the saying of a certain painter: 'Sit in the right place and get the perspective correct.'

I must settle myself at that point which my eyes take as their own so that it is the past centuries which form my vision; that point from which everything is seen through the eyes of a Frenchman. The totality of these proper relationships between given objects and a given subject, the Frenchman, that is French truth and French justice; French reason is the discovery of these relationships. And pure nationalism is simply the discovery of that point, searching for it, and when it is found, holding fast to it and receiving from it our art, our politics and the manner of living our life ...

All the great men who have gone before us and whom I have loved so well – not only the Hugos and the Michelets, but also those who have made possible the transition into the modern period, the Taines and the Renans – believed in the existence of an independent faculty of reason which enables us to reach the truth. I was passionately committed to this idea myself. The sovereign individual with his intelligence and his ability to seize on the laws of the universe! This idea must be destroyed. We are not in control of our own thinking. Our thoughts are not the products of our own individual intelligence; they are the physiological translations of primeval physiological dispositions. Our moral judgments and our reason are merely elaborations of these dispositions in particular circumstances. Human reason is in such bondage that we all follow the path of our ancestors. There are no truly personal ideas; even the most outrageous ideas, the most abstract judgments and the most bewitching sophistries of metaphysics are aspects of this general disposition and are to be found in every member of the same species under an enforced loyalty to the same set of symbols ...

A note on the terms 'French race' and 'French nation'. Let it be said once and for all: it is inaccurate to speak of a French race in the strict sense of the term. We are not a race but a nation; the nation is an ongoing thing, new each day, and it is our duty, we who are part of her, to protect her from the threat of destruction or the possibility of a decline into insignificance.

Of all the analogies which can convey a feeling for what a nation is, listen to the one which pleases me best.

I would most happily compare a nation to those compounds of small stones and mortar which occur naturally in running water. The mortar which binds these stones comes partly from the wear and tear on the stones themselves and partly from their movement. When the mass is dragged along by the water, other stones attach themselves to it and become buried in it. Layer forms upon layer. But if each separate element of the top layer can be identified, each none the less has the solidity, in the face of physical force, of all the component parts which have attached themselves to the original nucleus but which are today unseen. And that solidarity created the resistance of the whole to the forces of nature. If a single stone breaks off from the whole, it rolls quickly, gets worn down and becomes dust; even if it attaches itself to another mass, it is still half worn, diminished in value.

Thus it seems to me that the individual is bound to all his dead ancestors by the efforts and sacrifices of individuals in the past, just as the stone is bound to the mass by the mortar formed by the successive layers.

The State of the Dreyfus Question

Déroulède's Formula[1]

The campaign mounted by a certain group of people

[1] Paul Déroulède (1846–1914), author and right-wing deputy, anti-Dreyfusard and Boulangist. Founder member of the *Ligue des patriots* (1882), and attempted, in 1887, to stage a Boulangist *coup d'état* without Boulanger.

which is called 'the Dreyfus affair' is an example of the disassociation and decerebralization (*décérébration*) of France. At the same time it widens the division amongst us and troubles the spirit of the nation.

Déroulède's formula is really striking. He states: 'It is highly improbable that Dreyfus is innocent, but it is absolutely certain that France herself is innocent.'

Alfred Dreyfus is a Symbol. Very few Dreyfusards associate themselves closely with ... [those] who affirm the innocence of Dreyfus.

In any case, on what evidence does the suggestion of a miscarriage of justice rest? Neither you nor I have access to the full facts of the case (and we never will have); as a result, we cannot give an original opinion, but can only refer to the opinions of those who manipulate opinion.

'They are suspect,' a Dreyfusard replies.

'Suspect of what?'

'The General Staff has sacrificed Dreyfus to please the Jesuits.'

That cannot be a serious point. Another Dreyfusard tells me that the General Staff made a mistake in good faith and that it now persists in the error through *esprit de corps*.

Why should Billot,[1] Cavaignac,[2] Zurlinden,[3] etc., still

[1] Jean-Baptiste Billot (1828-1907), general and politician, Minister of War 1882-3, and again in 1896.

[2] Jacques Godefroy Cavaignac (1853-1905), general and politician, Minister of War 1895-6, and again in 1898. Anti-Dreyfusard and a leading member of Barrès's *Ligue de la Patrie Française*.

[3] Emile Thomas Zurlinden (1837-1929), general and politician, Minister of War 1895, and again in 1898, when he resigned because he wanted no part in the revision of the Dreyfus case.

side with the General Staff if the latter has committed
the crime of breaking an innocent man? No, let us leave
that to one side, it is mere speculation! You could speculate
just as easily, or even more easily, in the case of the first
condemned person that comes to mind, for Dreyfus had
not even got that peculiarly French way of pleading his
case to the imagination that other criminals have ...

Most Dreyfusards, I have seen it a thousand times, if
you examine their reasons for believing in the innocence of
Dreyfus, will quickly interrupt you:

'Ah! Dreyfus! That's the point! Suppose he were the
worst man on earth! It's possible, I grant you, but ... '

Here our Dreyfusard, with eyes alive with passion,
reveals his deepest thoughts, his real motive, the driving
force inside. Now he says:

'It's a disgrace to see how Dreyfus's so-called treason is
exploited by the clericals.'

Then:

'I can't stand by and see the due process of law perverted, even in a case involving the worst criminal.'

And again:

'We've never had such a good opportunity to destroy
the army.'

It is indeed a pity that such a master of the imaginative
moral inference as Anatole France, whose first step is
always to note the relationship between a sentiment
expressed and the facial expression, has not seen fit to
develop these three essential phrases into three little
comedies. If he were to use the physiognomy of the
speakers to throw light on the matter, you would certainly
be able to put everyone with whom you could possibly
quarrel with over the affair into one of the three categories
provided by the exercise.

The vast majority of the Dreyfusards are moved by

considerations which have nothing to do with the supposed innocence of Dreyfus.

For some it is a question of dealing a blow to anti-semitism. M. Joseph Reinach maintains that racial hatred has found a powerful means of increase in the Dreyfus affair; he hopes to calm down the anti-semitic agitation by rehabilitating Dreyfus and, much more to the point, by showing that Dreyfus is the victim of a treacherous fanaticism.

For others, it is a question of abolishing military jurisdiction. These gentlemen insist on a version of the case which they present as an absolute certainty, according to which a document was illegally handed over to the court martial. In the name of the rights of man and citizen, Protestants and liberals, with the occasional anarchist peeping out from amongst them ... deny that any consideration of a general nature justified an *acte d'exception*, or that particular cases require particular measures.

And for others, it is a question of destroying the army. M. Jaurès and his friends have taken it upon themselves to broadcast and exploit this aspect of the Dreyfus affair as loudly and as thoroughly as possible. Certainly there are important reforms to be dragged out of the army! And how useful would even the revolutionary audacity which M. Jaurès now deploys to the detriment of the Fatherland have been in the cause of saving the nation at the time of the Madagascar campaign! Yes, to the detriment of the Fatherland because he is attempting to destroy everything with the sole aim of rehabilitating a condemned man, and, let it be said, to the detriment of the Socialist Party because that party can win through only by taking a line totally different from its present anti-militarism, that is to say, by convincing people that the principal points in its programme are compatible with the needs of a great modern European state.

The Dreyfusards have been like this from the start. How do they know if their man is innocent or guilty? The only truth available is the judicial truth, but the socialist way of reasoning does not allow them to accept that this is the only truth possible. They have to make a social and political question out of a mere question of law. Why? So that certain obsessions dear to their hearts, can triumph. These considerations have nothing to do with the problem given to the judges of the court martial to solve. Also, they say that Dreyfus is a symbol. Be quite certain that these political operators have picked up this little Jew to use as a weapon, like picking up a knife from the gutter.

I judge Dreyfus as a Symbol in relation to France

If Dreyfus is a traitor, to release him would be an action of minimal importance; but if he is more than a traitor, if he is a symbol, the case is altered: now it becomes the Dreyfus affair! Stop there! The triumph of the Dreyfusard camp, the camp which supports Dreyfus as symbol, would put into power those men whose intention it is *to remake France in the image of their own prejudices*. And as for me, I want to preserve France.

The whole of nationalism is contained in that opposition. You are dreaming, and you want to lead us in the direction of your dreams. We are content to state the conditions which alone can save France, and we accept them. In fact, I am worried by the thought of what value might be put on your 'generous' preferences in the calm of the study!

In theory, one may support this or that point of view; one may, according to one's inclination, praise or condemn the army, military justice or race war. But it is not a question of one's own inclinations; it is a question of France and these questions should be treated in the light of the interests of France.

I beg you to believe that we must not suppress the army because a militia would not be enough in Lorraine.

We must not suppress a strictly military justice because certain insignificant faults in the civil sphere become, through their results, grave faults in the military sphere.

We must not complain about the rise of anti-semitism at the very moment the enormous power of the Jewish race becomes obvious, a power which threatens France with a total change in her nature.

It is precisely this that the intellectuals of the university, drunk with a pathological Kantianism, fail to understand. They chant, like Bouteiller: 'I must *always* act in such a way that my action could be a *universal rule.*' Not so, gentlemen! Leave aside those pretentious words *always* and *universal* and then you are true Frenchmen. Make it your business to act according to the interests of France at this time.

Dialogue on Absolute Truth and Judicial Truth
(Taking place under the following circumstances:)

The Criminal Chamber of the Court of Appeal was occupied with a petition for review. It was thought that the Chamber would acquit Dreyfus ... it was believed, on the other hand, that Colonel Piquart would be court-martialled.

'A court martial!' exclaims the one. 'Ah! so much the better. It will provide us with one truth, at least. But wait. This will not be absolute truth. No institution could provide that. No individual possesses it: it is not of this world. Only the crudest religious optimism would promise it. A court martial, like any other judicial power, provides us with judicial truth and we ought to respect it.'

'Certainly,' replied the other, 'society would not make sense if we failed to recognize the universality of relativism. Those who understand the function of law in a country expect the courts to find truth in law, not absolute truth. This truth is the more estimable because from it the police derive their power to act. But there is a difficulty: not long after the decision of the court martial, we will receive the decision of the Appeal Court. This court will also give us a judicial truth. So, I want to know, if the two decisions contradict one another, what happens then?'

'That is hypothetical.'

'It is feasible. What I know of the brief, of the military temper and of the desperate efforts of Piquart's counsel, induces me to believe that the accused will be condemned. At the same time, the practice of the Criminal Chamber when it examines what it has of the Dreyfus records, and the secret confidence of the friends of the ex-captain, makes me think that the court will annul the 1894 proceedings.'

'Piquart dishonoured and imprisoned, Dreyfus free and rehabilitated! The colonel guilty, the captain innocent; these are the two truths that we are leading to. Poor country!'

'Indeed! What are they going to do for the poor country in such an emergency – those who love it and who place its interests above money and faction?'

(Here a long silence.)

'What they must! I can now see the principle that should have been followed from the first. They should not have started proceedings against Dreyfus. Once his treason was proved, they should have demanded his resignation and sent him to be hanged somewhere else.'

'What! Undermine the rule of law! The rational principles of the state!'

'Forget about that old phrase *raison d'état* which merely rationalized the supreme power of the king over the rival factions in the nation. Today, there is neither reason nor power except in the nation itself. It is the "national interest" and the "common good" which must intervene and prevent any of those proceedings that would inevitably produce a situation too serious for France in its present uncoordinated, autistic state to resolve.'

'The idea of summarily dragging a criminal off to his punishment upsets me.'

'You would have been spared your unpleasant feelings. You would never have known. Ministers are not made just to dine at the hostess's right hand at table when there are no members of the Académie present and to entertain their old friends. They have to examine the facts carefully and enforce measures that answer the immediate need.'

'What have you got against General Mercier?'[1]

'Nothing at all. Everyone knows that in the delicate situation of running an army in a democracy, a military commander cannot make political decisions. General Mercier applied military law as an honest soldier without confusing it with the concerns of government where too often decisions are made only after bargaining and consultation.'

'Tell me now. Anyone can see that no one in France

[1] Auguste Mercier (1833–1929), general and politician, Minister of War 1893–5; it was he who had Dreyfus court-martialled; violently attacked after the revision, but absolutely refused to answer his accusers.

has the common good as his particular charge; no one embodies the ideal national order. What if there were a revision of the constitution? Could not the means be found of compelling someone to take the responsibility by redistributing power?'

'Oh yes! A revision of the constitution! This is always offered as the universal panacea. Certainly it would be reasonable to assume some authority at the head of government, to give the republic a head and a centre. But my idea is to regenerate France by seeking out the causes of her decadence. First, we have lost the sense of the relative. Then, we have got into the habit of using words that have lost their meaning ... Lavisse,[1] particularly – a fine fellow, isn't he? Well! When he wrote a letter to the press on the affair, he ended with the assertion that if the court martial released Piquart, *France would once again take her place as the leader of the nations*. Weigh these words! They are empty. What would they mean in the mouth of a historian? Even coming from a speaker in a farmer's cooperative ... But from a Lavisse! The same general causes in the political and philosophical order that make such a good mind content itself with empty words made us decide in the Dreyfus affair to punish the traitor when we were not certain of our strength to use the law, and then to free him without considering whether a civil war would ensue. In the name of public safety the Dreyfus case should never have happened, or rather the body politic should have been prepared for the shock by various conditioning exercises.'

'Well, as things are, what is the best thing to do?'

'There are Frenchmen cleaning their guns. There are

[1] Ernest Lavisse (1842–92), professor of history at the Sorbonne, and director of two huge projects of historical research, a *History of France* in ten volumes and a *History of Contemporary France* in nine volumes.

others, in small committees, drawing up proscription lists. I will wait for the decisions of the court martial and the Court of Appeal. I acknowledge these institutions implicitly because I was born of French parents, and I support them year in and year out because they give me the truths I need.

'You talk like a sane man, but a little under stress. Just now you agreed that these truths were sometimes contradictory, didn't you?'

(Silence for a while.)

'Well, my dear fellow, I think I can find it in myself to accept these contradictions, and by accepting the processes of the national reason bring into subjection the demands of my own particular reason.'

(Another silence.)

'Perhaps you have to be this kind of hero. But, for many, the difficulty of respecting two legal truths that contradict one another is complicated by many different feelings. Imagine the suspicions that would be sown among the interests that suffered! To redouble opposition to civil and military justice we have ready to hand personal hatreds, party rancour, racial hostility. France is very, very sick.'

'The worst she has ever been. In this frame of mind you could explain the most remarkable atrocities in history: the guillotining of Lavoisier or the shooting of Bonjean.'

'How can you talk like that? I can only think that you hope to keep your peace of mind by suppressing your own feelings in the national interest. In this crisis where we are all out of our minds, you satisfy your natural instincts which are to understand, and, when our fists are clenched, you channel your energies into wistful studies of social psychology.

'Be careful you do not attribute sadistic motives to me! I am not so naïve as to stake my own development on the decadence of my country. Besides, France could hardly value an account of the present cultural ferment in which every soul is writhing under our sorrowing eyes. Would it tell us how societies disintegrate? Huh! We know well enough what death looks like. The rare, the unpublished, the unheard, the unknown – these should be offered, for they promote life. (At the moment we cannot even understand the eras when our nation, united, purposeful and flourishing, played a part of the highest significance in the world.) These are the elements of which young historians too preoccupied with explaining the past by the present are deprived. The kind of history that is unwholesome, injurious, is not the history that will fill the gaps in our education.

What is an intellectual? What does one expect from an 'intellectual' – on one side or the other – in the Dreyfus affair?

M. Albert Metin wrote to me in '98 when he was still a student (he has since published an excellent study of socialism in Australia), after reading the articles that I am reproducing: 'Why do you, like the unfortunate Taine, employ scientific terms in an unscientific and derogatory manner? Remember the imagery and the analogies in the *Origins of Contemporary France*. When an intelligent man uses the word "superficial" or "degenerate", he does not admit the pejorative sense that these words have in ordinary conversation.' Well, let us give the word 'intellectual' a simple label and regain something of its true meaning. Take the definition in *Rosmersholm*. Ulrik Brendel says to

Rosmer: 'Montensgaard is a shrewd man: he wants only what he can get.' The intellectual, on the other hand, is a man from the sciences or the humanities who has no power but who still upholds a social ideal. Should journalists and deputies who control the principal mechanisms of power have the last word in matters of public concern? Must the intellectual who prefers to study rather than to govern submit to authority without discussion? This would lead to the ruin of our beautiful and grand conception of a vital and organized France.

On the other hand, Anatole France writes (I summarize): 'In calling us intellectuals, you cast aspersions on intelligence and ridicule those who have understanding. You defame them, you offer violence to them. You claim that they are meddling in affairs that do not concern them. Are there, indeed, things which the faculty of understanding should not grapple with? I am sorry to have to quarrel with our opponents, but there is not a single object which intelligence should not consider fairly and squarely. Everything is its concern. Those men who have devoted their lives to the discovery of scientific truth, those working in laboratories or libraries, are better suited than the common man to distinguish the true from the false in matters affecting the established order and the public interest. Since they are so beneficial to the common good, their duty is to make themselves available.'

So, the intellectual defines himself as a cultivated individual without a mandate who aims to apply his intelligence to resolve effectively the various problems that arise from the Dreyfus affair.

My objection is that in this affair there is no place where intelligence could gain a firm hold. We do not possess the elements necessary for a comprehensive knowledge of the subject: only some of them are known. We could build

only by hypotheses. How do you think that you, a cultivated man, disciplined by training in methods of analysis,
could undertake to solve a problem when you have not all
the data?

After listening to our most implacable opponents, I
suggest that this should be put on the label which they
have devised for themselves:

*Intellectual: an individual who convinces himself that
society should be founded on a basis of logic; and who fails
to see that it rests on past exigencies that are perhaps foreign
to the individual reason.*

We think that we do not falsely represent the thinking
of the 'intellectuals' in this definition. At least we use the
word in this sense and no other.

As for ourselves, we are happier to be intelligent rather
than intellectual, and we would cherish the pure belief —
in any contingency — that everyone has a role to play in
the social order according to his proper function.

In this as in every other case our wisdom is in agreement
with popular opinion which says to those in libraries and
laboratories: 'Let everyone stick to his own skill and the
sheep will be well cared for.'

The Protest of the Intellectuals

In November 1898 a certain number of people, among
whom there were some who were intelligent, began a
campaign to sign a document affirming their sympathies
for the ex-captain Dreyfus. Clemenceau, who published
their names in *L'Aurore*, coined the phrase: 'It is the
protest of the intellectuals.' Or 'the register of the elite'.
Who would not wish to be involved! The university graduates supported it; they marched in close order with their
professors.

'Intellectual' used in this sense is bad French, says Anatole France. This word, defined as 'that which pertains to the intellect, cannot be used in any sense other than as a reference to a faculty of mind. Those who have attempted to make it a description of a certain kind of person do not know their own language.'

Leaving aside the question of the meaning of the term, nothing could be worse than the thing itself. We have described this above. A partial culture destroys instinct without substituting a true consciousness for it. These aristocrats of thought advertise the fact that they do noι think like the stinking mass. It is only too obvious. They no longer instinctively identify themselves with their own class and they never achieve the clarity of vision which would enable them to reflect the common view of the masses.

These intellectuals are a fatal flaw in the attempt that society makes to create an elite. In every operation there are always a number of sacrifices. A glass-blower used to tell me often that he lost a number of pots for every one that was a success. In rejecting the intellectuals, we should pity them rather than offer them ill-will. In their way they cooperate with that wholesome rationality that is peculiarly French, though it is missing in them. A dog whose brain has been made useless still provides a valuable service in the study of psycho-physiology; the poor animal, even with a vacant mind, still helps the study of the functioning of the intelligence more than anyone else.

How justly did the Spartans lavish the pleasures of drinking on the helots! (Those who, as every reader knows, made up the academic body of Sparta, and so may be compared to the university graduates who signed the Dreyfus protest.)

I rejoice in the fact that the helots both gave instruction to the young and enjoyed the pleasures of the bottle. It was a master stroke in educational administration. However, we are not always in the position to distribute such largess [*pots-de-vin*]. Then too, some sensitive nature might recoil from accepting it. Yet the Dreyfus brigade does not strike me as being in the least inferior to Lycurgus and I congratulate their resourceful recruiting sergeants for saying: 'Give me your name and I will give you the title of "intellectual" ... '

Our Professors of Philosophy

Previous generations hoped to achieve a tremendous advance in the development of the human mind by passing from the high realms of the absolute into the plain of the relative, but now the professors and their students are holding back this advance by using empty words fit only for politicians. They talk about justice and truth when any thinking man knows that they ought to confine their attention to considering whether a given account of the facts of a situation is the right one in relation to the people concerned at that particular time and in those particular circumstances. Where does this error among the professors and notably among the majority of our leading philosophers come from?

In France there is an official philosophy. This state ethic is Kantianism. M. André Cresson, a distinguished professor at the college in Alençon, writes: 'Kant's ethics, with a little modification, are the basis of almost every course in moral philosophy that is taught, particularly in France. It is to be found in most manuals on children's education. Thus, it takes on an official character.'

This Kantian doctrine taught in our classes claims to lay down a rule for man seen as an abstract universal entity. It does not consider individual differences. It has the effect of moulding the youth of the present day Lorraine, Provence, Brittany or Paris after a constant, abstract, ideal type. Yet what we need are men who are strictly rooted in our soil, in our history and in the national consciousness; men who are fitted to the immediate requirements of the country. The philosophy that at present instructs the state is responsible more than anything else for the belief that the intellectual despises the ordinary unthinking citizen and makes intelligence operate at a level of pure abstraction, beyond the plain of real things.

Caught up in mere words a child is cut off from all reality: Kantian doctrine uproots him from the soil of his ancestors. A surplus of diplomas creates what we may call, after Bismarck, a 'proletariat of graduates'. This is our indictment of the universities: what happens to their product, the 'intellectual', is that he becomes an enemy of society.

My attribution of the power to mislead youth to the professors is confirmed by the attitude of a great number of them during the events of the Dreyfus affair. This affair demonstrates beautifully the behaviour of that earlier generation without roots. Bouteiller, for example, is a natural intellectual and at the same time is an agent in the process of uprooting: he belongs to a higher order among those who have no roots. What happens when he tries to alight on the plain of reality? *L'Appel au Soldat*, *Leurs Figures* ... these show us Bouteiller in a political role. His philosophy does not stop him. There is an epigram from Venice mentioned in Goethe: 'If only every zealot was crucified in his thirtieth year! Once he has got to know the world the dupe becomes a scoundrel.' Our Bouteiller who can speak only of sacrificing everything to justice and who would willingly prefer, in common with our other Kantian intellectuals, to destroy society rather than endorse injustice, turns out to be a fraud.

I do not mean that every rhetorician of the absolute necessarily ends up as a swindler. But it is an observable fact, confirmed time and again in the Dreyfus affair, that every absolutist comes to grief in public affairs.

Protestantism in France

Within an interval of fifteen months, the *Revue du Midi* (January 1st, 1899) and *L'Action Française* (May 15th, 1900) conducted an inquiry into the relative merits of Protestantism and Catholicism for the future of France.

Would it be a good idea to make France all Protestant?
I replied:

'I am from Lorraine. One of the most important dates in Lorraine is the year 1525 when the Duke Antoine cut the Rustands to pieces at Saverne.

'If that band of Protestants had won, would not the destiny of Lorraine have been directed towards Germany? (It is worth recalling that the German Rustands swore to avenge their Protestant brothers who were condemned to death by the magistrates of Metz; that, furthermore, it was the Catholic party who a little while afterwards handed Metz over to France.)'

This victory of Duke Antoine (called 'Antoine the Good') revived the loyal enthusiasm of the subjects of Lorraine. For they believed that the survival and welfare of the nation depended on the outcome of that struggle. This extended to the whole of France. M. Fornenon, in his *History of the Dukes of Guise*, a pamphlet against the princes of Lorraine, reproaches Claude de Guise, who commanded six thousand French troops, for this victory. 'The public coffers were empty, the soldiers either prisoners or demoralized, the people ruined or discontented. Guise risked the last of the armed forces, the last of the knights remaining in France to support the interests of the princes of Lorraine.' M. Fornenon recognizes, however, that François I considered himself deeply indebted to Claude de Guise: 'When he returned from captivity, François I thought it necessary to treat him as a prince of the blood royal and conferred on him the rank of duke and peer. Until then this had belonged to only three princes.'

As a result of the victory of Saverne and the policy of the Guise family, Lorraine and her larger neighbour France developed free from the influence of Protestantism. I do not want to involve myself in theological controversy; I am not inspired by religious zeal. I have no desire to enter into a discussion on the nature of true religion. The claim that something is good and true always needs to be clarified with a reply to this question: in answer to what exigency is it true or good? The Catholic world is where my forbears grew to maturity and prepared the way for me. As a consequence I find it the least jarring to my nature: it can best accommodate my various roles and best promote the life suited to my nature. That is why I honour the Guise family, and why I regard the destruction of the Protestant forces as one of the most fortunate occurrences in my distant past. I intend to preserve the benefits of this victory with all the power at my command, for it enables the tree of which I am one leaf to continue to be.

Jews and Protestants considered 'in the abstract'

Every instinct makes me a part of the Lorraine tradition.

In addition, it is a discipline that my reason accepts. Other hereditary influences confirm this repugnance I feel towards Protestantism (with its secular education so different from my own) and towards Judaism (a race antagonistic to my own).

Can it be said that I cannot make out a good case for an ethnic character peculiar to a particular race or breed? That is another question. The Jews have no native land in the sense that we understand it. For us, a homeland implies the soil, our ancestors, the land of our dead. For them it is only the place where they find the greatest profits. So their intellectuals arrive at the celebrated definition: 'The Fatherland is an idea.' But what idea? Simply that which is most useful to them. For example, the idea that all men are brothers, that nationality is a prejudice to be destroyed, that military honour corrupts the blood, that a country should disarm (and not recognize any power other than money), etc.

Does it follow that you should call them 'dirty Jews' or the highest aristocracy in the world? You can do what you like, according to your own inclinations and your circumstances. It does not matter. But do not deny that the Jew is a creature apart.

Obedience to the law is the mark of the greatest moral sensibility. The case of Socrates illustrates this incontrovertible statement. But I could never accept a law with which my spirit could not identify itself. I feel greater antipathy if the law is not the law of my race.

The relativist seeks to distinguish the ideas appropriate to each human type. Those excellent men who closed the borders of Lorraine to the Protestants had a real feeling for the relative. So too those who pacified the discordant elements and assured stability among the dissident forces affected by the Edict of Nantes.

Reply to the Intellectuals

Taine and Renan saved the honour of the intellectuals in France. They knew their duty: to assist in the development of a national self-awareness.

It should be understood that the Dreyfus affair did not arise by chance, but is a result of the conditions in which we live. I believe that with study they could be modified. I am sure that this is the only way of guarding against the crisis that would inevitably develop from this affair – as it did in the Wilson affair and the Panama scandal.

What spiritual illness causes these criminal conspiracies? And by what remedy or rather by what method could we build up a resistance against it? This is what the *Patrie Française* should study if that organization is to be the mind of the country.

By such a study, whether they realize it or not, they would be following the path along which Renan[1] travelled when he wrote *Réforme intellectuelle et morale*, or Taine when he went in search of the characteristics of the national edifice which both nature and history have built up and which they have to maintain.

This homage that I have offered to the method of Renan, evident in his estimable works, does not mean that I accept all the contentions of this philosopher who, for example, believes in the intoxicated dream world of the poet. Is it necessary to tell me, a man from Lorraine, who wrote *Les Déracinés*, that the definition: 'What is a nation? It is a spirit', is repugnant to the French people.

[1] Ernest Renan (1823–92), writer and historian, head of the *Collège de France* (1883). A defender of the republic, who left the Church but substituted for Catholicism, in an ambitious scheme of *Réforme intellectuelle et morale*, a civic religiosity, stressing the importance of spiritual values in national life. Author of a famous *Histoire du peuple d'Israël*.

This is a prescription from which it is possible to suffer – which, in fact, causes us to suffer the most abominable consequences. But the most serious differences of opinion should not prevent us from preserving our gratitude to a man who has done so much to give our nation a sense of the relative. And we have never felt the need for a sense of relativism so much as in the course of this Dreyfus affair, which is nothing but a metaphysician's orgy. They judge everything with reference to the abstract. We judge everything as it accords with France.

Proposal for a Doctrine to the Patrie Française

I was invited to attend the third conference of the *Patrie Française*. I set about to define nationalism, or rather to look for its principles and its tenor.

We must begin by discovering the causes of our decadence.

The Dreyfus affair is, merely, the tragic intimation of the general condition. A wound that will not heal leads a doctor to diagnose diabetes. Look beyond the symptom to the root cause of the condition.

Our serious disease is the divisions troubled by a thousand separate wills and a thousand individualistic imaginations. We are crumbling, we do not have a collective knowledge of our goal or our resources or our soul.

Those nations are fortunate whose movements are knit together in such a way that their efforts are coordinated as if designed by a superior intelligence.

There are many ways that a country can achieve this moral unity. Loyalty to a sovereign can unite a nation. In default of a dynasty, traditional institutions can provide a centre. (But our excellent country abruptly renounced and annihilated its royal house and institutions.) Other races succeeded in drawing their consciousness from their own organic natures. This is true of Anglo-Saxon and Teutonic groups who are progressively on the way to creating themselves as a race. (Unfortunately there is no such thing as a French race, only a French people or a French nation: in effect a political unit.)

Yes, but unfortunately, speaking of groups that are inevitably rival and hostile in their struggle for life, ours has not yet reached a clear sense of identity. That we acknowledge this implicitly is seen from the fact that we are sometimes Latins, sometimes Gauls, sometimes 'soldiers of the Church', or the 'great nation', the 'emancipators of the people'.

In default of moral unity, of a common identity for the whole of France, we have contradictory catch-phrases as the various standards under which zealous men of influence are able to gather their followers.

The aim of nationalism is to resolve each question in the best interest of France. But how can we do this if we have no national identity and no idea common to us all?

When a critical situation arises it is interpreted by each party according to its own notion of what constitutes the distinct identity of the nation. And so the explanation of the significance of the Dreyfus affair; instead of being determined by the movement of a common spirit; by Frenchmen who identify their idea of the good with the country they live in; conflicting solutions are produced from the analyses of ideologues who use as their guide the axioms they fancy.

Given this lack of moral unity in France which has no royal house or traditional institutions and is not a race, it is quite natural that the unscrupulous metaphysicians, provided that they are eloquent, persuasive and generous, capture our imaginations. In proposing an ideal to us, they are obliged to supply this moral unity. But far from delivering us from our doubts, they succeed only in multiplying them by their many contradictory assertions.

What is the remedy? Only a sluggish sensibility and a spirit severely corrupted by anarchy could be happy in a France so disunited, so lacking in guiding intelligence.

But what means is there of precipitating the consciousness that the country lacks?

First of all, let us reject philosophical systems and the groups that generate them. Let us direct all our efforts not to a *notion* of our spirit, but to reality.

We are men of good will; whatever the origin of the opinions that exercised a formative influence on us – our family, our education, our environment, and the thousand intimate details of the circumstances of our lives – we have decided to take as our point of departure what we are and not some ideal of the mind. Some of us may well feel that the Revolution turned us away from a most pleasant and happy way of life; others may regret that the First Consul, under the Concordat, placed France back under the influence of Rome. Others still may be sure that the destiny of our country is closely connected with that of Catholicism. Everyone has his own interpretation of French history. But let us relinquish these fantasies: why should we propel ourselves down the conjectured paths where France should supposedly have gone? We might find a more positive profit by engrossing ourselves in French history, by living with all its dead, instead of placing ourselves out of the reach of any of its experiences.

Among all these developments that seem to have been in conflict with one another, what moral anguish there would be if the preferences of our peculiar nature held sway. All the different Frances – France under the Consulate, France under the monarchy, France of 1830 or 1848, France of the Empire with its authoritarian or liberal government – though they show a prodigious instability and vacillate between contradictory extremes, they still proceed from the same origin and move towards the same end. They grew from the same seed and are the fruit of different seasons from the same tree.

Without doubt the individual reason is not equal to these oscillations. It might seem that this reason would profit more by not developing under such uncertain and contradictory conditions. Indeed! Do we expect nature to be an eternal spring? And the accumulated experience of generations to have succeeded in making us believe that the snows of winter and the rains of autumn are simply necessary for the spring?

In the past, did not the champion of the good whose mantle we have now taken play his part in the face of even harsher contradictions?

I am from Lorraine, gentlemen; but my small country has been French for only a century. Let us speak frankly, as historians do. We did not become French territory because this was our inclination; in fact we joined France because France trampled on us, because Germany trampled on us, because our dukes, not knowing how to organize our resources, failed to defend us, and because after the outrages by which France succeeded in crushing us, there was no order or peace in our country.

You would find it hard to imagine a worse history than this one of Lorraine, subject of a dispute between France and Germany since the tenth century. She has never been allowed to live a whole and vital life. We would have had a fine independent sovereignty, with our customs and institutions. We had all that is needed to win a place in history, or at least to be assured of order and security, and to create a nationality. Unfortunately our ducal house was inferior in political acumen to that of the Capetians. Our dukes defended us badly, and then abandoned us.

We received the first intimations of the Revolution with enthusiasm, a little after our union with France.

From 1786 to 1789 our little country, under a misapprehension, hoped for a government composed of Lorrainers. But in the seventeenth century nearly three-quarters of a population totalling four hundred thousand died as a result of the atrocities of the French occupation. This provided France with an auspicious opportunity for substituting the French way of life for that of Lorraine, which had been repopulated with French people. What made the union decisive however were the material advantages gained by the peasants and the middle class from the Revolution, together with the comradeship in battle and glory secured in the republican and imperial wars. In 1814 Blücher made an appeal to separatist ideas. He said, to the municipality of Nancy, 'If only I could recall the palmy days which your ancestors enjoyed under the gentle and paternal rule of the dukes.'

In a word – and this will show my point – we in Lorraine are French not because France is 'the eldest daughter of the Church' or because she gave to the world the Declaration of the Rights of Man; we are not loyal to the country as to a spirit, a group of principles. In fact, we joined France because we needed order and peace and because we could not find it elsewhere. Our patriotism does not carry with it any idealism or philosophy. And indeed it was more sensible that we should turn towards France instead of Germany, because France is a Catholic country. It is also true that the civil achievements of the Revolution and the military honours of the Empire won the hearts of our people. So our patriotism is comprised of all the elements that dialecticians insist on keeping separate and opposed to one another. This brief table of chance occurrences which associated Lorraine with the fortunes of France proves that history heals all breaches. Logic, the analytic distinctions of thinkers, perpetuate the difficulties which the natural dynamism of things undertakes to remove. Men who continually keep systems before them are puerile and morbid. They insist on condemning whatever does not please their imaginations. No *conception* of France can prevail, in our decisions, over the France of flesh and blood.

If the *Patrie Française* succeeded in giving to its adherents a sense of the real and the relative, if it could convince the most honourable and dedicated professors (who from time to time cause us a lot of trouble) that by judging things as historians rather than as metaphysicians they would effect a transformation of what is obnoxious in the political spirit of our nations and would restore our moral unity, it would create a national consciousness.

To achieve this reasonable and realistic view of our Fatherland, we should develop ways of knowing what exists in the nature of the country. We should not combine ideas at a purely rational level. They should be reinforced by feeling. Sensibility lies at the root of everything. It is useless to try to force truth into existence by reason alone, for intelligence can always find a motive for replacing whatever you may have adopted. To create a national consciousness, we must bring that superior intellectualism whose method has been shown us by historians into association with an element that is less conscious and less voluntary.

Led astray by a university culture, that could speak only of man and humanity, I, for my part, would have been roused into supporting anarchy, if certain sentiments of respect had not engaged my feelings.

One day, I was at Metz. The Prussians, who radically transformed Strasbourg, have not succeeded up to this moment in changing that ancient city of Lorraine in the slightest. Once she had accommodated herself to the immense burdens that were inflicted on her, she seemed the same in her state of subjection as she had been in the past. How much more moving: a slave who retains the alluring qualities of a free woman! The Prussian faces, the uniforms, the official inscriptions, all indicate clearly enough that we are a conquered people. I visited the cemetery of Chambière where there is a monument to the 7,200 French soldiers who died in the field hospitals in 1870. There is a high pyramid in the middle of the German military graves. The arresting inscription is a complete revelation: 'What utter wretchedness! Was I born to see the ruin of my people, the ruin of the city? And to remain among them while they are delivered to the hand of the enemy? What sorrow!'

A passing Frenchman will accept this lament, this imprecation, with all its implications, and having pondered over it, turn in the direction of France and shout, 'You wretched country! Your people could not accept this country's glory or its land!'

But should not we accept a certain community of interest and responsibility for neglect when, after so many years during which children have grown into men, nothing has been done to deliver the Metz and Strasbourg abandoned by our fathers?

The bodies of young men of twenty and twenty-five are piled together under the stones of this captured country. Their lives would have had no meaning had one refused to look for it in the idea of the homeland. But now, today, they will live again. Their death was powerless to redeem the territory, but it enables the nation to look at the record without total shame during this dismal year. It is a fitting consummation of a sacrifice that they should yield while still hating to lose so ineluctably their frail identity. The Prussian trumpets and tambourines which resound without respite over the tombs of Chambière from a neighbouring field do not deter us from tenderly spelling out the names inscribed on the tombs, the names of our brothers.

In the same cemetery the commemorative stone which the Germans themselves consecrated to their own dead opens and hurls the insult, 'God is with us.'

A crime, this, that makes nothing of those young men who lie defeated, whose eyes were closed by the women of Metz.

It does not require the High Command of the German forces to decide irrevocably that our soldiers are at war with God. France has played too important a part in establishing the basis of civilization. She has rendered too many services in the cause of the highest notions of the world, extending the range of ideals and making them more precise. Or, in another language, she has developed the idea of God. No free spirit would ever subscribe to the vulgar dream of a corporal, who allows himself to believe that God – that is to say the direction imposed on the rhythm of humanity – is effecting the decline of this nation. It entered into the crusades in a spirit of freedom and fraternity, and, through the Revolution, proclaimed the right of people to manage their own affairs.

But consider the pretentiousness of the whole of Germany from the merest drudge among her soldiers to the most thoughtful of her professors. It is no matter of chance but the result of the development of a national attitude that they write an inscription claiming God as their own ally, a few yards away from the heap of bones belonging to our compatriots. These they placed outside the paradise of the children of Jesus, if they were Christian, and, if they were atheists, remote from the affirmations of the beauty and goodness glimpsed by humanity. They repulsed our armies by their barbarous fighting methods and banned the thought of France as if it were utterly noxious.

In that small area, the bodies of Frenchmen and Germans are heaped together to promote a vigorous growth of vegetation: some thirty trees spring up to heaven. Germany may wish so self-consciously that the spirit of France and the spirit of the Fatherland unite only in the ultimate state of a common humanity, or in the bosom of God. But in reality they place us beyond the pale, they campaign for the destruction of our tongue and our thought. This is a holy war.

In the land of Metz and Strasbourg, Germans, more cruel than orientals, who cut down olive trees and fill up wells, are realizing their dream of destruction.

They prevent the minds of little French children from thinking like Frenchmen. They overwhelm them with German novels and German ideas, and like brushwood burying a living source, choke a sensibility which for centuries had refreshed the race and which these children receive from their parents.

Well, gentlemen, it is not by throwing a little earth on to bodies, or an insulting formula at centuries of history, or so many words as a sop to our conscience that one placates the conscience, past events or the corpses. At Chambière, before the dead stopped up with sand, with a winning gesture of veneration, our heart convinces our reason of the grand destiny that awaits France and imposes a moral unity on all. This voice of our ancestors, this lesson of the soil that Metz knows so well how to make us understand, is worth more than anything in forming the consciousness of a people. The soil gives us the discipline we need: we are the extension in time of our dead. This is the concept of reality upon which to base our existence.

In order to allow the consciousness of a country such as France to free itself, each person must be rooted in the soil and in the earth. This may seem too material an idea to anyone who thinks he has attained an ideal whose loftiness he judges according to the degree to which he has succeeded in suppressing the voice of his blood and the instincts of the earth.

But what splendid benefits to society and what excellent individuals would be produced, by implementing the principle I have put forward with all the legislation it necessarily entails.

This attitude to the dead directs us to a law on applications for naturalization. The dead! Yes, indeed! How then would a man regard himself if he represented only himself? When each of us looks over his shoulder, he sees a succession of indefinable mysteries, which in more recent times have come to be called France. We are the sum of a collective life that speaks in us. May the influence of our ancestors be permanent, the sons of the soil vital and upstanding, the nation one.

The view that we have of the soil compels us to envisage an organization of the country by regions. The soil speaks to us and works with the nation's consciousness quite as much as it cooperates with the dead. The soil gives the active life of the dead its efficacy. Our ancestors pass on as a whole the heritage accumulated in their souls only by the immutable vital activity of the soil.

In this assembly where each person has such a clear

idea of the nature of our country, I do not propose to over-excite your feeling for that place in France where you were born and where the doleful vale of your parents' resting place lies. Why should I trouble your souls? I really wish to address my words to your reason and particularly to your political reason.

It is only by drawing your attention to the resources of French soil, the efforts it demands of us, the services it renders, the conditions, in short, in which our race of foresters, farmers and winegrowers has developed, that you will come to understand our national traditions as realities and not mere words. In this way too you will appreciate the new forces that have come to maturity on our soil. In order to distinguish what is necessary and legitimate among contemporary aspirations, for example among those who demand legislation on labour matters, it is a good idea to grasp the differences between conditions under a monarchy in a democratic (and, alas, plutocratic) and industrial France.

To be productive, this knowledge need not be theoretic. Anyone who feels himself naturally part of the national consciousness, who is in harmony with the country's destiny, may, even if he cannot put it in words, still follow its barely perceptible rhythm of development. The administrator and the legislator might well take this grand principle as their inspiration: the spirit of our country is stronger in the soul of a man who has roots than in the soul of one who is rootless.

No Frenchman would ever intend to meddle with the state. But the state that suffered from the lack of a national consciousness would be mad to neglect that sense of its own identity which every one of our regions has preserved. From a large number of administrative questions I single out the problem of education for your special attention.

The provinces, whose spirit some superficial minds think to be extinct, have furnished and will still furnish France with some distinguished luminaries that may provide it with light and inspiration. We see the stamp of Ardennes in Taine, of Brittany in Renan, of Provence in Mistral, of Alsace-Lorraine in Erekmann-Chatrian. Independent universities enable us to gather what remains of the spirit of the ancient countries and at the same time they bring a universal culture to those parts. This circular movement is of the greatest importance. It develops us in harmony with what was prepared for us by our ancestors and is transmitted by the instincts of the soil, and prevents us from succumbing to the torpor of provincialism.

The minimum programme that I propose for your consideration is not the product of *a priori* computations which you are obliged to prefer to the facts of the case. There is a prevailing mood that demands greater severity with regard to laws on naturalization. The great cities, with their wealth and ambitions, are clearly designed to become points of centralization and could shift responsibility for those niggling cares, that at present distract the state, to the territories and to the citizens themselves, and leave the state to attend to her principal concern, our collective security.

We are ready for these two reforms; one light stroke would be enough to cause the chemical precipitation.

The Principle of Authority. Now, in order that the national consciousness may gain in efficacy, should it not express itself in some kind of authoritative office?

Such an authority will appear of its own accord, as soon as our country has come to know what it is and can consequently discern its future role. If we agree in the value we place on our powers, the energy we have accumulated will take one direction quite naturally, and without violent effort an organ of the national will will be created.

The *Patrie Française* has acted very wisely in refraining from the direct pursuit of a political goal. Our basic principle and our membership hardly permit it. Let us confine our political activity to within the limits of the statutes and restrict ourselves to the work of 'clarifying opinion on the principal interests of the country'. This is the most useful work imaginable, for the best institutions have the greatest effectiveness and durability only when they are able to take root in a political climate that has been radically transformed.

THE UNDYING SPIRIT OF FRANCE[1]

(An address delivered in London, at the Hall of the Royal Society, under the auspices of the British Academy, July 12th, 1916.)

Ladies and Gentlemen:

In his 'Litany of Nations' your poet Swinburne puts these words into the mouth of France apostrophizing Liberty:

I am she that was thy sign and standard-bearer,
Thy voice and cry;
She that washed thee with her blood and left thee
    fairer,
The same was I.
Were not these the hands that raised thee fallen and
    fed thee,
These hands defiled?
Was not I thy tongue that spake, thine that led thee,
Not I thy child?

How many men and how many nations, since 1870, have believed that we were unworthy of this eulogy that so touched our hearts. We were mistrusted. They said of us: 'They are no longer what they were ... France is a nation grown old, an ancient nation.'

Especial stress was laid upon the idea of France as an *old nation*. And therein they expressed but the truth; France was when no such thing existed as Germanic consciousness,

[1] Translated from *Les Traits éternels de la France* by Margaret W. B. Corwin (Yale University Press, 1917).

or Italian or English consciousness; in truth we were the first nation of all Europe to grasp the idea of constituting a homeland; but there seems no reason why claims of such a nature should work to our discredit with nations of more recent origin.

Among those who thus spoke there were many who looked upon us without animosity, sometimes even with sympathy. According to them France had in the past laid up a vast store of virtues, noble deeds and glorious achievements beyond compare, but today is seated in the midst of these like an old man in the evening of the most successful of lives, or still more like certain worldly aristocrats of illustrious lineage, who have preserved of their inheritance only their titles of nobility, charming manners, superb portraits, regal tapestries and books adorned with coats of arms, all denoting sumptuous but trivial luxury.

It was in this wise, as we well understand, that we had come to be regarded as jaded triflers, far too affluent and light-hearted, with pleasure as our only concern; the French people were supposed to allow impulse and passion to determine the course of their lives, pleasure being the supreme good sought, and to Paris came representatives from every nation to share in this pleasure.

Small wonder that the undiscerning foreigner, intoxicated by the easy and cosmopolitan pleasures of Paris, failed to recognize the underlying force present at every French fireside, which prides itself upon keeping remote and isolated from the passing crowd, or what was stirring in hearts ever hearkening the call to a crusade and needing, as it were, but the voice from a supernatural world to bring forth and reveal to themselves their inherent heroism.

August 1914. The call to arms resounds. The bells in every village echo in the towers of the ancient churches whose foundations arise from amidst the dead. These bells have suddenly become the voice of the land of France. They call together the men, they express compassion for the women; their clamour is so stupendous that it seems as if the very tombs would crumble, and all at once the French heart is unlocked and all the tenderness that has so long been kept concealed comes forth.

Women, old men and children flock about the soldier, following him to the train. This is the hour of departure, not as Rude has depicted it, carried along in the storm and stress of the '*Marseillaise*', but a departure even more tragic in tone, in which the soldier mutters through set teeth: 'Since they will have it, we must end it for ever.'

The departure! We cannot be at the same moment in all the railway stations of Paris and of all our cities, towns and villages, on all the docks, nor upon all the boats bringing back loyal Frenchmen from abroad. Suppose we go to the very heart of military France, to the school of St Cyr where the young officers receive their training.

Every year at St Cyr the *Fête du Triomphe* is celebrated with great pomp. Upon this occasion is performed a traditional ceremony in which the young men who have just finished their two years' course at the school proceed to christen the class following it and to bestow a name upon their juniors.

In July 1914, this ceremony came just at the time of the events which in their hasty course brought on the war, and for that reason was to assume a more than usually serious character.

On the thirty-first of the month the general in command at the school made known to the *Montmirails* (the name of the graduating class) that they would have to christen their juniors that same evening, and only according to military regulations, without the accustomed festivities.

All understood that perhaps during the night they would have to join their respective regiments.

Listen to the words of a young poet of the *Montmirail* class, Jean Allard-Mécus, as he tells his mother of the events of this evening, already become legendary among his compatriots: 'After dinner the Assumption of Arms (*prise d'armes*) before the captain and the lieutenant on guard duty, the only officers entitled to witness this sacred rite. A lovely evening; the air is filled with almost oppressive fragrance; the most perfect order prevails amidst unbroken silence. The *Montmirails* are drawn up, officers with swords, "men" with guns. The two classes take their places on the parade ground under command of the major of the higher class. Excellent patriotic addresses, then, in the midst of growing emotion, I recited:

"Tomorrow"

Soldiers of our illustrious race,
    Sleep, for your memories are sublime.
Old time erases not the trace
    Of famous names graved on the tomb.
Sleep; beyond the frontier line
    Ye soon will sleep, once more at home.

'Never again, dearest mother, shall I repeat those lines, for never again shall I be on the eve of departure for out there, amongst a thousand young men trembling with feverish excitement, pride and hatred. Through my own emotion I must have touched upon a responsive chord, for I ended my verses amidst a general thrill. Oh, why did not the clarion sound the Call to Arms at their close! We should all have carried its echoes with us as far as the Rhine.'

It was surrounded by this atmosphere of enthusiasm that the young officers received the title of *Croix du Drapeau* for their class upon their promotion and it was at this juncture that one of the *Montmirails*, Gaston Voizard, cried out: 'Let us swear to go into battle in full-dress uniform, with white gloves and the plume (*casoar*) in our hats.'

'We swear it,' made answer the five hundred of the *Montmirail*.

'We swear it,' echoed the voices of the five hundred of the *Croix du Drapeau*.

A terrible scene and far too characteristically French, permeated by the admirable innocence and readiness to serve of these young men, and permeated, likewise, with disastrous consequences.

They kept their rash vow. It is not permissible for me to tell you the proportion of those who thus met death. These attractive boys of whom I have been telling you are no more. How have they fallen?

There were not witnesses in all cases, but they all met death in the same way as did Lieutenant de Fayolle.

On the twenty-second of August Alain de Fayolle of the *Croix du Drapeau* was at Charleroi leading a section. His men hesitate. The young sub-lieutenant has put on his white gloves but discovers that he has forgotten his plume. He draws from his saddle-bag the red and white plume and fastens it to his shako.

'You will get killed, my lieutenant,' protested a corporal.

'Forward!' shouts the young officer.

His men follow him, electrified. A few moments later a bullet strikes him in the middle of his forehead, just below the plume.

On the same day, August 22nd, 1914, fell Jean Allard-Mécus, the poet of the *Montmirail*, struck by two bullets.

Gaston Voizard, the youth who suggested the vow, outlived them by only a few months ...

Ah, how dearly has France ever paid for the flaunting of these bits of bravery in the face of the foe! One can but approve the austere severity of the great commanders who discouraged the generous impulse of these boys thus lavish of the treasure of their lives. War provides the leaders of men with enough occasions for useful sacrifice without taking it upon themselves to invite a fatal ending. But we must not overlook the fact that these leaders of men are but boys. Sudden stress of circumstances has called them to the battlefront. They feel a necessity for establishing their leadership. But how? By their superior knowledge or experience? No means is open to them except through gallantry in attempting some deed of exceptional daring.

That is evidently the idea which one of them, Georges Bosredon, a twenty-year-old St-Cyrien, had in mind when in writing to his sister he puts the matter thus forcibly: 'Say nothing about it to Father and Mother, but, as an officer, I run small chance of returning. I fully recognize this and gladly from this hour offer my life as a sacrifice. We shall arrive at the front very young, with nothing especial to recommend us, to be put in command of men who have seen service, already old soldiers. To keep them going we shall have to give all we have and we shall give it.'

Generous-hearted youth, who makes no mention of mistakes made just before he was born, and who, just arriving upon the scene, accepts as only natural that he should pay with his life for victory!

In all our great schools and in all our colleges the boys are brothers to these young military commanders. To them all one thing alone is of importance: that France should no longer remain a vanquished nation. These are the young, the pure, the source of new life, the sacrificial offering of their native land. They stand ready to accept any burden laid upon them to render them worthy of their forefathers, to fulfil their destiny and to ransom France.

The college professors made no mistake in judging of them. For some years they had heralded the oncoming of a generation of clear-eyed youths, with confident bearing and hearts knowing no fear. Destiny was preparing deliverers for France. 'Whence issues the France of August 2nd?' exclaims one of the masters of the Lycée Janson-de-Sailly. 'From beneath the threat of Germany under which it has been bowed for forty years. This anguish, this prolonged humiliation, gives place at last to highest hopes.'

Such are the young men of our nation. But war has brought together into the army the entire male population from eighteen to forty-eight years of age.

Naturally a man of forty does not leave home with that intoxication of happiness that we have just observed in our young St-Cyriens. He no longer feels that 'criminal love of danger' which Tolstoy, talking near the end of his life with Déroulède, acknowledged to have himself felt in his youth. This is due in part to the cooling of the blood; it is also due to the opening up of a new horizon.

In starting a home of his own the young man of yester-day has taken upon himself certain duties of protection toward his family. How can he be expected to show the magnificent impetuosity of the St-Cyrien who says: 'To be a young officer during the war is truly the career in which are to be reaped one after another the rewards of honour, energy and devotion.' The father of a family has already gathered to himself the rewards of life; he has to forsake them and, if he fails in the beauty of alacrity, what he manifests is the beauty of a sacrifice always contemplated. This sense of the sacrifice he is making is felt also by the younger man, but he hastily dismisses apprehension on this score, will not admit it so much as to himself, and meeting it face to face, rejects it with anger. The older soldier, on the contrary, welcomes it and regards it as meritorious, it may be as an offering to God, or it may be as an offering to his native land.

Germens spero was the motto assumed in the mud of the Artois trenches by the soldier François Laurentie, the father of six children. He indeed suffered, but was cheered by the hope that his offspring would not have to suffer. All testamentary letters issuing from the trenches echo the same refrain. The Territorial fights that his children may not be called upon to fight. He makes war to abolish war.

But he fights also for his native land. What must have been the feeling of the men of the Twentieth Corps shedding their blood before Nancy and before Verdun! And we can picture the emotion of the men of Péguy, those citizens of the Belleville and Bercy quarters of Paris, when, at the end of their retreat in September 1914, they caught sight of the great city enveloped in mist, Paris, to whose defence they were hastening. One of these, Victor Boudon, who had been wounded at the Battle of the Ourcq, writes on that occasion: 'From afar we could discern the white rays of the searchlights on the forts of Paris and, from time to time, through the foliage the lights of the capital itself. Our hearts beat violently with joy and with dread.'

Another soldier, a shrewd observer of these beginnings of the campaign, thus sums up his testimony: 'An all-pervading atmosphere of devout offering.'

And what does the war make of these youths and old men? A brotherhood. Binet-Valmer, enlisted as a volunteer for the duration of the war, sends me from the front where he is fighting this most wonderful phrase, which echoes the feeling of all: 'Our men are worthy of unstinted admiration, *and we all love one another.*'

The men are admirable, that is to say, they are ready to sacrifice themselves. Behold these soldiers volunteering for the most perilous services, soldiers who go of their own motion to carry off wounded comrades from between the trenches and to bury the dead; it is needless to enumerate such occurrences or to present proof of them. It is recognized that the sons of France are brave. And throughout the world everyone knows about the battle which has been going on for five months and which we may rightfully call the victory of Verdun.

In the midst of the carnage these sons of France constantly recall to mind that they are men with souls. The best of them raise their bloody hands towards Heaven each invoking his God. Each one of them is taken up with trying to show the nobility of his thought through his gallantry and self-sacrifice. Each acts as if he knew (and he does know) that the people of his faith throughout all France have entrusted to his safe-keeping their honour and the fortunes of the ideal for which they all are striving. Our schoolmasters vie with our priests in their efforts, while the elite of the nation and their brothers in arms join in admiration equally apportioned between them.

All are actuated by a lofty moral purpose: the pride and necessity of shedding their blood only in a just cause.

The soil of the trenches is holy ground; it is saturated with blood, it is saturated with spirituality.

Today throughout the world everyone knows about an incident which innumerable newspaper and magazine articles, prints and poems have brought before the public. Doubtless you will recall it. The Germans had entered a trench and shattered all resistance; our soldiers lay stretched to earth, when, suddenly, from this heap of dead and wounded, one arises and, seizing a sack of grenades within reach of his hand, cries out: 'To your feet, ye dead men.' With a rush the invader is swept back. The inspired word had caused a resurrection.

I was anxious to know the hero of this immortal deed, Lieutenant Péricard. Here is the tale as he told it to me:

It was at the Bois-Brulé early in April 1915. We had been fighting for three days; there was only a handful of worn-out men left of us in the trench, absolutely cut off, with a rain of grenades descending upon our heads. If the Boches had known how few we were! Their artillery raged incessantly. A lieutenant, whose name I cannot now recall, and who had come to my support, stood puffing at his cigarette and laughing at the projectiles, when a bullet struck him just above the temple. He leaned against the parapet, his arms crossed behind him, his head bent slightly forward. From the wound the blood gushes out describing a parabola, like wine through a gimlet hole in the cask. The head drops further and further forward, then the body, then, all at once, he drops.

You should have seen the anguish of his men, who threw themselves sobbing upon his body!... It was impossible to take a step without treading upon a corpse. Suddenly the precariousness of my situation comes over me. The frenzy which had transported me drops away. I am afraid. I throw myself behind a heap of sacks. The soldier Bonnot remains alone. He gives no heed to anything, but continues to fight like a lion, single-handed against what numbers!

I pull myself together; his example has shamed me. A few comrades rejoin us. The day draws to a close. We cannot remain as we are. To the right there is still no one in sight. I can look along the trench for a distance of thirty metres, where it is broken into by an enormous bomb-proof shelter. Supposing I should go and see what is going on beyond it! I hesitate. Then, with one resolute effort, the decision is made.

The trench is filled with bodies of French soldiers. Blood everywhere. At the first I step forward warily, very uneasy. What! I alone among all these dead men. I venture to look at these bodies and I seem to see their eyes fixed upon me. From our own trench, behind me, men are gazing at me with horror in their eyes in which I can read: 'He will surely get killed.' It is true that from the screen of their shelter trenches the Boches are redoubling their efforts. Their grenades are falling all about and the avalanche is fast approaching. I turn back towards the bodies stretched out on the earth. I can but think: 'Then their sacrifice is all to be in vain. It will have been to no avail that these men have fallen. And the Boches will come back. And they will steal our dead from us!' ... I was transported with rage. Of what I did or precisely what I said I no longer have any clear recollection. I only know that I called out something more or less like this: 'Come on there! Get up! What are you doing lying there? Let's chase these swine out of here.'

'To your feet, ye dead men!' Was it raving madness? No. *For the dead replied.* They said to me: 'We follow you.' And, rising at my call, their souls mingled with mine and formed a flaming mass, a mighty stream of molten metal. Nothing could now astonish or hinder me. I had the faith which removes mountains. My voice, hoarse and frayed with calling out orders during the two days and nights, had come back to me, clear and strong.

What took place then? Since I want to tell you only of what I can myself recall, leaving out of account what has been related to me afterwards, I must frankly own that I do not know. There is a gap in my recollections; action has consumed memory. I have but a vague idea of a disordered offensive attack in which Bonnot, always in the front rank, stands out clearly from the others. One of the men of my section, though wounded in the arm, never ceased hurling upon the enemy grenades stained with his blood. As for myself it seems as if I had been given a body which had grown and expanded inordinately, the body of a giant, with superabundant, limitless energy, extraordinary facility of thought which enabled me to have my eye in ten places at a time, to fire a gun and protect myself at the same time from a threatening grenade.

A prodigious intensity of life coupled with extraordinary episodes! On two occasions we ran completely out of grenades, and on two occasions we discovered full sacks of them at our feet, mixed in with the sandbags. All day long we had been walking over them without seeing them. But no doubt it was the dead who had placed them there! ...

At last the Boches began to calm down; we had a chance to consolidate our barricade of sacks farther along in the trench. We were again masters of the situation in our angle.

Throughout the evening and for several days following I remained under the influence of the spiritual emotion by which I had been carried away at the time of the summons to the dead. I had something of the same feeling that one has after partaking fervently of the communion. I recognized that I had just been living through such hours as I should never see again, during which my head, having by violent exertion broken an opening through the ceiling, had risen into the region of the supernatural, into the invisible world peopled by gods and heroes. The summons was not mine alone, it was that of us all. The more you sink my part in the whole mass, the nearer you will come to actual fact. I am firmly persuaded of having been only an instrument in the hands of a power above.

For more than a thousand years now this mighty stream of feats of valour has been flowing in undiminished volume. We have just been dipping into it; we could carry away from the passing flood only what could be contained in our two hands held together. And what about it all? What is proved by these entrancing and heroic achievements, this life beneath the surface, this overflowing French spirit?

The French make war as a religious duty. They were the first to formulate the idea of a holy war. The soldier of the Year II, believing himself the bearer of liberty and equality to a captive world, dedicated himself with the same zeal and in the same spirit as the crusaders to Jerusalem. When the crusader shouts 'God wills it', when the volunteer at Valmy shouts 'The Republic calls us', it is but another form of the same battle-cry. The idea is that of bringing about more of justice and more of beauty in the world. To both a voice from Heaven or their conscience speaks, saying: 'If you die, you will be holy martyrs.'

It is not in France that wars are entered upon for the sake of the spoils. Wars for the sake of honour and glory? Yes, at times. But to carry the nation with it the people must feel itself a champion in the cause of God, a knight upholding justice. We have to be convinced that we are contending against barbarians, in former days against Islam, at the present time against pan-Germanism, or against the despotic Prussian militarism and German imperialism.

Frenchmen fighting in defence of their country have believed almost always that they were suffering and enduring that all humanity might be the better. They fight for their territory filled with sepulchres and for Heaven where Christ reigns, and up to which at least our aspirations rise. They die for France, as far as the purposes of France may be identified with the purposes of God or indeed with those of humanity. Thus it is that they wage war in the spirit of martyrs.

Would you have me present to your minds a wonderful theme; would you know how our forefathers, nine centuries ago, were persuaded to go on crusade? You would learn at the same time how our soldiers of the present day ought to be addressed. Listen to the words of Pope Urban II (a native of France, born in Champagne) as he preached before the Council of Clermont in Auvergne: 'People of France,' he said, 'nation elect of God, as is shown by your deeds, and beloved of God, distinguished above all others by your devotion to the holy faith and to the Church, it is to you that our word and our exhortation is directed ... Upon whom may be laid the task of avenging the outrageous acts of the unbelievers if not upon you, Frenchmen, to whom God has vouchsafed more than to any other people, illustrious distinction in arms, exalted hearts and agile bodies with the power to bend those who oppose you? May your souls be stirred and quickened by the deeds of your ancestors, the valour and might of your King Charlemagne, of his son Louis, and of your other kings, who have overthrown the dominion of the heathen and extended the confines of the Holy Church! ... O very valiant knights, offspring of an invincible lineage, recall to mind the prowess of your fathers!' That was the right way to put things before our noble ancestors. And that is how they were pleaded with by Jeanne d'Arc, who called herself the 'Daughter of God' (*Fille Dieu*). Bonaparte adopted the same tone and with him the republican generals, and it is still the same spirit with which the hearts of our soldiers are kindled when they rush forward out of the trenches singing the '*Marseillaise*' under the benison of their chaplains.

Doubtless reason does its part in affecting and convincing us. The argument is used that France is a real and tangible masterpiece whose outline must be perfected and maintained, that Strasbourg and Metz are essential to her existence, that she needs to establish the balance to her southern population by accessions to the north and east, that she will be as if disarmed and open to attack as long as she remains deprived of her natural frontiers. But this would still leave many apathetic. To be ready to sacrifice their lives the sons of France demand that they shall not die for the cause of France alone.

There came a time when France burst the chain of her traditions and lost from sight even her memories of the past; nevertheless to her spiritual nature she still remained faithful. In each succeeding generation she has brought forth Rolands, Godfreys of Bouillon, Bayards, Turennes, Marceaus, unfamiliar as these names might have become, and at all times she is elated with sentiments which vary only in form of expression.

The epic drowses at times, but never, from the beginning, was it more fired by brotherly love and zeal for religion than at the present hour. Many passages from the Old Testament, obscure and of small moment in themselves, do not reveal their full meaning except in the light of the New, so the feats of valour performed by knights of old and our revered ancestors seem but the figuration of richer and holier things of today. The entire history of our nation would appear to have been leading up to what we have witnessed during the past two years.

Millions of Frenchmen have entered this war with a fervour of heroism and martyrdom which formerly, in the most exalted epochs of our history, characterized only the flower of the combatants. Young or old, poor or rich, and whatever his religious faith, the French soldier of 1916 knows that his is a nation which intervenes when injustice prevails upon the earth, and in his muddy trench, gun in hand, he knows that he is carrying onward the *Gesta Dei per Francos*.

Roland, on the evening after Roncevalles, murmurs with dying breath: 'O Land of France, most sweet art thou, my country.' It is with similar expressions and the same love that our soldiers of today are dying. '*Au revoir*,' writes Jean Cherlomey to his wife, 'promise me to bear no grudge against France if she requires all of me.'

CHARLES MAURRAS
(1868–1952)

In many ways, Maurras is a tragic figure. A monarchist, he was rejected by both his kings as 'not our interpreter'; spokesman of the Catholic nationalist right, five of his works and the *Action Française* were placed on the Index in 1926. His capacity for self-deception was almost limitless – he could believe that a small literary coterie, the *École Romane*, was an important intellectual movement or that Pétain's government really did have the freedom of action it claimed to have and that the National Revolution would succeed. Not a single *Action Française* candidate ever won an election in its own name. He was, as the Pope remarked, 'A very fine brain, but alas, only a brain.'

After the invasion of 1940, Maurras supported Vichy and was purged as its ideologue. The charge was that he had passed information to the enemy by public denunciation of various individuals. Maurras defended himself on the grounds that the one consistent political position in all his writings is hatred of Germany. His position is precarious, but not without a certain rigour. He hated the same things that the Nazis hated – democracy, the republic, certain kinds of socialism, Jews and individualism. But whereas the Nazis were claiming that democracy was foreign to the spirit of Germany, being a foreign import from Jerusalem and Paris, Maurras was saying the same thing, only blamed Jerusalem and those Teutonic forests where Tacitus had first descried the seeds of a rough, Germanic liberty. The Nazis claimed that Marxism was Jewish, Maurras claimed it was both Jewish and German.

213

Again, Maurras claimed to support Pétain because it was through him alone that he saw a hope for a new France. Pétain was Boulanger all over again. *Revanche* would live on in the spirit of the Marshal. The whole debate is absurd, and in showing this absurdity may lie its historical usefulness, but it does point to a consistency in Maurras's position. That consistency was precarious. In the 1930s Maurras was forced by his nationalism to denounce the rise of German and Italian fascism in so far as they tended to weaken France's position in Europe generally, but he was also forced by his hatred of democracy to oppose anti-fascism as well. Maurras was gaoled in 1936 for threatening a member of parliament who supported sanctions against Mussolini.

Maurras was *Action Française*. In Maurras and Vichy its absurdities meet. As Michael Curtis has so perceptively remarked, despite a certain grandeur in his writing, 'In politics he was always to be the *éminence grise* of a coterie.' Maurras was sentenced to life imprisonment and national degradation after the liberation; he was released in 1951 for medical reasons. The President of the Republic thus showed to Maurras a generosity of spirit which he had never shown to his own political opponents.

The selections from Maurras are taken from volume II of the *Oeuvres Capitales,* published in 1954 by Flammarion in four volumes. The translation is by John Frears.

DICTATOR AND KING

(*This declaration which bears the title* Dictator and King *was drafted by me in the summer of 1899 with the intention of mobilizing the support of a certain number of royalist writers ... What follows is the essence of that document.*)

Royalist Dictatorship: Its Principles

The undersigned, being royalist writers, expressing their personal views only, but drawing not only upon the tra-ditions and constitutions of the former monarchy of France, but in particular upon the speeches and writings of the Count of Chambord, of my Lord the Count of Paris, and of his Grace the Duke of Orleans, and especially the recent declarations of the latter, affirm that the head of the House of France is in their opinion the dictator which the nation needs as well as being its legitimate king.

They affirm, secondly, that the government of the King of France will, at the commencement of its dictatorship, inevitably be obliged to take repressive and retributive measures in order to make possible subsequent acts designed to restore order and justice.

Finally they affirm that the acts of repression which the king will be compelled to carry out will in no way result in the useless multiplication of grievances. No new party of outcasts and the defeated must be permitted to form in France. Public vengeance must strike at the ringleaders of the present troubles, all the ringleaders, but them alone: to the misled and the misguided the king will bring peace and a fresh start. His ancestor Henry IV overlooked the sedition in the common people but had no hesitation in executing fifty gentlemen in a single province who were guilty of plotting civil war. Thus the royal hand must strike only at the real criminals, but it must seek them out with cold and methodical determination, prompted by no other feeling than the love of France and hatred of the nation's enemies. After the Commune thousands of workers were shot and the leaders escaped scot-free: a King of France would have struck down the leaders without pity but spared the people ...

The Royal Regime

Royalist dictatorship having resolved this crisis, we now have to define what form the normal government of the kingdom would take. We see it as the rule of order. We see that order conforming to the nature of the French nation and to the rules of universal reason.

In other words, we see a regime which is exactly the opposite of the one now inflicted upon us.

Today freedom and its dangers are to be found so to speak 'at the top', that is to say in the elaboration of high-level policy on matters which affect the future and the security of the nation. Authority, however, in its most rigorous form has been pointlessly set up 'at the bottom', to deal authoritatively with matters in which discussion, difference of opinion, and the initiative of every citizen would have been not only harmless but positively advantageous; this sovereign and decisive authority has been applied to the minutest details of the relationship between individuals and the administration.

To turn this kind of order upside down, to bring freedoms downstairs to the people and restore authority at the top, would be to reconstitute in a proper manner the natural and rational order of things; the royalist constitution is thus the proper, natural and rational constitution of the country at last restored, and the reign of the king is no more than the return to our true order.

'Liberties for the people'

There is no interference, legal or illegal, which the French administration does not consider itself entitled to inflict upon the taxpayer and those whom it administers. There is no limit to the insolence that officials dare to use in their dealings with the citizen. An anonymous and impersonal Caesar, all-powerful, but irresponsible and unaware of the effect of his actions, applies himself diligently to the task of molesting the Frenchman from the cradle to the grave. Whether he wishes to live alone or to associate, the French citizen is certain to encounter at every step the Caesar-state, the Caesar-office ready to impose its directives (with prohibitions) or its wares (with subsidies).

Those aspects of public affairs that the citizen knows are under the supervision of, or at the convenience of, the state. Without the state, a parent, town council, a board of directors, or even a simple village fête committee can decide practically nothing in matters that are of the closest and most direct concern to themselves. Voluntary associations, like political or intellectual societies, or natural associations like the family, town or province – all gatherings of citizens are either overcome with inertia thanks to the laws of the state or else banned at the whim of those who happen at that moment to be the masters of the state ...

Not only does the state irritate and pester the French citizen, it inflicts upon him some very insidious comforts. It helps him in situations where he ought to help himself. It weans him from the habit of thought or personal initiative. Thus, thanks to the state, the civic function of the citizen falls into disuse and atrophies. The citizen becomes ignorant, lazy and cowardly. He loses civic sense and civic spirit. Treated as a minor, he becomes fit only to follow docilely his guardians. He neither responds to nor cares about the basic interests of his community. Wardens look after the communal good and he lets them get on with it; he stands apart from his fellow citizens. He returns to the individualist condition of the primitive savage.

As a natural result of this regime, cities of ten thousand souls often contain not one citizen worthy of his community. Why have citizens in places where the centralized state takes over outright every civic task? Unfortunately, it is true, these tasks are badly performed by the state because the state is badly equipped to perform them. Thus our different communities slide into irretrievable decadence, and the state itself follows. Poor in men, France will soon be poor in all things.

Considering that the eras of true and stable national well being in France were those in which the power of the throne, independent as it was, and master of the proper prerogatives of the state, placed no impediment to the free control of their own interests by the different bodies, guilds and communities;

Considering that the shining example given to the king and to France by eight centuries of historical experience will not be lost upon either France or the king;

Royal power cannot fail to lead, with firmness and wisdom (taking into account the time and indispensable precautions required for such a task) to the re-establishment in practice of liberties in every sphere where the higher interests of the nation and of the state do not require the exercise of authority.

That is to say:

Families will arrange their own affairs as it seems best to them. They can leave their property to whoever they wish. Fathers who wish to provide succeeding generations of their descendants with hereditary assets that are neither transferable nor distrainable will have entire liberty so to do. Recognized at last as the natural associations that they are, families will be able to acquire rights analogous to those of the citizen, to possess in common an honorary and moral title, just as they can possess a title to property.

Towns and villages (or districts) will, as a result of a judicious series of liberating measures, become the masters of their own affairs to be managed as they think best, assuring their own internal law and order without state intervention, deciding all domestic matters or matters which affect any of their members, and being restrained in the exercise of this honest and reasonable liberty only by the common good and the security of the realm.

The important hinterland regions linked to our great cities (Lyon, Bordeaux, Marseilles, Lille, Nancy, Toulouse, Nantes, Rouen, Montpellier, Grenoble, Besançon, Limoges, Clermont, and so on) will be recognized in law and freed from the artificial divisions into departments, which is absurd and irrational.[1] The regions which look to these cities as their natural capitals will progressively obtain autonomy in all that affects their own particular interests and does not compromise the national interest. Great provincial councils, under the ultimate but distant control

[1] These lines were written more than twenty years before the restitution of Metz and Strasbourg posed problems for the French Republic which it has been unable to resolve, but to which its frenzied and fatal spirit of centralization has added needless complexities. (Maurras's footnote.)

of the state, will collaborate in the reawakening and renewal of the whole body of the nation now shrivelled by the Jacobin policy of centralization.

Professional, religious and intellectual associations, enjoying total liberty, will be subject to common law and considered as autonomous legal entities, but creating their own rules of conduct by that *esprit de corps* which is the fount of all progress; they will be entitled to own, to acquire and to transfer property, to be under obligation to pay taxes and fines, and may be, in the event of legal misdemeanour, either temporarily or permanently suspended.

To sum up, the citizen, in every sphere where he is competent and directly affected, where he is capable of knowing and therefore judging, is, at the present time, no more than a slave. Royal power will restore to him the sovereignty and freedom of action in this domain which was seized from him illegally, uselessly and to the detriment of the nation's strength.

This is what the king will do for liberties. He will restore them to the citizens. He will be their guarantor, their defender, their policeman. Let us now examine what he will do for authority, once he has chased it out of the internal details of civil life.

'Authority at the Top'

He will set authority on its feet, define it and use it for purely national objectives.

The French state, which meddles in everything today, even in schooling and the sale of matches, and which, as a result, does everything infinitely badly, distributing non-inflammable matches and hare-brained education, is powerless to fulfil its true function as a state. It has been handed over lock, stock and barrel to the representatives of the legislative. Ministers are nothing but clerks and servants to the senators and deputies and devote themselves exclusively to obeying these their masters in order to preserve the portfolios. As a forceful aphorism has it: 'The elector begs favours from the deputy, the deputy begs favours from the minister, the minister begs votes from the deputy, the deputy begs votes from the elector.' A class of citizens, heartily despised by the entire country, makes its living by a trade in influence and intrigue; senators, deputies, vote-jobbers – it is only by chance that one finds one single independent character in a thousand such individuals in that profession. Those of their number who pass for having clean hands merely testify to their own stupidity. On the very day of the Loubet election, one of our masters could write that the future representative in congress was distinguished above all by his intellectual inadequacy.

Invariably ignorant and limited, often impoverished and corrupt, these are the masters of France. We are told they can be changed. A change of personnel serves no purpose. A parliament, composed by some chance of enlightened men, would of necessity be very quickly replaced, like the Assembly of 1871, by a horde of agitators, catchers of the popular vote. If these newcomers are honest on their arrival, they will soon be corrupted by the working of the regime. The Count of Paris has rightly observed: 'These institutions corrupt their men, whoever they may be.'

What then is such a government? A shadow, a juxtaposition of meaningless syllables! One set of leaders is too much like another for any to stand out or prevail for long. Ten, twenty or thirty months is as long as the victory of any of their ministerial groups can endure: a republican cabinet, charged with the task of providing for the grave political and economic necessities of the nation, is incapable of lasting any longer. What department store or corner shop, what vegetable stall or shoeshine stand would survive this continual and systematic change of management? What industry would not be ruined if the board of directors was overthrown every ten, twenty or thirty months?

No minister has the time to study the services he is supposed to direct. It is only by good luck if he knows what they are. And so the poor fellow leaves his head civil servants to decide everything. From time to time, upon the command of some parliamentary group, he pushes them around with ignorant and violent passion. Thus we pass from routine to revolution with no possible happy medium. Neither genuine, stable and personal control, nor dependable tradition. Neither does our administration make any progress: it is only too happy to avoid its own downfall.

For this unstable ministerial direction is, furthermore, divided against itself to the point of madness. You do not even achieve unity of view in one minister. He has his political friends to satisfy, his adversaries to placate. Thus parliamentary manœuvre clashes with his general policy aims; the latter is totally subordinated to the former. As most ministers are drawn from the shameful class which lives on public funds, just as they exist only by courtesy of the class of their own vote-gathering pimps, the resources of the nations are put to the sack. Useless expenditure, electorally inspired, increases daily and the revenue declines for the same reasons. National defence, the industrial and commercial life of the nation, everything is sacrificed to the petty interests of the vote manufacturers.

If a port is built, it is for them. It is for them that roads are laid. It is for them that railways are constructed. The general interest has but a miserable share in it. Our financial power is dissipated to satisfy the electoral clientele of influential deputies and senators just as our political power is frittered away in cementing the foundations of influence and in defending it with tenacity. Powerless to act in the public good, the regime, when it supposes itself to be in a position of strength, lavishes its fiscal resources and its powers of control upon the task of establishing its own supporters or consolidating the anarchy which reigns at their side.

This wastefulness and the lack of competent and continuous direction causes industry and commerce to dwindle, despite the artless illusion created by the 1900 Exhibition. Agriculture cannot sell its produce or only at low prices, and the political prestige of France follows the same curve of depression as her economic power. A power, without force to sustain it, which feebly administers rather than commands the army, has allowed itself to be flouted for two years now. This power, having at a diplomatic level and not without incoherence committed itself to the Fashoda[1] venture, has been unable to extract itself from the mire except at the price of our collective shame. The Russian alliance has even ceased to figure in the vocabulary of Europe's conversations.

Bismarck undoubtedly foresaw many of our present misfortunes when he did all he could to dedicate us to the republican system. Bismarck was not ignorant of the fact that the strength of a state presupposes unity of view and

[1] In 1898, French troops under Marchand occupied Fashoda at the headwaters of the Nile; Kitchener arrived with a British force, but Marchand refused to leave. Eventually the French did leave, and this was taken to be a grave humiliation for France.

the spirit of continuity, cohesion and organization. As a republican regime is synonymous with the absence of a master will and continuity of thought at the centre of power, he sensed the extent to which such a regime divides and condemns to perpetual upheaval any people that abandons itself to its tender mercies.

We are told by the parliamentary republicans as well as by the proponents of plebiscite, that this unstable and feeble power rests upon a solid base. The base they find so solid is the national will, as expressed by parliamentary elections or referenda.

From the national will springs, since in the national will resides, government authority. The very people who refuse the citizen the right to deal with the matters he knows best and to look after his own closest interests, the very people who refuse the municipal elector the right to change a public fountain or lay a path without state permission, are the ones who accord to the same citizen, the same elector, by the most astonishing of constitutional fictions, absolute power to make a judicious choice, to express a valid opinion on the most remote, the most profound, the most complex questions of general policy. This elector and citizen, whose competence to make the humblest decision was but a moment ago regarded as suspect, is suddenly supposed to possess all the intellectual powers of the Académie Française for he is called upon to choose between radical policy and opportunism, between authoritarian and liberal, between socialism and capitalism, and to acknowledge his right, by his choice and by his vote, to guide the direction of legislation, supreme justice, diplomacy, and the military and naval organization of the whole nation!

So staggering an illusion could never be fulfilled with integrity. Instead of complaining about it, we must recognize that it is unattainable and assert clearly that however independent, however honest, however intelligent the elector may be, he can never be competent to decide the majority of the questions put to him. This disability makes him either violent and blind or hesitant and fickle, or all simultaneously.

The French elector spends his time giving blank cheques to men he does not know, with no other guarantee than the fine shades of meaning written into the election posters upon which candidates publish their intentions. This system is an incentive, a stimulant, an imperative to the opposition parties (even the honest ones though it applies much more forcibly to the less honest) to provoke the greatest possible number of scandals and disasters in order to bring about as many changes as possible at each new election. In this way party interest replaces the public interest. In this way France sinks into decay.

What becomes of the state in all this? It becomes a slave. The slave of parliament. The slave of the parliamentary parties, of electoral deals. The slave of unforeseen events even, events which under such a regime unleash both panic and opinion changes, hence ministerial changes, changes of direction, events which are precisely those requiring for the public good the maximum possible of firmness, stability and self-control. At the very moment when it is most necessary to stand firm, the system compels the foundations to be shaken; Varron is kicked out at the very moment when, however incompetent or unworthy he may be, he should have received from the state an overwhelming demonstration of confidence. Subject to these multiple forms of slavery within, the French state finds itself similarly enslaved in its external relations. Other states tolerate its apparent independence solely for the purpose of giving it the maximum opportunity to decline, to degenerate and to disintegrate on its own.

Since the undersigned writers are prompted by their knowledge of political necessities which may have escaped the attention of their fellow citizens, and since they act as spokesmen and elders of their race, in the full exercise of the rights and duties conferred upon them by the present deplorable state of affairs;

Since they are fully aware of their obligation to minister and to watch over the common good;

Since the common good, precondition of every right, imposes upon all a fundamental obligation towards the national community;

Since the national community, the motherland, the state, are not associations stemming from the personal choice of their members, but the handiwork of nature and necessity;

Since the unity of France, furthermore, is not the product of a certain number of individuals living at one given moment and having in common certain ideas, certain passing fancies, but of a certain number of families reaching out from age to age and having in common certain permanent interests: the land to be defended, the continuity of the race to be assured, a fund of moral and economic capital to be developed;

Since under the republican regime, the fatal absence of all permanent authority threatens and compromises these deep and constant interests which are the generating force of France's strength, of the decisions, ideas and sentiments appropriate to Frenchmen;

The French citizen will hand over to the surviving branch of the House of Capet, by solemn and irrevocable covenant,[1] the exercise of sovereignty. By this means, authority will be reconstituted at the head of the state. Central power will be freed from the rivalry of parties, assemblies and electoral caprice: the state will have a free rein. On his own responsibility, in the inseparable interests of his family and his people, the king, as head of state, will reign and govern. Carefully weighed, legal and responsible, the royal arbitration of both him and his successors, will assure the unity, steadfastness and continuity of aims – always taking into consideration the help of competent persons sitting on technical committees and in local assemblies.

Let us now explain the details of this latter function of the state:

There will be no more Westminster-type parliament. The parliamentary experiment, tried during the monarchies of 1815 to 1830 and of 1830 to 1848 by the most honest and even the most enlightened of men, was a failure. Even if considerable progress was achieved under the Restoration and the July monarchy, even if it is true that our moral and economic capital was replenished at that time and that we are still living on it, nevertheless history shows us that these benefits emerged 'despite' the parliamentary constitution thanks to the politically gifted

[1] It will no doubt be objected that this covenant or handing over of sovereignty is itself an act of the popular will and therefore a feature of the system we condemn.

This logical-sounding objection will however not be made by competent logicians. A doctrine of political mythology is one thing – a doctrine by which the popular will is sovereign merely because it is the popular will. Quite another is any act, determined by that same will, exercised once only and founded upon reason and the public interest instead of upon itself. The value of this particular act of the popular will is determined by the value of that reason and public interest: and this value will logically precede and supersede the act of the popular will. (Maurras's footnote.)

princes or to the virtual ministerial dictatorships of the Duke of Richelieu, Villêle and Guizot – dictatorships incidentally which would have been possible only under a monarchy.

The prince must have a clearly defined sphere of responsibility. As Renan observed: 'Royalty symbolizes a whole nation concentrated in one individual, or, if you will, in one family, and aspiring thereby to the highest expression of the national conscience since no conscience can equal that which results from one single mind,' whatever, one might add, the individual worth of that one mind. The ministers will be directly responsible to the prince. Every year delegates from the provincial assemblies will meet in Paris to vote and control the financial budget. Paris will be the normal seat of court and the permanent meeting-place for all the great public services.

We consider under this heading all bodies worthy of the title of public services: Chambers of Commerce and Industry, the Union of Guilds, the Agricultural Association, Académie Française, etc. The king's councils will naturally be recruited from these highly qualified technical bodies, which are the true representatives of the activity and production of France, and have nothing in common with that pack of scoundrels, intriguers and gossips who, under the pretext of an electoral mandate, jam the corridors of the Palais Bourbon or the Luxembourg: irrelevant to the nation, isolated from the nation, in terms of both its interests and its needs.

The part of the nation that works and produces will thus be in permanent touch with the political power. This political power as a specialized institution will be the master of its own special competences. Advice and enlightenment will be afforded to it, but its right to act will be unfettered. The throne's technical councils, these professional associations, can later on form the elements of some new senate; but, apart from the fact that senates are historical creations and not improvised, it is perhaps better if the technical councils, which represent particular skills, are normally kept separate from one another so that each may fully exercise its respective authority: if the need arose, they could always be either assembled for some congress, or be drawn upon for the formation of various inter-professional commissions, the deliberations of which would be moderated, initiated and arbitrated by the king, in person or through his representatives.

Any possible encroachment by local assemblies or professional bodies upon the royal prerogative of the state will be made impossible, or at least be quashed with extreme severity, by the sanctions determined by the laws of the kingdom. Similarly any citizen who suffers injury by subordinate authorities, will be able, as appeal of last resort, to invoke the authority of the prince as supreme arbiter and high judge of his case. His role will be to decide between conflicting opinions, to act as conciliator and moderator between the parties. He will not, however, interfere in their affairs except as a last resort and upon the express appeal of the interested parties, for there will be more important considerations to which he will have to direct his attention.

To sum up, the state, represented by royal power in all remote and lofty questions of general policy which lie beyond the capacity and the knowledge of individual citizens, will be re-established in its natural and rational prerogatives – namely independence and authority. The citizen will delegate them to the state willingly since it is impossible for him to exercise the necessary powers for himself and he is therefore, under today's conditions, the first to suffer, in well-being and in national pride, from the lack of protection for himself and of guidance for the nation.

The state will have many advisers but henceforth one single master.

Thus in the new kingdom of France, in conformity with national tradition, will be reconciled that authority and those liberties which are both of equal necessity.

Comparison of Royalist and Republican Regimes

We have republican government and autocratic administration: the public good requires that this paradoxical situation be reversed.

The administration should be republican, because it should serve the public; the government autocratic because it has to govern it. What is important to the life of the taxpayer is liberty; what is important to the political life of the nation is authority, the precondition of the spirit of continuity, decision and responsibility.

'Authority at the top, liberty below' is the basic maxim of royalist constitutions.

The ridiculous republic, one and indivisible, that we know so well, will no longer be the prey of ten thousand invisible, uncontrollable little tyrants; instead thousands of little republics of every sort, 'domestic' republics like families, 'local' republics like towns and provinces, 'intellectual' and 'professional' republics like associations, will freely administer their own affairs, guaranteed, coordinated and directed as a whole by one sole power which is permanent, that is to say personal and hereditary and with an interest in the preservation and development of the state.

It is to be noted that such a state, so powerful in its proper function of government, will be extremely feeble from the point of view of acting against the interests of the citizen. Whereas the citizen of the French Republic

is left only with his own meagre individual powers to protect him against the mighty state machine, the citizen
of the new kingdom of France will find himself a member
of all kinds of strong and free communities (family,
town, province, professional organization, etc.) which
will deploy their strength to protect him from any injustice.

The guarantees made to citizens in the republican state
are entirely theoretical. They are, in fact, derived from a
theory (the rights of man) which leads to the repudiation
of the state's prerogatives. In practice these guarantees
entirely disappear. Respecting the paramount prerogatives
of the state, monarchist theory confers upon the citizen
practical guarantees, guarantees *of fact*: not only are they
theoretically inviolable, they are in practice very difficult
to violate.

Liberty is a right under the republic, but only a right:
under the sovereignty of the royal throne liberties will
relate to actual practice – certain, real, tangible, matters of
fact.

Consequences – Royalist Party

From this royal authority, thus placed at the apex of the
whole structure of civil liberties, will of necessity flow
greater freedom for the individual and greater strength for
the nation. We will attempt to specify how the three most
thorny problems of French politics will, in all probability,
be settled.

1. The religious question. The freedom of association
and the rebirth of traditional autonomous bodies, com-
panies and communities will tend to lead inevitably to
the suppression of subsidies for religious denominations
and universities, who must learn to provide for their own
needs.

Roman Catholicism, France's traditional religion, will be restored to all the honours to which it is entitled. Only a government of illiterate lunatics could grudge it them and, for example, ban from the Sorbonne of Louis IX and of Gerson all teaching of theology. This regime of paltry meddling will be declared closed. However it is clear that total intellectual freedom will reign on French soil. Far from disturbing the work of scientific and philosophical research, the state must support it and promote its advance, by granting dignity and funds to all who have distinguished themselves in these fields. Moreover, on the firm ground of organization and direction there can be no conflict between the religious spirit and the scientific spirit. Catholic political thought rejects revolutionary ideology – which is equally abhorrent to the positivists. As for positivist political ideas, their sympathetic affinity with Catholicism is obvious. The state will have only to impose upon itself and observe the strict injunction neither to foster nor to subsidize (unlike the present inimitable republic) theories whose ultimate objective or immediate aim is the overthrow of the state: political anarchy and its theorists will therefore be carefully controlled and if any religious organizations exist with a tendency to lead towards anarchy, they too will be subject to the same supervision, which stems from natural law. The same rule will apply to religions which might tend to be detrimental to the national interest by serving the interests of foreigners.

2. The military question. The King of France, who alone will possess the authority to undertake such a reform, will create the living symbol of his power and our unity, a professional army as large and well-trained as possible. The remaining national contingents would be formed, trained, drilled and put into a state of readiness

by the appropriate methods and as quickly as possible.[1]
The principle of the division of labour invalidates the
concept of the whole nation under arms, based in its theory
upon a historical error of grave proportions (the volunteers
of 1792) and realized in practice by a botched and detest-
able imitation of the German system.

3. Economic questions. Usury will be outlawed.

While firmly rejecting all hypocritical notion of philan-
thropy, we shall defend the working man against agitators
and demagogues – and speculators too. The abuses of the
private ownership of capital, which serves as the pretext
for revolutionary agitation, will be vigilantly watched.
National industry and national labour will be protected
not only against the inroads of foreign industry and foreign
labour, but also against international speculators based in
our midst. A strong and healthy nation eliminates these
parasites on its own. 'Sound policy' will restore to it its
finances. The administration, wrenched at last from the
turbulent control of parliament and from the somnolent
routine of officials, will be able to give useful assistance.

Responsible to the crown for administration, the various
ministers will be encouraged to introduce reforms desired
by the public. Financial controls will be set up on the same
lines as the system of political checks and balances, not
with the object of slowing down transactions but of sparing
citizens from those unexpected financial disasters whose
effects rebound upon the whole country. Property will be

[1] It is perhaps worth emphasizing that, in so crucial an area,
the will of the royal dictator will be exercised with even more
independence than over other matters. We merely indicate the
principle. In a republic, the interests of the state and of the army
are in contradiction. In a monarchy they are in harmony. The
state can apply itself to the task of building up a stronger and
higher quality army at the same time as that of alienating the
economic and social burden of militarism. (Maurras's footnote.)

safeguarded and encouraged in all its forms from the humble savings account, the simplest and most fundamental means of personal protection, to the landed estates which form the physical basis of the motherland.

Conclusion – The King of France

Whatever critics may say, this hope of a French renaissance is no chimera, for the nation's vitality, if menaced, does not seem to us to be fundamentally impaired, morally, physically and economically; we are still extremely richly endowed; the trouble is that our wealth is being frittered away by incompetent administration. He who can cure the two political maladies which have afflicted us for two hundred years, 'the administration ruled by all, the state ruled by none; the administration master of all, the state with no master at all', will remove the root cause of our misfortunes. We are royalist because we consider that hereditary monarchy alone is capable of administering the necessary treatment.

A parliament, created by elections and dependent upon them, confers upon the state neither authority nor independence. A head of state elected by universal suffrage is in the same position as a parliament. Nominate him in good time, and what an incentive you give for the most tremendous electoral agitation! And what periodic upheavals you ensure for the state! The President of the United States of America dare not, even in the gravest of situations, take a single decision, settle a single question, give a single precise directive, when the date of the presidential election is looming up: the unfortunate man fears, in effect, that by expressing any opinion whatever, he will alienate some section or other of the electorate.[1] If the

[1] These six lines from 'The President of the United States ... ' onward were written by Frédéric Amouretti. (Maurras's footnote.)

president is elected for life, what an incentive you give to the would-be assassin, and, in any case, consider what revolutions, what agitation, what transports of political fever you are hatching for the day of his succession! This is the type of regime that ruined unhappy Poland; instead of reducing and limiting rivalry for power to a single class, or caste, or family, such a system extends it to cover the entire country.

In addition this type of dictator is responsible only for a certain length of time – at maximum for the duration of his life. If he avoids errors and risks of a too direct and too immediate a nature, there is nothing to prevent him from compromising, mortgaging or sacrificing the future of the country. This is the danger of personal dictatorship. And this is why we demand sovereign power not for one man, not for a whole people, but for one family which represents the people and is itself represented by one man. We hope that no one will reply with any nonsense about the hazard of birth. As if elections contained no hazard! As if these were not worse than the first! A dauphin is brought up in preparation for the throne; there is no special upbringing for presidential candidates. Besides which, the natural hazards of heredity have never, in any country, nor even in the most primitive tribes, placed upon the throne a succession of mediocrities remotely comparable to the series: Carnot, Périer, Faure, Loubet. The presidential honour was nevertheless conferred upon these four abysmal nonentities by the 'choice' of both Houses, meeting in solemn Congress.

The system of hereditary monarchy assumes, upon the basis of natural feelings of consideration for the family's future (which will be there nine times out of ten, even if once it is lacking), that the head of state will not gamble idly away the future of his dynasty and that in all his plans he will feel obliged to exercise prudence and thought. It is precisely these truly paternal qualities, appropriate to fathers and to heads of families, which have distinguished the House of Capet in its task of representing France. Its principles, applied from one reign to the next, have been never to stake too much on a single enterprise so as not to risk too great an ultimate loss — as was the case with the Napoleons. In contrast to Napoleon I and Napoleon III, who both left France smaller than they found it, the descendants of Hugh Capet all handed down their heritage just as they received it from their predecessors or increased by a province or two.

If then, in order to spare ourselves fruitless and dangerous electoral contests, to forestall the periodic recurrence of political agitation, and finally to ensure peace, if, we repeat, it is agreed that power must be entrusted to a family, it is obvious that it is to the finest, the oldest and the most illustrious of French families that such an honour must fall. Neither the Bonapartes, however 'glorious' their historic role may have been, nor any other French family, whatever 'services' they may have rendered to the nation, can offer guarantees comparable to those of the race of Capet. It is the oldest royal line in Europe, and it belongs to us. Even better, 'It is us.' Its history is our history. The face of our land everywhere records their name and memory. Just as Ivan the Terrible came to be known as the founding father of Russia, so this dynasty can be called the founding father of France.[1] Without it there is no France. This is an unchangeable statement of fact.

Memories of the Roman Empire created Italian unity. The realities of the Germanic race and tongue, linked to the traditions of Charlemagne and of the Holy Roman Empire, created German unity. The unity of the British

[1] The phrase is Frédéric Amouretti's. (Maurras's footnote.)

stems from their island nature. But the unity of the French, a political achievement, created by the long exercise of the gentlest and the firmest of authoritarian policies, is the result and exclusively the result of a thousand years of unswerving dedication by the House of France. This unity as solid as today it 'seems' spontaneous and natural, is the sole creation of our princely line. It sufficed that nature made such unity possible, not obligatory, not inevitable: our princes formed it and shaped it like an artist moulding according to his own personal inspiration the material he has selected.

A dynasty that is truly of the *earth* and of the *soil*, since it rounded out our *land* and shaped our *country*, and yet one for whom one cannot really assert which of the words boldness or wisdom best serves to describe its qualities! The policy of the Hohenzollerns, so disastrous for France, but so advantageous for the whole German people, has itself been but a competent copy and a thoughtful plagiary of the policy of the House of Capet.

Starting from one corner of the country, this popular and warlike dynasty gradually extended its sway to the limits of ancient Gaul. Its traditions are inextricably blended with all of ours. The liberties which a hundred years of Caesarism and anarchy have made us lose are the liberties that our forefathers conquered for us in days gone by under the rule of the House of Capet. This royal line of kings recognized those liberties in countless acts of solemn consecration. Liberty died with royalty. We now herald their twin rebirth.

The speechmakers, of English, German or Swiss extraction, who preside over the Holy Republican Church, say, in one of their own odious expressions, that there exists an 'ideal' France. We are citizens of a real France. When we talk of France, we refer to the most cherished and beautiful of realities, and not to some abstract idea. *Pulcherrima rerum*, as the Roman said of his own fatherland: we mean the soil of France and its varied riches, the blood of France and its subtly blended riches, the traditions of France, the interests of France, the thought and feeling of France. We think of the houses, of the altars, of the tombs where holy remains lie sleeping. That real France, being what she is and needing kingship, belongs by definition, having been what she was, to the kingship of the head of the House of France. He, being who he is, matches this need and these traditions. The people are ready to awaken to the same needs and traditions. May all cultivated minds recognize the natural ties of blood between a great nation and a princely line, and at last comprehend this watch-word for the future of our nation.

'Guided now by the sure foot and clear vision of science, by reason and by determination, let us continue on the road built for us by the traditions and instincts of our ancestors.'

ROMANTICISM AND REVOLUTION

(This passage forms the general preface to a collection of essays under the title Romanticism and Revolution, *published by Nouvelle Librairie Nationale, Paris 1922.)*

Common Origin

A combatant from the barricades of July 1830 is said to have rushed victorious and powder-blackened to a friend's and cried, 'We have beaten the romantics.' For this particular hero of the republic, no distinction existed between the armed defenders of the legitimate monarchy and the poets who sang of the Catholic Middle Ages: he seemed to recognize in the language of Thiers, of Béranger,[1] of Paul-Louis Courier,[2] the pure classical spirit. It is very much in this sense that Taine sees the spirit of revolution take form and grow within the classical tradition.

This superficial similarity need trouble us no longer: friend and foe of romanticism agree that its identity with revolution is close and deep. Romanticism and revolution resemble nothing so much as two stems, which, though they look different, grow from the same root. The movement

---

[1] Pierre-Jean Béranger (1780–1857), writer of popular verses and at one time considered the national poet of France. Imprisonment under the Restoration for his satirical poetry only increased his popularity, and a fine of 10,000 francs was paid by popular subscription.

[2] Paul-Louis Courier (1772–1825), scholar and pamphleteer who, under the pseudonym Paul-Louis Vigneron, upheld the rights of the peasantry against clerical and governmental oppression. His best pamphlets are considered not much inferior to the *Provinciales* of Pascal.

239

of ideas or rather of dreams, of which 1750, 1789, 1830, 1848, 1898 are the landmarks, is something which obtains or which can be sustained in every field of action or of the imagination: morality, politics, poetry, history, philosophy, religion. We never fail to discover in this profuse entangled undergrowth of the complexity of man and events the unity of the human spirit. If difficulties there be, they can be resolved: the classicist in Béranger or Thiers poses us perhaps a problem no greater than that of Chateaubriand's loyalist monarchism, no objection more embarrassing that the legitimist fervour of the young Hugo or the revolutionary action of the most classical of our contemporaries, Anatole France.

Taine's error astounds us! It has been lightheartedly pointed out that we must look in Rousseau's *Social Contract* rather than in Boileau's *Art Poétique* to find the ideas that guided Robespierre. The analytical approach, the confidence in reason, the passion for the continuum of thought, the clear, the intelligible, the Greek and Roman vocabulary, the decor of antiquity, oratorical passages taken from the *Conciones,* examples from *De Viris,* these characteristic modes of expression, even if inherited from the age of classicism, possessed in themselves not one element of the genius of revolution. The oratorical, discursive form was but an instrument of the mind as long as it remained uncorrupted by the service of special interests. It is this corruption that has to be explained.

In the same way, eager study of the republican orators of Athens and Rome would have continued to throw a favourable light upon the monarchy, the aristocracy and tradition, if illuminated by the study of the historical circumstances of the experiments in popular government of classical antiquity: they include special conditions — slavery is an instance — and these favourable conditions could not protect a rash regime from consequences that have the appearance of retribution; through its natural spokesman, a Corneille for example, or a Bossuet, the classical spirit observed and related this aspect of retribution long before a very different spirit, of different origin, could take its place and obscure or contest this finding. This democratic deviation is an effect and must not be confused with its causes.

Democratic deviation – undergone by the classical spirit, not perpetrated by it. On its own the classical spirit gives us no guide in this question.

Auguste Comte, whose gaze is penetrating but in a different direction, found this explanation but Taine took no note of it. In a margin note of a copy in the Bibliothèque Nationale, Taine boasts, I am told, of not having been able to complete the endurance test of *Système de politique positive*. So much the worse for him: whether idleness or spite, it has cost him dear. A little more perseverance would have led him to those conclusions in which, having defined the Reformation Movement as 'systematic sedition by the individual against the species', Comte senses the central thread of revolutionary thought and action. The traditions of Athens and Rome are as innocent of revolutionary content as was the inspiration of the medieval Catholic Church. The ancestors of the Revolution are to be found in Geneva, in Wittenberg – more distantly in Jerusalem. They spring from the Jewish spirit and from the varieties of independent Christianity that grow wild in the deserts of the East, or in the dark Teutonic forest, wherever barbarians meet. Comte's hypothesis, curiously enough, is confirmed by wiser revolutionaries who claim descent from every medieval dissident, Vaudois or Albigensian, who came to the West from Asia and Africa long before the Bibles of Jan Hus, Wyclif or Luther had undermined the faith of the northern and eastern peoples. But faith, no less than the 'Eternal Gospel', found a ready audience in the civilized nations of the south and west of Europe. For the German and Anglo-Saxon world it was different: ill-infused by Catholic humanism, Judaism could penetrate unchecked.

The German mind, reading the Holy Word, could not but hear in it the cry of those violent effusions of the senses that civilization attempts to moderate: the cry of love and hate, of hope and despair, of servitude and liberty, that hysterical yearning for independence of one who, in Guizot's phrase, 'flails in all directions with no other goal than his own satisfaction'. The inner turmoil let loose! This unbridled fundamentalism first of all swept away, or perhaps merely overturned, the discipline – mental, moral, aesthetic discipline – reason, law, order, taste in which was embodied all the civilizing influence of the classical spirit. The prompt reaction of our French humanists, Ronsard and his group, to what Jaurès called the 'Religious Revolution' – the gift of Luther the German to sixteenth century Europe – throws immediate light on this point: Calvin was forced to flee, Henry IV to convert to Rome, and the whole Reformation to withdraw from the Latin countries.

Where Taine saw affinity, there was therefore but contradiction: perpetual and logical contradiction. Affinity there was, but it is to be found between what we call Germanic individualism (the empire of the imagination over unsugared reason, the precedence of the particular over the general, of the private over the communal) and the heated, disordered preaching of those heroes of the theological revolt … Luther and the reformers found followers as Arminius had: their own race said, 'You are of our blood.' Through them Europe returned to the darkness of the isolated conscience as if to the recesses of the caves from whence its ancestors had sprung. Almost at once our continent paid the price in the devastation of religious conflict and the Thirty Years War. France was the first to be free of conflict and the greatest century of French thought and of the French genius began, the high point of the nation's order and the nation's soul: a state under one monarch, a Catholic faith, and for these an art fit to give expression to their golden age.

The visits of Montesquieu and Voltaire to London mark the first important encounter of the classical French spirit with that Hebrew and German spirit by which England recently had been troubled. The intellectual curiosity of these two great writers should have been accompanied by vigilance. Mediocre novelty more than it should caught their eye. They brought home to Bordeaux some seeds of foreign anarchy and unrest, without being greatly affected by it themselves: in their great works both bear the marks of fever while remaining free from its rage: the oriental graft has left their blooms unwithered. However feeble they might have been in general philosophy, Montesquieu and Voltaire possessed the advantages of wide knowledge, the exercise of reason, good taste, common sense and that natural sense of the proportions of man's powers: the first a renowned gentleman of the robe, and the second a wealthy bourgeois. But the wretched Rousseau!

A creature that nothing could or might restrain. He came from a part of the world where for two hundred years had hung the stench of decomposition. Neither family feeling, nor party loyalty, nor even that political self-interest which would have been a moderating influence upon any other man from Geneva, nothing could temper the mystical fury of that low-born footpad, driven hither and thither by an old spinster, hopelessly overspoilt by the

friends of his early years. Fit for all trades, including the
most degrading ones, in succession lackey and lapdog,
master of music, parasite and kept man, he acquired his
education on his own; in him a moral basis, like the
intellectual, was lacking; as he fashioned his own science,
he constructed his own standards of taste, his own code of
decorum, from a blend of experience and reading or from
a succession of lessons from those mistresses he has described with such baseness. Reasoning came easily to him:
but, sensitive and versatile as he was, and quite incapable
of holding fast to the truth, his diverse arguments have no
common thread but the rhythm of his own whining
complaints, and we find in him in almost equal measure
the criminal, the savage and the lunatic. Madness,
savagery and crime, the adventurer, fed on Jew-inspired
revolt, called that virtue. Virtue, incarnate in a 'me' of
dingy quality, was declared the right and proper judge
of the human race. This virtue put forward for us as a
model his own unschooled vicious and limited nature.
His outraged and plaintive sensibility, set up as the law,
was in last resort the court of appeal against the universe. The more sincerely abject, the more naturally
slavelike he became, the more he claimed that men
should accept all he said, should obey him, should worship
him.

At that time, on our side of the French frontier,
flourished the seventh or eighth century of modern
civilization. He came in to France, like one of those false
prophets, spewed up by the desert, fixed up with an old
sack, girt in camel-hide, head covered with filthy ashes,
who used to trail their mournful wailings up and down
the streets of Zion: tearing their hair in their rages,
eating filth, and fouling the people with their hate and
scorn. But the Paris of 1750 was nothing like an Asiatic

shanty-town full of grubby Jews. Thoughtful and gracious capital of the intellectual world, seat of a still powerful monarchy, whatever happened in Paris spread out in glory throughout the rest of the known world. It was the walls of this magnificent seat of wisdom that he cast down.

The glory of France and the dominance of Paris were used to spread abroad the ravings of a madman. This wild subhuman thing, this life-form scarce emerged from the principal swamp, seduced the world by the paradox and the principal challenge of his primitive intellectual equipment. Hearts too sensitive, minds too cultivated, found it interesting; inevitably those parts of the world that were least advanced were more responsible: unsophisticated Europe could hardly fail to see itself and to admire itself in that child of nature that sophisticated Paris had made its adored idol. So much so that, in one segment of his audience, the most wooden of all, the German, his teaching was adopted word for word: time-honoured ideas were thrown out; what was regarded hitherto as ignorance, imperfection or weakness to be corrected, claimed, by the fresh bloom of its barbarian simplicity, superiority over the desiccated exhaustion of inspiration imputed to any educated, cultivated, mature race. The arts, literature, science, tradition, the past, in a word anything that had been made, all were of no further account – pure nature led direct to the divine: it alone could speak to the world the infallible language of the future. Among men, the ignorant, among peoples, the backward – these alone were listened to. Thus sang in unison democracy and the German race to claim their insolent right to conquer.

So savage natures and the savage nations followed Rousseau, adopted him as their model. It was in a different way that the French spirit had first contemplated him. The most human of peoples, the French were a little tired of the pleasures and the powers of man. As Voltaire had seen, illuminated as he was by the anti-semitic genius of the Western world, France was yearning to go on all fours and munch hay. She went on all fours. She munched. To satisfy these unnatural appetites, she stuffed herself with Rousseau.

In Rousseau then (and it is the one point we can clearly distinguish in this disordered individual) is to be found the break in France with certain principles of the spirit, certain standards of taste, certain customs and traditions of the state: his *Héloïse*, his *Confessions*, his attitude and way of life lead us back (and retrogressive it is) to that reign of 'nature' the affectation of which produces romantic sensibility; his profession of faith reduces religious life to the god within oneself, without ritual or priest, that is the culmination of Protestant logic; his political ideas are soon to subject France to the doctrine which destroys monarchies and which dreams up republics.

I prefer at this point to demonstrate these facts rather than give them general names. For they are visible, tangible. There is nothing more clear, more certain, than the coincidence of his three themes; literary, religious and political. This harmony will be challenged – paper and the air have to put up with anything; but when we look closely at the efforts of those muddlers who strain themselves to chase Rousseau from his natural position, we find little of substance.

'As a writer he employed the cadences of Bossuet?'

'He could do no other than use what already existed.'

Further, he could not ruin everything at once. Finally, to be effective, he needed to take over the most effective tool that lay to hand. But wait for what follows, and for what follows from that, wait until you see his successors and disciples. If you have eyes, watch the evolution, in verse and prose, in philosophy and in the novel, of that new-born principle – the absolute sovereignty of any human will and of its conscience – which is nothing more than the most arbitrary of feelings. Wait for crazed Xanthippe to assume the mantle of Socrates, and for Socrates to usurp the mantle of Jupiter. As it should, the mode of expression will follow the same evolution as the theme to be expressed. You will see growing not greater but clearer the distance that separates Rousseau from Bossuet. It is noticeable from Chateaubriand on. Sainte-Beuve was not deceived.

'The Catholicism of Rousseau?' ...

Men are not solid blocks of matter. Yet the more nature and history appear complex, varied and ever-shifting, the more striking and significant it is that at moments of crisis when events themselves judge and allot to each spirit its rank and function, the tenacious roots of the literary and of the political revolution have almost simultaneously put forth their shoots and yielded fruit. Often it suffices that one appears for the tip of the other to be at once descried: the first revolution caused the first ferment of romanticism. Romanticism, in its turn, has inspired our other revolutions. The young writers of the years before 1830 furnish an admirable example; their literary taste, which turned them away from classical ideas and principles, shook their loyalty to the established crown; hardly had it begun than the government of Charles X provoked their hostility which grew ever stronger; July answered their prayer, released them. Rebels, who were the contemporaries of this more or less continuous development, failed to take note of it, but we can never see very well what is too near.

Let us cite a further proof of this long established truth. Sixty years later, when Jean Moréas[1] created the Roman school, the critique of romanticism led to a critique of revolution. The point was that the damage inflicted upon art by the former led to awareness, understanding and definition of the damage inflicted upon public order by the latter. Just as decadence in literature had disposed man to permit the decadence of the country, so the renaissance of the classical techniques produced hopes and desires for reconstruction in fields quite removed from art and language. The degradation of our tongue, the tortured rhythms, that kingdom of words where subversion engenders total dislocation, all this reminds us of the subversion born of other crises. Sibling in blood to what philologists call 'a personal style', the literature of personal individualism tended to consign to oblivion all readers but the author himself. How could such a literature not be slanted in favour of a social system which puts the citizen in opposition to the state and, in the name of a state which would preside over its own destruction, incites its citizens now to the frenzy of insurrection, now to the torpor of civic indifference.

Following, as we have, the cause and chain up two or three parallel paths, we find before us every time the same body of false ideas as ill-proportioned to the human spirit as they are pernicious, deadly poison for the human race. We can use the same terms to qualify them. The vocabularies of literary criticism and of politics unite, the one to complement the other: the sacred freedom of the word, the sovereign liberty of the individual, equal-

[1] Jean Moréas (1856–1910), name adopted by Iannis Pappadiamantipoulos, a Greek poet of wholly French tastes and sensibility who, with Maurras and Ernest Raynaud, launched the *Ecole romane*, a return to the Greco-Roman roots of French culture.

ity in literary ideas, equality of all elements of society, a vague fraternity which creates the 'rights' of all and their right to all. These precepts intermingle, exchange images, echoing in reverse the imagery of the 'Reply to the Accused'.

J'ai dit aux mots: Soyez république, Soyez
La fourmilière immense, et travaillez, croyez ...

I told my pen: be a republic if you like,
Draw me that giant ant-heap; work, believe ...

The great political error, now recognized as such, illustrates the great aesthetic error, now beyond dispute, and conversely the latter sheds light upon the former. Let those industrialists who are troubled and embarrassed by the truth of this statement yet are unable to contest it, put it confusedly down, if they wish, to party political spleen – which, in fact, is in themselves alone.

It is not my fault, as Fustel[1] has already expressed it, if things are arranged according to a certain order. I have to put up with it.

Everyone has to live – including the impostor, the parasite, the charlatan. But he who looks at the double image reflected by these two mirrors juxtaposed cannot fail to see the totally objective truth of our proposition. The active study of ideas has been dependent upon those ideas themselves. Are they true? Are they false? Today, as in the past, the author of these essays can only repeat his sole preoccupation: to be right.

---

[1] Numa-Denis Fustel de Coulanges (1830–89), the outstanding historian of the second half of the nineteenth century; he taught the Empress Eugénie her history. Her husband, Napoleon III, knew his too well already.

Nature and Reason

The sovereign freedom of a state makes it externally independent of its neighbours, but internally renders it subject to the disciplines of strength, fruitful endeavour, justice and peace. The freedom of the different associations, institutions, and groups of which it is composed consists in remaining in control of their own rules of conduct: it cannot mean the freedom to disintegrate in internal strife. Finally the freedom of the citizens themselves, according to their different roles and stations in life, is but a proposition to each that he should pursue a mode of life which is appropriate to what he must do, and wishes to do. Freedom cannot authorize them to break ranks in disorder, it is the binding force against death, it is the defensive force against division.

In contrast, the political freedom of revolutionary doctrine utters without distinction one single appeal for the general liberation of every section of society, supposedly all equal, states, enterprises, persons, entirely without taking account of their different functions. The level of this indeterminate freedom is pitched so low that men bear no other label but that which they share with every plant or animal: individuality. Individual liberty, social individualism, such is the vocabulary of progressive doctrine. How ironical it is. A dog, a donkey, even a blade of grass are all individuals. Naturally, the jostling throng of disorganized 'individuals' will willingly accept from the revolutionary spirits its dazzling promises of power and happiness: but if the mob falls for these promises, it is the task of reason to challenge them and of experience to give them the lie. Reason foresees that the quality of life will decline when the unbridled individual is granted, under the direction of the state, his dreary freedom to think only of himself and to live only for himself. Posterity when it pays the price will declare this prediction all too well justified. In close parallel to this, the critical mind of the future will challenge the libertarian aspirations of romanticism, and literary history will see clearly the damaging effect they had upon the poet and his work: enslavement, decomposition.

Thus we find, in politics as in art, the harmony of nature and reason. Criticism and logic, history and philosophy, far from being in conflict, come to the aid of each other. We have had to dwell on this point before. Foreign influences (English mainly) at work in reverse upon the French conservative spirit, tended to represent the principles of the Revolution as an expression of the rational, and the principles of reaction as the voice of the natural world. Abstract reason had erred. Experience, with its clear view of the concrete, rectified the spirit's error, embodying thus the triumph of practical good sense (mental error being the child of pure theory!). This amounted to saying that all theories are false, all generalizations suspect. With one accord we have rejected this contradictory system and refused to dismiss all ideas simply because they are ideas. This rejection applies equally to the gratuitous notion that some special honour is due to an undefined 'idealism' which admits any old system of ideas if it seems to oppose reality. In fact reality and ideas are in no sense opposite or incompatible. There are ideas which are consistent with reality and these are the true ideas. There are realities which are consistent with the noblest ideas and these we call great men, beauty, sacred things. If contradiction we must establish, it is between true ideas and false ideas, between good reality and bad reality. No man of sense will condemn revolutionary ideas merely because they are abstract or generalized. Let us throw light upon this confusion.

The abstract and general nature of these ideas does earn for them a legitimate reproach but of a different kind altogether. When our foremost political philosopher, infuriated by the constant talk of man, of his rights, of his obligations, protested that he knew Frenchmen, Englishmen, Germans and Russians, that nowhere had he encountered abstract man, he was denouncing by so apt an outburst the methodological error of those legislators who thought that the destinies of a whole people could be settled by aphorisms which did not apply to it. Politics is not morality. The science and art of the conduct of the state is not the science and art of man's own conduct. What satisfies general man, can be profoundly disagreeable for the particular state. By losing its head in these metaphysical clouds, concentrating upon these insubstantial wraiths, the Constituent Assembly managed to overlook entirely the problem it was called upon to resolve. Its mind wandered and what followed is the proof.

Furthermore, as if it were not enough for the Assembly to use a pair of scales to measure out a gallon of water, it compounded the error by using false weights. From the standpoint of reason as invoked by itself, the general ideas of the Revolution are the antithesis of truth. In drawing up the French constitution, it felt inclined to speak of an ideal and absolute type of man in Article 1 of the Declaration of the Rights of Man: that they be born and live free and equal before the law. 'What,' exclaimed Frédéric Amouretti,[1] 'a child five minutes old is a free man!' And, of course, it logically follows from the declara-

[1] Joseph-François-Frédéric Amouretti (1863–1903), like Maurras a Provençal; disciple of Mistral who led a movement (*Le Félibrige*) for the revival of the Provençal language. His passionate provincialism influenced both Barrès and Maurras. He contributed frequently to the *Cocarde* when it was run by Barrès.

tion that this infant has the same freedom as its mother and father!

In exactly the same way, if the Assembly was disposed, when dealing with a tangible entity called France, to reason in terms of political society in general, it should have avoided the pitfall of holding that the social group is an 'association' of individual wills whose 'aim' is to 'conserve' 'rights' (as Article 2 has it) since society is in being before the will to associate, since man is a part of society even before he is born, and since the rights of man would in any case be inconceivable without the existence of society. Any affirmation to the contrary, belied in nature, is totally untenable in reason. Whoever drafted such articles produced a mere collection of words without having examined what they meant. There is nothing more irrational.

Nor is it rational that all men should command everyone to be sovereign: this is yet another contradiction in terms so characteristic of the pure and unadulterated irrational. It is not rational that men should meet to elect their leaders, for leaders have to command and an elected leader is little obeyed; elected authority is an instrument which bears no relation to its intended function, an instrument first ridiculous then defunct. If it is not rational, it is contradictory, that the state, founded for the purpose of building unity amongst men, unity in time which we call continuity, unity in space which we call concord, should be legally constituted by competition and discord between parties which by their very nature are divisive. All those liberal and democratic concepts, principles of the revolutionary spirit, are no more than an essay in squaring the circle.

It should not be supposed that even at the outset the needle of reason failed to pierce the skin of revolutionary principle and expose its weakness. Its first critics were not just simple practical men like Burke whose sense of politics and history had been somewhat shocked. Good critical minds, clear vigorous spirits like Rivarol[1] and Maistre, found intolerable the absurd because it was absurd; in the unreason of liberal and Jacobin they foresaw disasters to come; error and catastrophe.

The catastrophes they predicted came to pass. Revolutionary legality has broken up the family, revolutionary centralism has killed community life, the elective system has bloated the state and burst it asunder. While the enfeeblement of peaceful crafts has brought about the recession of the economy, five invasions, each more severe than the last, have demonstrated, both in defeat and in victory, despite the immense sacrifices of our nation, the total inadequacy of the New Spirit and the New State.

Of the three revolutionary ideas now written up on every wall, the first, the principle of political liberty, essence of the republican system, has destroyed not only the citizen's respect for the laws of the state which he regards as the commonplace expression of a passing whim (no whim is permanent), but also and above all his respect for those other laws, profound and solemn; *leges naturae*, offspring of nature's union with reason, laws in which the caprices of man or the citizen count for less than nothing. Oblivious, negligent and disdainful of these natural and spiritual laws, the French state threw discretion to the winds and exposed itself to the gravest dangers and corruptions.

The second of the revolutionary ideas, the principle of equality, essence of the democratic system, handed over power to the most numerous, that is to say the most

[1] Antoine de Rivarol (1753–1801), man of letters, journalist and pamphleteer, famous for the saying, '*Ce qui n'est pas clair n'est pas français.*' 'If it's not clear, it's not French.' Respectfully received in England by Pitt and Burke.

inferior elements of the nation, to the least vigorous producers, to the most voracious consumers, who do the least work and the most damage.

The Frenchman is continually discouraged, if he is enterprising, by a meddling administration legally representative of the greatest number, but finds himself, if he is meek and humdrum, in receipt of the favours with which the same administration gratefully blesses his idleness, and so he has resigned himself to being an office parasite to such an extent that the flame of French national life burnt low and almost died because individuals are not helped to become people or rather because people are dragged down to the level of a herd of individual sheep.

Finally the third revolutionary idea, the principle of fraternity, the essence of cosmopolitan brotherhood, imposed on the one hand a limitless indulgence towards all men, provided they lived far enough away from us, were unknown to us, spoke a different language, or, better still, had a skin of different colour. On the other hand this splendid principle allowed us to regard anyone, be he even fellow citizen or brother, as a monster and a villain if he failed to share with us even our mildest attack of philanthropic fever. The principle of universal fraternity which was supposed to establish peace among nations, has taken that frenzy of anger and aggression built by nature into the secret mechanism of that political animal, that political carnivore rather, called man, and turned each nation upon itself, upon its own compatriots. Frenchmen have been instructed in the arts of civil war.

And that is not all. The same ideas, distributed worldwide as French merchandise to all our customers, brought great harm to them and returned with interest upon our own heads. Happy lands, that had been protected from Luther by the Inquisition or some other stroke of good

fortune, were contaminated by our own disease of biblio-
mania. Spain, Italy, the little nations of the south and east,
the people of Asia and Latin America, all those who in
faith entrusted to us the upbringing of their young generations and the guidance of their understanding, today are all
the more gravely infected as if by a new species of virus for
which no preventive inoculation exists. These nations have
suffered the consequences of our errors. While revolutionary ideas forged in France their three-pronged fork of
anarchy, the same ideas, supposed French though not so,
produced in the minds of France's satellites the conviction
that the civilizing role of France consisted solely of instruction in anarchy. Today this grievously impedes our
efforts to propagate the notion of order. We are hard put
to it for a reply to President Wilson when he quotes to us
the ideas of Victor Hugo.

The dissensions among these new nations are but the
echo of our own. Their weaknesses are ours. For they
dispose of resources infinitesimal by comparison with ours
and so, long before us, they will reach bankruptcy. To us
they will attribute that bankruptcy, the more so since to us
they attribute what they have the kindness to call progress.
They give themselves impossible constitutions: French
ideas! They enunciate ideal programmes of perfect
absurdity: French ideas! They conceive of no civic energy
but that which resides in opposition and sedition, they
attach ludicrous majesty to the notion of revolution:
French ideas again! In the world's loveliest places, beneath
happy skies, among ancient ruins which are most fit to
inspire us with nostalgia, with the hope for the universal
harmony of the old order, or with that soaring feeling of
the natural inequality of man, in Athens, in Florence, by
the peaceful waters of Genoa, I have talked with men in the
fullness of their mature years, when reason puts forth

its fruit, men formed in the pure physical mould of humanity at its highest and most magnificent, and I have heard such men blabbering such dreary rubbish, blaspheming so savagely against all the normal conditions of prosperous life that tears of pity have welled into my eyes. Revolutionary ideas had been there before me. In the temples of order, they have set upon the altar, under a French pseudonym, the graven images of anarchy and barbarism.

There is worse to come. Even in the midst of the nations that flourish today, nations whose true interests, understood at last, have set them free from the barbaric ideas whose cradle they once were, in the midst of nations which, though seemingly attached to the Reformation, do not always administer their affairs along Protestant lines, we find men from the dregs of the population setting themselves up as rebels against their national institutions. These factions, wherever they form, regard us as their accomplices, their natural mentors, let alone as their eventual protectors. They imagine they honour us in attributing to us the chief responsibility for their crimes and their follies. With pride they promise us gratitude and even help should the need arise. This holy alliance of the plebs which, in our honour, has been going for a hundred years, has never yielded us any profit save that of the reputation of perpetual agitator and the mistrust of the whole of Europe which flows naturally from such an honour. The strong, the rulers, the few who could have stood by us in the hour of trial, have long kept their distance, as though we were dangerous lepers or pathetic weaklings of no account.

As for the triumph of the revolutionary rabble who lift up their eyes to France, the result of its long awaited coming was for France to be forgotten, neglected, and soon openly derided by their former friends. When they became powerful in their turn, they sought only the friendship of the powerful amongst whom we were no longer included. Such is the story of French relations with other revolutionaries as soon as they found themselves in possession. We saw that clearly enough in the 1914–18 war. Lenin, like Bonaparte before him, had no further thought, once swept to power, but to secure his position by seeking agreement with those he judged to be the masters of the world. And so he left us alone, and, in the interests of his people and of himself, applied himself as best he could to dealing with our enemies. This is the fifth benefit which we have derived from revolutionary ideas: the seeds of anarchy they sow have reaped for France the enmity of the entire human race.

All this might as well have been inscribed on the title page of the new principles. So easy was it to foresee that the whole of the preceding page, practically to the name of Lenin himself, appears in a piece I wrote twenty-three years ago. But what is a mere quarter century of prophecy by us in comparison to the majestic predictions of the wisest contemporaries of the Constituent Assembly or of Napoleon! No effects had yet appeared but from cause alone, from the basis of the principles invoked, the chaos of ordeal and ruin to come could be prefigured, even defined. Since those principles were judged false in themselves and ludicrous in their legal application, their pernicious consequences in practice were clearly foreseen. The pure spirit had seen and had reacted. Wise before the event not after, reason rebelled: *a priori*. By a process of induction we have followed the route back to the historical causes of our misfortunes, but the political observers who saw these causes originate, deduced that whole subsequent chain of misfortunes to come. So honourable a truth deserves to be recorded with emphasis and with pride. The mere fact that the Revolution has laid claim to the sceptre of reason does not oblige the counter-revolution to hand it over and to limit itself to a kind of *a posteriori* verification as for instance in Le Play[1] and others, which but prophesies the past. Our gift for empirical organization has not forgotten Comte who did not fear to philosophize with all his heart and soul and who put to such wise use all the forces of the spirit.

Man, the two-legged animal without feathers, has always applied reason to politics and social morality. If he has not always reasoned correctly, it is because historical criticism and logic do not always meet in one mind. Now in this type of research the logician needs the critic of history if he is to obtain an accurate and general purview upon which to base his reasoning. But when he has his purview, if he respects it and handles it well, he has at his disposal a degree of clarity and certitude which other sciences lack. Chemistry and physics study their field without penetrating the surface. They record the relationships which obtain between substances, but they are reduced to guessing at the reasons why. In precisely the same way as the other sciences of observation, politics drawn from historical criticism takes note of similarities in the recurrence of various phenomena in order with certainty to extract valid laws. Thus, the term democracy had only to appear for history to see the term centralization hard at its heels. It is

[1] Pierre-Guillaume-Frédéric Le Play (1806–82), social reformer, who in *La Réforme sociale* (1856) argued for the necessity of the authority of the Church and the state in an economic life whose basis was to be patriarchal; the industrialist was to be in the same relation to his workmen as the father to his children, exercising an authority based on love, not coercion. A classic paternalism which had some influence on French industrialists, and found echoes at Vichy.

a fact, hence a law. Its cause? Political science can see, can know, can tell. Because it is rooted in history, in man, politics can supply the reason for the inseparable link between democracy and centralization, ineluctably forged by the nature of things. Deep and close experience has revealed to the political scientist, in the most secret recesses of the human heart, how the interaction of passion and interest in a governing party wherever it may be, whatever it is, and providing it wishes to be re-elected, must compel the democratic state ceaselessly to keep watch upon, to renew, and to strengthen the cohesiveness of its electors, therefore to hold them fixed in a tight and more and more centralized framework of officials and hangers-on. And so the psychology of man offers us the rational explanation we cannot find in test tubes – the motive force is man-made! Once we have grasped the hidden cause of the effects we observe, we can predict or make deductions at will.

It is unquestionably at this point that theoretical reason becomes a matter of chance. Speaking of a methodology employed in higher mathematics, Leibnitz referred to it in grave terms as 'blind or symbolic'. All logic which uses abstract symbols gropes in the darkness of blind algebra. The vehicle leads the driver. All is well if the motor performs. All is well if no sign or series of signs is confused with another. If we stray from the firm surface of observable fact, we can put our trust only in the driver's skill and instinct. However, when the logician has the necessary feel, he can from time to time re-establish contact, either by observing directly, or by consulting that marvellous compendium of recorded experience to which historical criticism gives him access, and this comes like a ray of living daylight to illuminate the dark tunnel of deduction. Certainly he would fare less well if he denied to dialectical reason its soaring flight, but his advance would be less sure if repeatedly he failed to check its conclusions.

Note on the Classical Spirit

By a deplorable error, perhaps the result of schoolday or teacher prejudice, Taine, our master, has been misguided enough to qualify as classical the spirit which prepared the Revolution. Upon reflection we see how infinitesimal was the part played by classical antiquity. The revolutionary library scarcely includes any classical works except perhaps Plato's *Republic* and Plutarch's *Parallel Lives*; and even they are only present in so far as that father and learned doctor of revolutionary ideas, J.-J. Rousseau, has borrowed from them — and that more a question of language than of matter.

Furthermore Plutarch was well aware of semitic ideas, which, despite himself, had already penetrated his thought; for he was born almost at the very moment that the wind from the East was presaging the destruction of the great soul of classical antiquity. As for Plato, he is, of all the Greek sages, the one who brought back from Asia the most Asian ideas and the most singular of them; he, more than all his fellow Greek philosophers, was the object of commentary and distortion by the Alexandrian Jews. What is called Platonism and what could be called Plutarchism, if we isolate them from their context, could dangerously misrepresent the wisdom of Athens and Rome; there are some parts in the two doctrines which are barbarian more than Greco-Roman, and already 'romantic'.

But ancient Greece, with its physicians and geometricians, with its sophists, its artists, its logician-poets, with Phidas, with Aristotle who opened up a new world, laid the foundations of positive science, positive philosophy, positive religion; while ancient Rome, with its statesmen, historians and moralists, unfolded for us so powerful a lesson in realist politics that not even the English parliaments or the Capetian monarchy have surpassed its achievements. Neither in the family, nor in the city of the ancients, was anything left to anarchy; the judgment of leaders and the limits imposed by the laws moderate and complement one another to perfection. The unfortunate history of the last half century of Athenian liberty, the repeated warnings of the Aristophanes, the Xenophons, even the Platos, and of all the masters of the Greek genius, the rapid degeneration, the drama of the final eclipse, all these show the superiority of aristocracies and of other regimes based upon firm authority where, in any case, the institution of slavery makes democracy an illusion and any popular government unreal.

In modern times, the Catholic philosopher prefers to model himself on Aristotle; Catholic political thought appropriates to itself the methods of Roman politics. Such is the nature of the classical tradition. The classical spirit is the essence of the doctrines of humanity at its highest point. To call the spirit of the Revolution classical is therefore to strip the word of its true meaning and to open the way for unimaginable misunderstandings.

Revolution came from a different direction altogether: the Reformation Bible, the statutes of the Geneva Republic, the Calvinist theologians, the old individualist ferment of the Germanic race for which trilingual Switzerland already served as the European corn-exchange, the personal elan of a sensibility unrestrained by either hereditary morality, rigorous scholarship or healthy reason – these were the humble origins of the ideas which were born in the spirit of Rousseau. By the magic of eloquence, they entered with him into the long-established social order of France; far from seeing in these ideas any manifestation of the classical spirit, they led to the destruction of that spirit of progress and order. Who can deny that with Rousseau began the era of the romantics?

For the very reason that Taine has so just a claim to be respected by us all, it is important that we should explain why a detail of his terminology cannot be accepted and why, precisely, it is our duty to challenge it.

THE POLITICS OF NATURE

(This passage, dedicated to Madame la Marquise de Maillé, forms the preface to Mes Idées Politiques, *published by Fayard, Paris 1937.)*

1. *Protective Inequality*

A tiny chick breaks from its shell and at once begins to run about. It has virtually all it needs to claim 'I am free' ... But the infant man?

The infant man has nothing. Long before being able to run he has to be extracted from his mother's womb, washed, wrapped up, fed. Before being taught his first steps, his first words, he has to be protected from danger. What little instinct he does possess is incapable of providing for his needs; he has to get them from someone else, who has carefully made the necessary preparations.

He is born – but not his independent will, nor an individual basis for action. He will not for a long time be able to say 'I' or 'me', and yet already a circle of protection and care is drawn around him. Practically inert, the infant man, who would perish if he had to face alone the harsh world of nature, is received into the womb of another fussier, kindlier human world: and merely by virtue of the fact that he is its infant citizen, he remains alive.

His existence, thanks to this generous flood of free external services, has begun. His account is opened by generous subscriptions, which he never deserved, for which he never even asked, but from which he alone will profit. He can frame neither his demands nor his desires, his needs have yet to be revealed to him. Years will pass before memory and reason will be in a position to propose to him some act of compensation. Nevertheless, from the first moment of his first day, when any notion of personal existence is completely alien to his tiny body, which resembles that of some small animal, he attracts and concentrates upon himself the effort of a whole group upon whom he depends as much as he depended upon his mother when he was imprisoned inside her womb.

The first characteristic, then, of his social activity is to comprise no degree of reciprocity whatsoever. It is an activity which proceeds from one point only and which operates only in one direction. As for the other point represented by the child: it is mute, *infans*, as lacking in freedom as in power; the group to which he belongs is totally innocent of any notion of equality: no pact is possible, nothing which remotely resembles a contract. Moral agreements require two participants. One-man contracts do not yet exist. No description could be too explicit, no admiration too great, for this spectacle of pure authority, this image of hierarchy so perfectly defined.

It is thus and in no other way that the very first stroke of the brush outlines the rudiments of human society.

The character of man's entry into the world is so clear, so unambiguous, that it leads us immediately and irresistibly to the very serious conclusion that there is nothing so misguided as the philosophy of the 'immortal principles'. This philosophy describes the beginnings of human society as the fruit of covenants between jolly full-fledged fellows, crammed with awareness, life and freedom, acting on the basis of some kind of egalitarian principle, almost equals if not actual equals, almost contractually abandoning this or that part of their 'rights' with the express object of guaranteeing the respect of others. These dreams crumble to dust beneath the facts. Their liberty is an illusion, their equality a sham. Life is simply not like that, it offers nothing remotely similar; its normal pattern is quite unlike what this philosophy would have it be and develops in a way which is entirely contrary. Life plays and will go on playing, acts and will act, decides and will decide, proceeds and will proceed, according to rules laid down by authority and inequality – in a manner diametrically opposed to the dreamy hypotheses of liberals and democrats.

Let us suppose it were otherwise, and that the egalitarian hypothesis had some slender basis of plausibility. Ridiculous though it may be, let us imagine infant man, one hour or one day old, being greeted, as doctrine would have him greeted, by a choir of his equals – that is to say a choir composed of other infants one hour or one day old. What could they do? What service would they perform for him? If we want this helpless pygmy to survive, it is imperative that he be surrounded by giants whose strength can be used on his behalf, without control by him, according to their wishes, according to their hearts, entirely arbitrarily, with the sole object of preserving him from extinction: total inequality, unqualified necessity, these are the two inexorable laws of guardianship to the genius of which, to the power of which, he must, for his salvation, submit.

It is only within the framework of this order (graded and stratified like all hierarchical orders) that the infant man can achieve the stature of the one ideal type of progress; by the growth of his body and of his spirit.

He will grow by virtue of these same necessary inequalities.

The way in which infant man arrives in the world, the people who await his arrival, the manner of his reception among them – all this dates the advent of social life at a point considerably in advance of any manifestation of the smallest act of the individual will. The roots of this phenomenon reach down to the deepest mysteries of the physical world.

Yet, and this second point is perhaps even more important than the first, this physical world, so elaborate and so structured a hierarchy, is in no sense savage or cruel. Quite the reverse! Kindly and gentle, charitable and generous, it affords no instance of any spirit of hostility between those it brings together: if there has never been the shadow of a peace treaty, it is because there was never a trace of war, of a struggle for life, between the new arrival and those who receive him. Mutual aid and sustenance for life – that is what nature offers the tiny naked guest, so hungry and so tearful, without even a farthing to pay for his hospitality. Nature's only concern is to help him. He is in tears; she fondles him, comforts him and tries to make him smile.

In a world where the doleful multitude cries out for its most basic needs – and needs that those who hear never fail to qualify as disastrous and excessive – in this world where all good is supposed to flow from the blind conflict of self-interest and from the indomitable pursuit of individual advantage – here is something quite different, something that we cannot call chance encounter or accident; here we see the unchanging eternal law of the first day: this shower of kindness upon the new-born child. In contempt of all notions of natural law, he is fed without having first done work. He is forced, yes forced, to accept without having first given! If mothers reply that one can hardly refuse to give sustenance to the child one has caused to be born, such a feeling is still not to be classed as one of the severe axioms of justice, it flows from the gentler command of grace. Or, if we must talk of justice, it is justice that is indistinguishable from love. And so it is! No human life conducts its most vital function without being clothed in the glorious moment of tenderness. Contrary to the 'plaintive song' of the romantic poet, the 'mark of human society', which appears on the 'naked shoulder', is not, as he would have it, 'the scar of the branding-iron'. We see only the traces left by milk and kissing: fate is unmasked, and we are compelled to recognize the face of kindly providence.

... But the infant man is growing now: he continues along the same majestic path of undue kindness – yes, undue in the literal sense of the word; he never ceases for a moment to receive. Leaving aside the fact that a language is instilled into him – sometimes a rich, wise language with its own gift of weighty spiritual heritage – a whole new harvest, whose seeds he never sowed, day by day he gathers in – education, initiation, apprenticeship.

The pure receptive state of the new-born child diminishes as the disproportion of strength between himself and his entourage grows less; effort, now possible, is asked of him; the words, more serious now, that are addressed to him are tinged sometimes with severity. To that early gentleness, which cradled him, succeeds now a love more masculine, which stimulates him to work, prescribes that work, rewards it. Constraint is sometimes applied, because the child man, more docile in one sense, is less so in another: he becomes aware of his capacity to defend himself, even to resist what is for his own good. He can harm, now, and he must learn that it does not pay. But his own contribution to all this is amply covered and compensated by the sum and value of new gains – whose approximate balance we can here only half assess.

We must leave to one side the most precious gift of all:

the moulding of heart and character. This vast and complex chapter has become infested by fools, knaves and charlatans who seek to preserve in its pages sufficient basis for the quibble which sustains the contemptible notion of the child-king or the child-god. The sublime originality of this prodigy, it appears, would be corrupted by parents, obstructed by teachers, impoverished or disfigured by education, when in fact we all know such training is not only necessary, but also teaches a limit to selfishness, softens the harshness and cruelty of an animal nature, restrains passion and frenzy, and so transforms the 'little savage' into that freshest, most amiable, most charming of all creatures: the well brought up and civilized boy or girl in their adolescent years. Truth can turn the tables upon the most twisted of sophisms. But because the task of our factual exposition here is to demonstrate rather than to describe, we shall have to neglect an important part in order to spare the tedium of a laborious debate. Let us limit ourselves to the incontrovertible, the irrefutable: in the domain of the human spirit the ample evidence of unilateral bounty bestowed by predecessor upon successor will suffice. Here, the child cannot be accused of being able to purchase or to recompense one iota of the immense inheritance built up by his ancestors, richer in centuries than he in years, to which he now has access. His friendly pasture, now a source of energy and wisdom, is infinitely enlarged, and still nothing appears within its confines which remotely resembles any notion of contractual equality. We can say that a change takes place. It is the change from ignorance to knowledge, from the inexperience of the senses, the clumsiness of the limbs, the physical underdevelopment of the body, to instruction in arts and skills: the gift, pure and true, offered to labourer's child and proprietor's child alike, to the needy as well as to the privileged; the poorest child receives his share. In a sense this share is infinite for it requires no subsequent recompense.

The infant man, thus nourished, endowed, enriched and adorned, is quite right to take note of his worth and, if he has 'got eyes in his head', to apply his careful judgment to the brilliant new ideas he sees around him in a world where he himself aspires to be the innovator when his day comes. But, until he has proved their worth, until he has begun his own work, he can scarcely do otherwise than to yield to the joyful abundance of the cornucopia presented to him. Since he had taken the trouble to be born, the very least he can do is to take the trouble to gather and to relish the golden fruit that an unknown god may strew before his feet.

Liberty plus Necessity

Now fully grown, he is reborn. From infant man springs the adult. Awareness, intelligence, the will, all appear, are exercised. He is in full possession of his powers. It is his turn to live, his persona now able to render to others all or part, or at least the greater or the less part, of what was once knocked down to him without a bid.

His personal endeavour is like that of his forefathers, it tends to the same ends of eternal melancholy, of universal discontent, which compel all men to try to change the face of the world, an effort ever accompanied by ecstasy and despair. The giddiness of youth is of little help in opening his eyes to the truth about his own life. Let us therefore begin by pretending to do as he does, and let us follow our young adult through the whirlwind of his activity by turns enravelled, disentangled and awakened by the promptings of desire and example.

The eternal workman, then, sets his hand to his task. He

does and undoes, tears out and replaces, destroys and rebuilds, unless he is that ignoble peddler and intermediary that merely traffics, buys and sells. He experiences all those vicissitudes of command and obedience which enable him to put himself to the test and sometimes lead to self-knowledge: true to himself or not, faithful to others or not, he cannot fail to measure himself against his fellows, superior or inferior, outstripping them or outstripped by them. Such as his work or his luck determine, but encountering very few equals although it will be customary, convenient and courteous for him to speak and act as though all were.

What he can recognize as true equality between himself and the men he meets will be more like something which is the *same* in all men. How can we describe this common identity?

It is a compound of knowledge and consciousness: something of the *same* in all men that makes them see, feel and retain in all objects that which is the *same*, invariable, unaltered and fixed; a faculty of spontaneous adherence to those universal axioms of numbers and shapes; the innate instinct to find refuge and repose in the perception and ageless accumulation of common sense and moral sense; the distinction of good and evil, the ability to choose the one or to refuse the other. In a word, that which, in all its differing forms and intensities, essentially constitutes the personal.

In order to clarify this idea somewhat, let us imagine the architect of the City of the Soul or his geometrician and surveyor busy with pen and pencil marking out the vast undefined spaces occupied and disputed by feelings, passions, images, memories, each a different element of the energy and courage natural to all men. The irregular curve with which he will delineate their different plots may form circles, ovals or any other shape, but will always be flexible, mobile, extensible, endowed as it is with the infinite and ceaselessly changing variety of life itself. Now let us see what makes this same practitioner use his compasses in the fixed position to draw a small circle with a hard and fast circumference: the circle will mark out the bastion where the treasure is stored and added to, the safe deposit for spiritual and moral values which reason and religion have agreed to make the attribute of humanity.

Each man, possessing that attribute, is, because of it, as good as every other man. That circle is the house of the impenetrable, the inviolable, the invariable, the un-coercible, the sacred. The nine-tenths of love which are physical find there their mysterious final tenth, half divine, the spark which renders it eternal or destroys it. It is the impregnable fortress of the highest point of our natures. And, as this circle is to be found in the geometry of every man of every different kind, we can say that it is their measure that we have at last discovered. How many times can this mental and moral measure be employed to assess the size and volume of the innumerable figures produced by human beings? The intensity of their passions! The vast extent of their needs! Their talents! Their strengths! Their vices! Those of their virtues that are of tangible or intangible origin! All that each person blends and combines of animal, vegetable and mineral within the living mould of his humanity!

From the vast map of the human universe emerges this one landmark. We must not suppose it to have been dis-covered by the moderns. Sophocles and Terence knew it well. Their audience was not ignorant of it. No abuses now perpetrated upon their texts can obscure the fact that the ancients never doubted that the personality was present in the slave no less than in his master. The little Platonist serving-boy carried within himself, like Socrates, all of geometry. This does not signify that he was the equal of Socrates, nor that he was considered, or is to be considered as such: which would be of as little value as asserting that we are all equal because we each possess a nose. It is enough that this general identity exists, that it serves and can serve as a basic unit of proportion: it submits the entire rational and moral activity of men to a single *set of laws*. If we approach by another route, we arrive at the same point. Whether personal action is dedicated to private life, or to social and political life, all that it *wills*, linked to the framework of rights and duties, falls within the criteria of the just and of the unjust, of good and evil.

Such is the little circle and its jurisdiction. It could never extend it to cover the whole living forest of unconscious and involuntary deeds which cover the vast teeming ill-defined area which surrounds it. The measure of moral laws will not suffice to police that immense expanse.

Here, first of all (and this, none disputes) we find the law of the body: wrap up warmly so as not to catch cold, lean on something firm so as not to fall down, eat so as not to perish. But there must exist other laws. A dowry of collective benefits has already been made available to the new-born human animal with his physical and moral development in view. If to grow and to mature frees him from his original ties, will he not find himself subjected to other conditions which will have their dimension of necessity as well? He is not destined for solitude which he would be unable to tolerate. The adult man, whatever restless torment sweeps him on, and often because of this restlessness, ceaselessly responds to his basic instinct: the impulse to seek out his fellow men and attach them to himself, or himself to them.

Now let us observe that, first of all, he makes no attempt

to propose or impose any conditions, any defined terms of agreement. His impulse will in time become *personal*: at the moment it is but *individual*.

His affinities are instinctive before becoming elective. They began by being fortuitous, even confused: often due to circumstance alone. The child plays a great deal and with many companions (usually the first that appear) before proceeding to the stage of expressing the charming 'Will you play with me?' that we hear in the public gardens of our cities. The habit of being together develops on its own; that *consuetudo* in which classical morality saw the character of amity. This is strengthened by the comradeships of adolescent years. Finally, as understanding of life grows, the reasons for behaving thus appear more sensible and good: '*From that time on everything occurs*', we may boldly assert, '*as though man had become fully aware of the prodigious advantages that his innate social function bestowed upon him and that he had decided to enrich them by imitating the work of nature, renewing it by his own art. Thus man, the creature of society, DEMANDS, in his turn, to invent and create association.*'

The reality is somewhat less clearly defined. An irrepressible wave of initial confidence makes him desire and solicit of his fellow man help and collaboration or the two together. But at this point, an instinct no less forceful generates the reverse movement, a wave of mistrust which impels him to desire and solicit guarantees and precautions to control the use of that help and collaboration. Either by some stroke of genius, or by more cautious steps, he seeks and finds how to eliminate from the association what he dreads most: the risk of variation, the danger of perversion. He seeks and finds how to associate security and durability. The binding force of contract will now be added to all the values of the association he first desired. Whether such a contract is sworn or not, by the spoken word or not, whether written on brick, stone, hide, bark or paper, it will be in terms of the mutual faith in one another of persons who at last decide to commit their free wills according to the light of the fully awakened, fully conscious spirit of each.

This first faith in the initial association should not surprise us; it springs from the sentiment of a common destiny of weakness and effort, of need and struggle, of defence and travail. 'Help me!' 'Give me a hand!' Nothing more natural in man than this: weak, he is always too alone; strong, he never feels adequately supported or served. Would he have sought out so avidly the collaboration of his fellow spirits, if they had not been different spirits, if all had been his equals, and if each had been as like him as one number is like another? What he wanted in others was what he could not quite find in himself. The inequality of work, the diversity of talents are the complementary elements which made possible and fruitful the exercise of functions day by day more rich, day by day more powerful. This stratification, born of the differences between people, is what fosters the success and progress of joint endeavour.

As for the mistrust between those who associate, it originates inevitably in the different forms of collaboration: in hiring and dismissal, in the timetable, in the seasons, in the interplay of favourable and unfavourable conditions; above all it originates in the products resulting from collective work; these are material objects which have to be shared out; they are therefore predestined to be the object of continuously disputed claims which every act of sharing engenders. Associates keep a watchful eye upon one another as naturally as they would upon a pickpocket or a pilferer.

If cooperation, then, is imposed by necessity, the risk of

antagonism will be ever present: the abundant production of the machine will make no difference. In conditions of universal affluence, there will still be the better and the less good; and these differences of quality will be valued, wanted, fought over. He to whose lot will fall the honour and the joy of satisfying basic needs will awaken new desires, numerous and keen, from which new disputes will spring. History teaches us that wars, civil or international, are by no means invariably the result of deprivation. Law suits too have other causes. Do not the richest people still squabble over what is superfluous to their needs? We try to prevent this universal evil by foreseeing it; we legislate, we bind ourselves to agreements. Contract in its turn produces problems: such is life and its never ending interplay of interests and passions. The seeds of war are eternal, like the need and will for peace.

To live we must associate. To live well we must contract. As if it arose from actual physical impulse, association is not unlike some pressing advice humbly advanced by our bodies which in common impoverishment form a united front. Contract, on the other hand, arises from the carefully weighed arguments of the mind whose aim is to confer the stability and identity of its own reasonable persona upon the changeable vagaries of that which is not itself. To illustrate the distinction, let us refer ourselves to the natural causes of the union of man and woman – as powerful, as profound, as moving as love itself – and compare them to the quite distinct reasons for the pact of marriage which gathers together these natural causes and refines them for the purpose of creating a union which will endure.

Bound and sealed by contract, association is justly regarded as the greatest miracle of that chemical synthesis of which human nature is capable. This miracle, undiscoverable at the outset of the social process, grows in the heart of the bloom this process puts forth, and is the fruit of it. Contractual association has been preceded, founded, and can therefore be sustained, by all that which has a share in 'the essential constituent elements of humanity': we must wish upon it that it rest with all its weight upon those pre-existing associations, half-natural, half-willed, that priceless legacy of the millennia of joyful history — home, city, province, guild, nation, religion.

In short, contract, the juridical instrument of social and political progress, transforms the personal initiatives of the man who would in his turn create new groupings, conforming to his own conceptions and needs, for the safeguarding of his own interests; in art, work, play, study, piety and charity. It is enough for us to think upon these groups and associations to feel to what extent person can multiply person, human transcend the human, promises and hopes rendering one another fruitful. An action which puts the edifices of nature to the service of the will of the human spirit confers upon its works the quality of superhuman authority.

Although the point has often been made, we must nevertheless not fall into the error of believing that premeditated association has made particular progress in our own time.

Its power has on the contrary decreased and the cause is not difficult to discover. This decline has its origin in the decadence of the person and of reason.

In the Middle Ages the contract of association embraced the entire edifice of life. The solemn oath sworn between man and man dictated the whole sequence of the innumerable bilateral services, the vast and profound efficacy of which made itself felt for centuries. Master statute of the will, contractual obligation was born beneath the plough, was upheld by the sword, and ruled the royal sceptre. But this noble concept of mutual obligation, sacred in law and given life by religion, was solidly anchored, one might even say grafted, upon the firm trunk of natural institutions: authority, hierarchy, property, community, personal ties to the soil, hereditary ties of blood. Instead of association and society being in opposition, they were combined. Without that the system would have withered fast, if it had ever emerged at all.

Since then, the constant attempt has been made to make man believe that he is a dependant or a beneficiary merely as a result of personal commitments: thus he can claim to decide everything by 'I want' or 'I do not want'. The impersonal creations of nature and of history are represented as considerably inferior to his own. The titles of correctness, usefulness and goodness are appropriated for what he himself has produced by the individual industry of his own brain, of the choice more or less personal of his own heart. However, was it he who, at birth, rescued himself from certain death? He was taken up and saved by the natural state of things which awaited his arrival. Was it he who invented the discipline of the sciences and crafts from which he so freely borrows? He received ready-made all these accumulated assets of the human race. If he does not complain of these assets, he thinks too little about them and distinguishes less and less clearly all that he must still receive of them, all that he must still draw from them.

Heredity and Will

For this lofty spring of superhuman energy is not dried up. Neither have we exhausted the possibilitiess of misfortune to which are exposed all men's lives from childhood through maturity to old age. As well as cold, hunger, deprivation and ignorance, other dangers come threatening a man and whether he will prevail or be overcome depends upon his courage, his intelligence and his skill. It depends upon the man himself. He can conduct himself according to the disorder of this and that organized principle which flatters his desires. Or he can grant serious attention to long-established customs and morals. There is a reason for the customary, and this reason is validated by experience.

Because the barbarian exists, ready for his chance to destroy societies and hold them to ransom – because these societies have within them the seeds of anarchy disposed to violence – because the compound of anarchy and the barbarian is perfect material for the task of bursting asunder all the contracts of social effort – because this two-edged sword is always suspended above us – our ancestors, citizens and soldiers, good citizens and good soldiers, closed ranks and took measures to preserve their peace, to protect their homes, and the outcome of all this is of some importance since, without it, we would not be where we are. Civil and military law is not born of the legislator's arbitrary will nor of the capricious will to dominate. Clear and tangible necessity dictated the construction of the pillars of order. It is not advisable to shake them on account of the disasters they hold in check. Other disasters would be spared us and great advantages obtained if only individual pride would less obstinately refuse to realize what are the normal conditions of human effort, the laws governing its successes, the order governing its progress, this whole code for good fortune rough-drafted, as it were, by nature in the half-light of the world's dawn but in which man can read clearly if he wants to. What has protected him, protects him now, and will protect him in the days to come. The mechanisms which guard him should be the object of his constant study: they would enable him to achieve by knowledge, and by knowledge of what he was achieving, what now he merely conceives of as pure routine. He could thus save himself the long and bitter process of learning by experience.

When we were young we were fascinated, I remember, by the poet-philosopher Maurice Maeterlinck's translation of Emerson's famous parable about the carpenter who made a point of never placing a plank above him that he wished to plane. He would place it at his feet so that his every effort might be multiplied by the weight of invisible worlds and the pull of a thousand galaxies. You can say that the carpenter was drunk, or mad; you can say that his idea of the force of gravity was false if it existed at all: but if he works overhead on something that could have been placed on the ground, exhaustion will overcome him before his work is done and he will have not only wasted time and immeasurable labour but also run a great risk of producing a shoddy result. That is what happens to the man who overlooks the friendly cooperation of the laws which could grant him economy of effort. He is RE-SOLVED to uproot everything of value. His closed mind and corrupt heart deny the truths that have been handed down in order to chase mere chimeras – and those not of his making.

However there is something else, something good and gentle that we have not named thus far: the family. Having opened the gates of life for a man, the family, wise council enriched by its concept of honour and its sense of dignity, directs his efforts towards the renewal of these bastions of providence on earth. Yet this is the very institution that many today are RESOLVED to challenge. The Russians, corrupted or perverted by German Jews, have recently reached the conclusion that they could do a great deal better than Mother Nature in the matter of children's birth and upbringing. Innovating spirits have always felt somewhat humiliated by the episode of their own birth. Liberal individualism and democratic collectivism have been no less shocked – and their attitude has the merit of logic – to see that the children of even the most independent-minded and emancipated workers are pitched into the world in this way without prior consultation nor being asked to vote on so important an operation! Though nothing could be done about that, the Russians have at least determined to make a vigorous effort to nationalize and centralize every home which until then, in Russia as elsewhere, formed little free republics, living by their own standards, following the laws of their ancestors modified more or less by the fantasies of their contemporaries. For this irrational system they have substituted administrations, services, ministries. Strong in the convictions of their 'pedologists' (inventors of a science superior to pedagogy, which, according to them was insufficiently Marxist and sometimes even anti-Marxist), they decreed that the children should be dragged from their parents as early as possible and handed over to kindergartens, play groups and public parks. Yesterday's last resort becomes today's new deal. The child is then invited to participate in his own development by electing his masters and monitors. Tremendous progress – leading straight to disaster. The little Russians grew all wrong. Their elders observed the emergence in footloose gangs of a weak, sick and criminal generation. They had to have many of them killed and to return to the old methods of upbringing, thus proving the validity of the old adage that cure costs more, and is less safe, than prevention. He who can make use of the waterfall, the tide and the wind has no need to search in the earth for artificial sources of energy. In politics, all the usable material is already to hand – and how powerful it is! From the moment that man sets himself to work *with* nature, the burden is lightened, the effort shared. The natural movement is resumed. The son finds it a simple matter to turn into a father; the infant into a nurse; the inheritor undertakes to preserve and increase his heritage so that he can pass it on when his time comes; the former student becomes the teacher, the former apprentice the master, the former initiate the initiator. All the care and duty from which one has benefited one directs towards new beneficiaries, guided by a blend of instinct and will in which we find such elements as habit, imitation, likes and dislikes, and, it must not be overlooked, gratification of self, for this latter is not necessarily in conflict with the social good ...

However, Mirabeau is the only revolutionary who ever understood any of that. Usually their dreams wander in the opposite directions: they are in a frenzy to rebuild the world poised upon the apex of a pyramid composed of selfless free wills. They are not prepared to accept the inconvenient evidence that things prefer to rest upon a wider and more natural base.

But what does nature have to say? In its ample wisdom, where all the resources of life meet and set to work, nothing takes precedence over the preservation and protection of the home for it is from thence, whether royal palace or log cabin, that all springs: work and art, nation and civilization. It has been insufficiently observed that in the Ten Commandments, the only time a reason is invoked in support is in the case of the fourth commandment [*sic*], 'Honour thy father and thy mother, that thy days may be long in the land that the Lord thy God giveth thee.' Is a particularly long life in fact accorded to those mortals who observe this commandment? We cannot tell, but this we do know – that long political life is granted to those nations which have conformed to it. No successful government has freed itself from it. We have seen all things but that. The history and geography of different peoples, in all that diversity, produce regimes whose outer form is equally diverse; but whether nominal power is exercised by one man or many, whether it is coopted, inherited, elected or chosen by lot, the only governments which last, which prosper, repose, in every case and everywhere, solidly and publicly upon the respect accorded to the institution of parenthood. For dynasties it goes without saying. But the great republics, too – all those which have conquered time – all were avowedly patriarchal: Rome, Venice, Carthage. Those republics that disavow these principles of nature, lose no time in disavowing themselves by the practice of unbridled nepotism – as is the case in our comrades' republic, which is first and foremost the daddy's boy republic, the son-in-law, nephew, brother-in-law and cousin's republic.

Since families are not equal in strength and property, a prejudiced man could accuse the dominion of the family of establishing unjust inequalities from the outset among the members of the same generation. Before we examine this complaint, let us look at the faces of those who make it. Either they are Jews, who for a century, have owed everything to the primacy of their race, or they are the instruments of the republican nobility. Their outrageous, if secret, oligarchism and the ignoble profits they have derived from it establish just what a tissue of lies enfolds their egalitarian maxims. But these same lies prove too that nature cannot be destroyed: nature gives birth to children of unequal blood, children strong and weak, handsome and ugly, weak and powerful, and she forbids the parents to wash their hands of their offspring to leave them alone to cast their dice upon the green table of competition or examination. Let the competition be controlled, let the examination be fair, let cheating and fraud be outlawed: so justice insists, and we must make it known that this can be depended upon. But it is by no means certain that justice insists upon competition in all things, nor that everything in life should be competitive. There is nothing to prove, either, that the weaknesses exposed on the race track do not find compensation elsewhere and that, in the final analysis, the champion's shield, the prize winner's diploma, the riband of the prime steer should be the only criteria upon which to classify humanity.

Jousting in the lists is a noble contest: but life includes others which are less sporting and from which all rules are absent. Personal merit, to which no dedication is too great, has a right to the highest honour for which no regard is too high; but precisely because of what it is, merit finds it easy and at heart not too unpleasant to equal and to surpass, in one field or another, the bearers of other, non-personal, assets. Personal merit will always have the last word. The man who has developed his own abilities acquires from them, together with a stable disposition and robust pride, his own personal blend of dignity. The man who knows what he owes to his forebears is animated by a rightful pride in their achievements. When these different powers unite in one person, he himself is infinitely enriched as is the community. When there is rivalry between them, that too can lead to excellence. But when they are locked in venomous hatred, let all beware. However, is hatred fatal?

Even the most moderate competition would be disastrous if the world had but one aim, if life offered desire and ambition but one objective and if, in particular, the first place in society or the state had automatically to be awarded to the winning winner, to the laureate of laureates, in a test to end all tests whose outcome publicly represented the supreme designation of the Best Man, who would thus be called upon to reign by virtue of his conquest of the Number One Position. But it is not like that. In the first place, healthy societies and well-constituted states do not put up their crowns for auction or contest; and, secondly, in the tremendous diversity of tasks and talents opportunities for conciliation, barter and compromise abound. It will be said that conflict abounds as well. But is it really supposed that some artificial means of selection for personal merit would be free of all painful friction? By leaving his empire 'to the worthiest man', Alexander merely consigned it to the battles of his lieutenants who tore it apart, naturally, in the name of the would-be dignity and superiority of each. Watchwords like 'to the worthiest man', when extended to cover the whole of civil life, merely spread strife and misery. In the end the whole population of competitors is infused with the spirit of a frantic emulation secreting bitter envy and jealousy. The health of the body politic is endangered, and the general standards of life and conduct begin gradually to disintegrate: even in the most gifted races democracy ends up as mediocracy.

Every tub-thumper insists upon the harmful effect of excessive inequality. Indeed, inequalities, if carried too far and perpetuated, tend to accumulate for some a great deal of surplus property rendering it useless and sterile. However, there is nothing so rare and so fraught with difficulty as the ability of great fortunes to endure and, when it does occur, often it is justified; in a country as active and highly-strung as ours, especially, such durability calls for exceptional qualities. Normally, vast fortunes are more easily made than preserved, more easily preserved than handed down. Great powers of dispossession and transfer seem to accompany the great estates which appear so stable. Idleness and dissipation are the daughters of excessive affluence. Poverty, on the other hand, contains a spur, energetic and healthy, which has only to prick a man for this affliction rapidly to be done away with. Does this natural swing of the pendulum, this compensatory movement, have as its final objective the establishment of some wiser equilibrium? Its effect for moderation and forbearance cannot be doubted. Whatever way the wheel of fortune may turn, the point is that it turns: envy and jealousy are not perpetually dazzled by the same objects.

The error is to talk of *justice*, which is the virtue or the discipline men impose upon their wills, when we refer to these dispositions which are superior (or inferior) to all arrangements resulting from man's will. In Marseilles they sing a song in which a docker complains that he was fathered by 'neither merchant nor lord'. Whom does he accuse? To whom can he protest? God is too high, nature indifferent.

The same fellow would be quite right to complain of not receiving what his labour entitled him to receive or of being the victim of some law which robs him of it or which prevents him from earning it. It is in this area that the lofty name of justice has a meaning.

The iniquities to be prosecuted, to be punished, to be suppressed are made by man's hand and it is upon them that are exercised the normal functions of a political state in a society which aims at justice. And although the state must, certainly, observe the imperatives of justice in the exercise of all its functions, it is not because of justice, but by virtue of other obligations, that it must direct its efforts, to the limited extent of its powers, to the moderation and regulation of the interplay of the individual or collective forces which are entrusted to it.

However it can undertake the management of the public interest only in so far as it makes use, with lucidity and with zeal, of all the infinitely varied mechanisms of social life, as they exist, as they interact, as they serve. The state must resolutely refrain from any claim to attempt the impossible task of revising or changing them: 'social justice' is a bad pretext: it is merely the pet name for equality. The political state must avoid any attack upon the infrastructure of the social state which it cannot and will never penetrate but in its foolish attempts against it it may cause grave wounds to its citizens and to itself. The imaginary changes made, in the name of equality, against a wholly irresponsible nature of things have the consistent effect of removing from sight the real wrongs perpetrated by criminals responsible for their acts: thieves, swindlers and cheats — those who profit, that is to say, by every revolution. The speculators who cream off public savings never exercise their vile commerce with such tranquil impunity as when popular envy is artfully diverted against 'inherited wealth' or mobilized against 'the two hundred families'. It is then that guilty Finance is most adept at making Agriculture, Industry and Commerce, quite innocent of conditions that derive from their natural state, pay for the wrongs its own treachery has perpetrated.

As for the imaginary benefits equality is expected to bestow, they will cause suffering to everyone. Democracy, by promising them, succeeds only in depriving the community of the tangible benefits which would flow, I will not say from the *free play*, but from the *healthy interaction* of natural inequalities and which would result in the profit and progress of all.

He who, for the sake of equality, suppresses all concentration of wealth, suppresses it with those indispensable reserves that any exceptional enterprise must demand and set to work. It is useless to replace this private treasury by the resources of the state – the swift and certain decline of all states burdened with such a responsibility demonstrates the inadequacy of this alternative.

He who, for the sake of equality, suppresses the normal patterns of inheritance for the property that remains undevoured suppresses with it, in one generation, one of the principal sources of this beneficial concentration of wealth: furthermore he suppresses all that composes and safeguards the moral capital that is even more beneficial. Manners of upbringing disappear: the trappings of social custom, its elegance, its perfection, its refinement. It is a barbarous and unhappy system that reduces all to the dimensions of the life of one single man or woman! You dream of attacking unjust personal privilege only? You imagine you will dispossess only a single bloated class? You will impoverish the entire community. A happy pattern of layers of influence superimposed one upon another produced benefits in which even the most disinherited had a share, raised the general level of the country and established in it a high standard of culture and good manners: and you would drag all that down to a single crude and uncivilized plateau.

The foreigners that visited our land in the days when we still had a monarchy used to admire the delicacy, the purity, the refinement of the French language spoken by the simple Paris workmen. Their speech reflected, like a polished surface, the orderly and natural distinction inherent in solidly based societies: *dispares ordines sane proprios bene constituae civitatis*, in the apt phrase of Catholic wisdom.

No social good exists but that culled from the rich and inexhaustible fields of human difference. Standardize and the harvest withers away. Justice is dishonoured and its interests betrayed when its name is ascribed to the smoke from blackened ruins.

Does the hate and envy of greatness make men prefer these ruins? Let us at least be clear that they cannot be avoided. Mediocrity cannot endure because it cannot preserve, cannot renew, for it lacks generosity, dedication, warmth. The ever-present threat of international violence, the internal decay resulting from an over-indulgent attitude to ignoble blunders, strain the meagre resources of such a regime: they destroy it, or rather it destroys itself. The future of humanity requires for its defence a certain heroism, a certain chivalry, which cannot belong equally to all. Exceptional men are indispensable to mankind. If they are derided, they dwindle and disappear and carry with them all of life that matters. There must be strong lords for there to be prosperous merchants, prosperous merchants for there to be active trade and flourishing crafts. Powerful and generous rulers are more than the honour and ornament of the world, they are above all its energy and its salvation.

This truth must not go undefended. We must have the courage to speak it out as loudly as possible, not uselessly regarding our own actions but fixing our eyes upon it alone, upon its light, upon its beneficence. The poor man honours himself in admitting the justice of wealth, firstly for what it *is* and then for its *proper* usage. The man without ancestors does no more than his duty when he accords rightful praise to the heritage of the centuries, to the historical and moral service, represented by the principle of heredity. This will deprive him of none of his dignity or pride. Rather it will justify his contempt for the baying of dogs whose trade is to think like dogs: those polemicists of anarchy are expressing an idea worthy of themselves when they claim that human relationships are bound to be strained and embittered by the experience of inequality; they are the more so by the proclamation of non-existent equalities. There are many children who do not suffer from their inability to equal their parents in stature. There are servants and masters whose clearly distinguished functions permit the establishment between them of the simplest of familiarities, of a kind of kinship. If the desirable objective of fraternity between men required that they should all be equal, so virtuous a goal could never achieve unity between actual brothers of flesh and blood because there would still be elder brothers and younger brothers. But from superior to inferior, as from inferior to superior, deference, respect, interest, affection, gratitude are all sentiments which climb and descend the rungs of the eternal ladder; nature interposes no substantial obstacle. On the contrary she encourages such movement by the diversity of the services that men feel impelled to offer, to seek and to render. Of such is the dialogue between the old and the young. Of such is the discourse of master and disciple. There is nothing warmer than the relationship between men and their leaders in a good army. Moreover, is the justifiable pride of some men, and the intolerable arrogance of some others, a reason to suffer or to cause to suffer? Error, passion and bitterness are in the final analysis less cruel than the permanent damage wrought by the insane myth of an impossible egalitarianism which would sharpen, intensify and perpetuate the chance conflicts that life by being alive, that the winds of destiny by blowing, would by the very nature of things soothe, dissipate, transform or melt away.

The evil in the world is as natural as the good, the natural evil is infinitely multiplied by the dream, the system, the artificial stimulants of democracy. Basically, however enviable the greatness of society may be, the

most burning feeling of all, for those who would understand the truths of the human heart, remains the feeling of
personal inferiority. Batté, 'the shame of the holy Mount
Parnassus', suffers incomparably more from being neither
Moréas nor Racine than the most fervent egalitarian does
from being born neither Rothschild nor Montmorency. It
is as hard for this imbecility to coexist with Mistral,
Barrès or Anatole France as it would be to live in suburban
modesty in the same district as the Duke of Villars.

Besides nothing obliges us to accept the smallest
injustice. There is no necessity to bend the knee before any
tyrant. The obsession with the possible *abuse* of power
blinds us to the fact that its overthrow is possible too.
Whatever powers there be, there are other powers close at
hand. But there is one supreme authority. The prime
function of this sovereign authority is to strike down the
powerful when they abuse their power.

Such a view will never be accepted, will in fact be
rejected *a priori*, by those who retain confidence in the
revolutionary commonplace that presupposes inalienable
hostility between governments and the governed. Nevertheless their interests coincide. And the strongest of all is
the interest in justice that the one 'dispenses' and the other
demands. Justice against the powerful is perhaps most
frequently and most easily realized when sovereignty,
properly constituted, is based neither upon election nor
upon money, but upon heredity. *Without* this disinterested
power, impunity and preponderance is assured to the
getter of ill-gotten gains, the possessors and inheritors of
the advantages of fortune. *With* hereditary power, social
abuses are judged and corrected by the rightful exercise of
the principle upon which they presume so excessively; the
punishment such abuse receives from hereditary power is
the most legitimate, the most sensitive, the most impartial,

the most effective: the way this principle was practised by the kings of France is the proof of its validity.

Authority in families, which is so little understood, is the most progressive of all forms of government. In the mid-nineteenth century, a French revolutionary, on a brief visit to London, was moved to indignation by the surprising spectacle, still notable a century later, in that so-called democracy of the institution of an extremely richly endowed hereditary peerage. A merchant of the City seeing his consternation replied: 'You would very possibly be correct, sir, for this or that individual member of the House of Lords, the Duke of such and such, for example, is well known for his narrowness of mind, Viscount so and so for his impenetrable ignorance, a third and a fourth for their drunkenness. All this represents a certain disadvantage to our community. But if the fifth or the tenth be a distinguished man, clearly worthy of his rank, the station to which birth has called him will enable him to repay us a hundredfold for all that the others could have cost us.'

There is nothing so practical and so true.

A community organized on these lines has the advantage, without revolution, in order not disorder, within the law and with no need of favours, of possessing a leadership assured of constant renewal and rejuvenation by brilliant successors, whose superior education has prepared them for great responsibilities they are ready to assume in the prime of manhood. Because he was the son of Philip, Alexander had conquered the world long before the demagogue Julius Caesar, despite his high patrician birth, had even thought of it in his republic. The social patterns of old France permitted the conquering genius of Rocroi[1] to manifest itself when he was only twenty years old. A

[1] The reference is to Condé's defeat of the Spaniards at Rocroi in 1643.

nation based on hereditary right is always rich in youthful leaders – and not merely once every half century as a result of ignoble adventures like our Panama scandal of 1892 or our Popular Front of 1936: these accidents apart, our democracy had well deserved its caption 'Rule by the Old'.

The benefits which flow from dynastic rule are not destined for a single party nor a single class. Clearly they are for the good of all – and in the interests of ordinary folk above all. Firstly, even if we suppose that 'elites' invariably place their own selfish interests first, the transitory 'interest for life' kind of elite has much longer teeth than the hereditary kind. A pack of sharks and vulgarians, it lacks, as Renan observed, the habit of those privileges and pleasures to which the 'man of quality' has become indifferent. This avid and excessive self-indulgence of unprincipled upstarts had the effect of reducing by the same measure the meagre share available to the common people. Further, democratic maladministration, with its defective organization and its low-grade managers, inevitably brings about the recurrence, at ever briefer intervals, of disasters which fall with the greatest severity upon the heads of those least able to withstand them. The French have been invaded six times since the dawn of this fine new democracy which represents so many houses destroyed, so many machines and household goods rifled, so many wives carried off, so many daughters raped.

The more violent the crisis of revolution or war, the more the 'little man' suffers while the wealthy man gets by. If the nation's humblest class have one overriding interest, it is the maintenance of peace and order, the time-honoured handing down of its meagre possessions. In so far as their modest proportions makes it possible, this class feels a special need not to be empty-handed at that solemn crucial moment of resource-straining expense – the arrival of the new-born child.

Here we see the virtuous and radiant splendours of inheritance – even in the humblest home. He who would diminish the value of this first offering around the cradle affronts the nature of society. He who would guard it and add to its treasure seals the bond between human and the superhuman. We sadly shake our heads over depopulation or the declining birthrate. But have we thought enough about the importance of these little bundles of private capital, decentralized unlike the state, grouped, so to speak, around the cradle? Every new life depends upon it.

'So you talk of capital, of the infant man's inheritance at the cradle. Do you mean for every child?'

'Of course.'

'In every cradle?'

'Every one! … On condition that you do not come running to me with set-square and ruler panting, "Equal shares for all."'

'Why not?'

'Have you forgotten already? Equality would bring down the whole edifice in ruins and there would be nothing left for anyone.'

THE FUTURE OF FRENCH NATIONALISM

'Nothing is done today, all
will be done tomorrow.'

All that remains for the thinking Frenchman to do is to see
that his will and not that of another be done: not the will of
the oligarchy, not the will of the foreigner.

There remains, that is to say, the imperative of rugged
effort in the field of real and practical action, the effort
that has tried to hold our country together, to preserve its
heritage, to save it from itself, to resolve its crises along the
way; this loyal effort is too old and proud a servant of
France to interrupt or slow down the work it has begun.
Those whose age has brought them near to death know
that this work depends on friends who are worthy of our
trust, because, for more than forty years, their slogan, and
ours, has been: 'Use every means, even legal.' Having
worked 'for 1950', they will work for the year 2000, for
they have never lost sight of their vision: 'For France to
have long life, long live the king!'

We could not have sustained our hope if our sense of
national pride had not been steadfastly in the forefront of
our minds. On that score, my mind is easy.

There is much talk of giving up in whole or in part our
national sovereignty. Mere words. Let us leave them to the
professors of law. These gentlemen have made their
quibbles so well respected, *intus et in cute*, these last years
that we can count on them to find something new to add
to all the most glorious dung-heaps of the intelligence. The
treasures of reality and fact are stronger than they. What

they consider to be outdated and ready to be thrown overboard has only to suffer the tiniest scratch, the shadow of a threat, and you will see the outraged reaction that will follow! Proof that there is nothing in the world today to equal the sense of national pride. Those who would like to give up a portion of it, will bring no benefit to the cosmopolis they dream of: with our heritage they will merely fatten other already overblown nationalities. The oustanding facts of our time are national facts: the astonishing persistence of England in the English soul during the years 1940 to 1945, the pan-Slav or rather pan-Russian evolution of the Soviets, the resistance that Russia encounters in the nations she thought to annex under the dual inspiration of race and creed, the awakening of the mighty conscience of America, the rebirth of German Nazism, all these are cases of acute nationalism. Not all are creditable. We would be mad to imitate or wish for them all. We would be even more insane not to take note of this evidence of a world-wide trend. In France, patriotism saw all this in many different colours after the victory of Foch: such enmity, such disgrace! Great parties characterized by their 'appeal to the masses' were sick or tired of the French language and had no time for anything but Marxist gibberish. The Germans had only to set up camp in France for all their offers to rebuild Europe to be rejected and Frenchmen, whether bourgeois, peasants, workers or noblemen, with very few exceptions saw only the hated 'Boche': in a twinkling the national spirit was re-established. The country had to stomach the humiliation of many an expedient hypocrisy. The universal use of this noble disguise is one more proof of its value and glaring necessity: we shall see.

The nationalism of my friends and myself bears witness to a passion and a doctrine. A holy passion, a doctrine motivated by ever increasing human needs. The majority of our fellow citizens see in this a virtue whose promptings are sometimes painful but always honourable. But, certain other Frenchmen, especially those in the legal world, to be found in all parties, find themselves, and will go on finding themselves, driven back upon nationalism as upon some necessary compromise. The more their divisions based on vested interest multiply and widen, the more they need an occasion to sound the note of the supreme duty, invoking the only means they have of prolonging their own power. These means are called France.

How can they escape it, divided as they are by everything else? Upon what argument, what honest common denominator can they reason together but that? There is no longer any yardstick common to both bourgeois economics and working-class economics. Working class and bourgeois are names of sects. The name of the country is France, so it is to that name that reference must be made. What is to the advantage of the country? If the criteria of the country first is accepted which presupposes the renunciation to a certain extent of partisan errors, it is found to contain the essence of our philosophy which consists of presenting, approaching and resolving all current political problems from the point of view of the national interest: we must select and reject what that openly acknowledged arbiter would select and reject.

Of course this imperative is strictly limited. The struggling parties will always do their utmost to grab as much as they decently can. But their alliances crumble if they cannot pretend at least to act in the name of motives which dare to go further than their own vested interests. Will they refuse to make this gesture? A refusal could sound the alarm for the body and the spirit of the real nation to arise, and even the electoral situation itself could be endangered. If, on the other hand, these specialists in disunity pretend to believe in the unifying power of the nationalist consensus, all onlookers of good will and reasonable intelligence will be satisfied.

So gently, violently, slowly or hastily the carnivorous parties, all equally ruinous, will either perish from their own excessive appetites or, as parties, will have to give way to some extent to the imperative of nationalism – or at the very least to a recognition of its existence. Practice will strengthen it. Exercise may not create new limbs but it loosens up and fortifies the ones already there. The various party doctrines will gradually be stripped down to their basic elements of empty promises and threats upon which their failures will inflict ever-increasing ridicule. Their faith will soon be no more than a memory without the redeeming virtue of relevance, the physical trace of which has long since been lost and men will jeer more and more contemptuously at these quaint relics, these false principles which sought the allegiance of empire and nation and who now pronounce their own obsequies.

Then a task of real significance can be restarted: the realization of the nation's great hope of setting aside a class and merging its parties.

French nationalism as a movement will not satisfy its aspirations without the return of the king. While we wait for this day to come, the dominance of the parties will have slackened, and, because of abuses perpetrated by them, mortality will once again belong to the French people, and French instincts and interests will have been restored to their former state.

We must not throw up our hands in horror at this word 'interest'. However uncouth it may sound, it has the merit of being appropriate. This word is full of the strength to preserve us from a grave error which could ruin everything.

If, instead of placating opposing factions and bringing them together on the basis of common interest, we are shamefaced and hesitant, if we try to find nobler criteria in the sphere of moral and sacred principles appropriate to the realms of morality and religion, this is what will happen: since, in social and political life, the genuine antagonisms of the modern conscience are deep and numerous, since the false dogma of individualism on the essentials of family, marriage and association is in direct contradiction with the rich customs and traditions of prosperous peoples which are also those that conform to the moral teachings of Catholicism, it will be particularly difficult if not impossible to achieve unity or even union in the sphere of moral principles. If we were to undertake such a venture, we would merely encounter the same contradiction in terms which we have so often experienced in the past.

These conflicting principles can submit to compromise but cannot produce one or create one, nor transform their divided and divisive natures into principles of compromise or agreement.

The bases for conciliation are few in number. I know only one.

When, in an argument over divorce or the family or association, you have exhausted all the fundamental pros and cons, drawn from reason and morality, without having achieved a shred of agreement, there is left to you only one neutral avenue to explore – that of examining the value of divorce or marriage or whatever from the point of view of the practical public interest. I do not assert that this examination is an easy one to make, or that it is clear or that it leaves no room for doubt. It can contribute some elements of light and harmony. But if, when you reach this point, you slander the notion of the public interest, if you disavow, humiliate, reject this vulgar compromise of the public good, you lose the precious and positive element of union which could result from it, and, having deprived yourself of this benefit, you find yourself once again in the presence of all the bitterness which will stem from the return to those violent disputes that should have been allayed by the common interest in social harmony.

It is all very well to accuse national and civic interest of artfully tending to eliminate what is called, not without a certain hypocrisy, the spiritual: it is simply not true. The truth is quite different. We have named and honoured as the highest inspiration of our guardian laws and ideas all the different forms of the spiritual, especially the Catholic. We have opened the gates of the city to them. We have begged them to enter it, purify it, pacify it, exalt it and bless it. By asking of each its prayers, by honouring and acknowledging their benefits, we have thereby given thanks for all the blessings of social and international emulation that these spirits could by their acts encourage. If, in addition, we have not asked them to give us the harmony we desire, it is because they do not possess it, being opposed to one another: the spiritual, unless it be reduced to a mere form of words, is an element of controversy. The God of Robespierre and Rousseau is not the God of Clotilde and of St Remy. The social and moral principles of Rome are not those of London or Moscow. To aspire to their fusion, by covering up what contradictions they contain, is to begin by mutilating them and to end by suppressing them all. From the moment unity of conscience disappears, as it has done in France, the only way left of respecting the spiritual is to welcome every worthy manifestation of it, under its proper names, in its purest and most divergent form, without altering the meaning of words, without using words to improvise empty agreement. The spiritual that was neither Catholic, Protestant nor Jewish would have neither vigour nor virtue. It must be one or the other, if the fruitfulness of the fruitful and the good deeds of the good are to be safeguarded; of such is the grandeur of humanity and of the superhuman. There exists a natural religion and a natural morality. This is a fact. But it is also a fact that their cardinal principles, as defined by Catholicism, are not acknowledged by other faiths. Nothing I can do will alter this. I cannot make Reformation morality reject individualism or the Calvinists accept the correct notion of religious worship. We can refuse to see reality, but reality, in the social order, confronts us nevertheless with clearly differentiated choices which we cannot avoid.

We can hope for all things from the abundance, the variety, the contrast of the moral ideas presented to us, except the creation of their opposite — uniformity. Therefore it will be impossible for anyone, be he Catholic, Jew, Huguenot or Freemason, to impose his own individual concepts as standard for the whole community. His concepts apply to him, whereas the standard must be the same for all. And so the members of the community will be obliged to find something else to serve as a common standard, something which applies equally to all and is capable of creating unity between them all. What can they find? We still see only one answer: that imperative whose commands, needs and simple conventions oblige them to share one common lot.

In other words, we must once again break off the discussion of the true and the beautiful to turn our attention to the humble and positive good. Good will not be an absolute, but the good of the French people at that level of politics where we find what Plato called the royal art, where we find set aside all schools of thought, all

Churches, all sects, where divorce, for example, would be considered no longer in relationship to this or that right or obligation, to this or that divine authorization or prohibition, but solely in terms of the common interest of the family and the good of the city. So much the better for those, such as the Catholics, who are already in agreement with this concept of the public good. They will do well not to speak disdainfully of it. For in the final analysis we do not present for thought and action too unworthy or inferior an object. Let us remember that peace is a noble state: the social well-being of a nation, the material and moral interest each citizen has in its preservation, these are things which lift man up and sustain him in the highest spheres of his finest and proudest actions. St Augustine's 'tranquillity of order' is a majestic aim. He who pursues and contemplates it will never wander from the ascending path of positive human progress. To leave the plane of ethics is not to disregard it provided one follows the true path of politics. No young conscript to the patriotic virtues is diminished by drawing his inspiration from 'the eternal France'; no veteran of the law, in a kingdom that even in the sixth century the Pope had placed above all other kingdoms, can be attacked for asserting that 'the King of France never dies'. All this is a part of our heritage which we find in its rightful place as the supreme inspiration of our human nature.

The generation of the young may possibly feel these lofty sentiments to be somewhat remote. That is because this generation has seen so many shifts and somersaults. They have some difficulty in distinguishing what is firm and immutable: they have never been shown it thanks to an apparently never-ending cycle of instability and ruin. This cycle must not be regarded as more fundamental than it really is. It is an accident which stems almost entirely from the classical debilitating effect of a cancer which has been well-known since men first reasoned about the state of society, since the golden days of Athens and then from age to age for more than two thousand years, ever since the Visigoth kingdoms of Spain were handed over to the Saracens, or the Italian republics to their convulsions, all by the common effect of anarchy. The experience of Poland gave us bitter proof of this truth only shortly before our own cruel ordeal began, and our last one hundred and fifty years are an instructive lesson in themselves.

The cancer is a serious one but it can be cured – and quickly. We will find it much easier to tackle if we take care not to embellish it with names other than its own. If we say 'the prevailing idea' instead of 'the revolutionary idea', we are saying nothing for we are defining nothing. If we say 'demagogy' instead of 'democracy', our shaft is misaimed. What we risk regarding as abuse or excess, is, in fact, fundamental and inherent. That is why I have devoted so much attention to exactness of terminology. Only a sane policy framed in clear and precise language can emerge unscathed from the Tower of Babel. That is how I emerged unscathed. That is how France will do likewise, and how French nationalism will by force of circumstance be reaffirmed. Nothing is finished; if nothing lasts for ever, nothing is lost for ever.

Above and beyond hope there exists a certain faith and trust which, though unrelated to religious faith, are not unlike it at the humble level of our earthbound certainties. I will never cease to repeat that Frenchmen have two natural obligations: one is to count upon the patriotism of their country, the other is to have faith in its genius; they will be redeemed by both for the second is ever more profoundly imbued with the first. It will be infinitely more difficult to destroy these two great French qualities than for them to endure and reawaken. Such qualities would find their own extinction a more arduous task than the most dogged effort to survive or the most painful pangs of rebirth.

Clairvaux, 1950

PAUL CLAUDEL
(1868–1955)

Claudel's ode, 'Words to the Marshal', shows how wary one must be of calling his kind of right-wing Catholic nationalism fascist. A declared anti-antisemite and opponent of Hitler, Claudel supported and welcomed Pétain in 1940 with one ode and de Gaulle in 1944 with another.

The motives for its composition remain problematic. Claudel had been a Third Republic diplomat, and Martin du Gard said he wrote the ode in order to get Pétain's old job as ambassador at Madrid. Yet, while the charge of opportunism against Claudel cannot lightly be dismissed, too much of the ode is familiar and rings true for it to be only an opportunist piece. The attack on the Third Republic (the hovel where France lived for seventy years), on politics and politicians (the madmen), the first salute to Pétain as the end of political corruption and the final exhortation to survival mirrors Vichy too faithfully for it to have been written tongue in cheek.

The translation is by the editor.

WORDS TO THE MARSHAL

Marshal, this poem is about someone coming back to life.
It is no small thing, coming back from the dead! In the
Bible the prophet lay all his length seven times on the
reluctant corpse, mouth to mouth.

Suddenly, his eyes have opened, he sees, and even before he
has begun to breathe we realize that he can hear.

To give life to someone who was dead at a single stroke,
you have to be the son of God!

But how beautiful it already is, how beautiful! that great
sigh and that vision which gradually comes to recognize
the light!

Marshal, here is that France in your arms, who has only
you and who is coming slowly back to life, slowly and with
a low voice.

She has not the right to speak out yet, except to make you
understand that she is weary.

That immense body, so heavy on him who is its only
support, which bears down with all its weight – all the
France of today and tomorrow, that same France of days
gone by!

The France of yesterday too, bleeding and ashamed, which
all the same cries that she has done her best!

'It is true that I was humiliated!' she says. 'It is true that I
was defeated!'

In place of my shining head there is only mud and gore.
Gone the sword in my hand; gone the shield hanging from
my neck.

I was left lying by the wayside, and the most cowardly
were allowed to insult me,

But all the same I still have my body which is pure and my soul which is without dishonour!

And no doubt I lived in that hovel for seventy years as in a fantastic dream,

But all the same I had to mother them a little, so that I could have their love as children!

Not a single one stopped loving me when I was dying, And not a single one failed to choose me again for the first place in his heart when I was reeling from the right.

Not one who failed to repeat, in a low voice, weeping, the oath which he had already sworn!

Dearer to him on the day of humiliation than I was on the day of victory! – I whose face could no longer be seen in the darkness of the hour.

My mother! but, in spite of everything, how good it is to be able to embrace her at the end!

You were no longer recognizable in the rags those madmen had wrapped you in!

But at this moment you are no longer false to the womb where Joan of Arc was conceived!

Let me cover your naked limbs with my devotion.

We are alone now, and it is good! and no one can see us.

No one can take from us the secret I share with you, my mother!

Marshal, remember, and it did not happen very long ago, The crowds on all the roads, like a stream become a torrent,

Women and children and men, like a herd of panic-stricken cattle,

And the howl of despair which met our decimated troops!

France! the whole of Europe, their defences breached, flowed into you, daughter of God!

And who wanted any other shelter than your roof which had already caught fire!

'You asked me for bread', said France, 'and I gave you my flesh.

You asked me for shelter, and I opened everything to you!
Let everyone come, now that my frontiers are broken down! come right to the depths of my gaping heart!
If what I may call my own is small, my heart is great.
Come and cling to me, come, numberless and trembling flock,
And share with me the most sacred bread, soaked with tears and blood!'

Marshal, the dead have a duty and that is to return to the living.
Certainly we will all come back to life on the day of the Last Judgment.
But it is now, even today, that we are needed, that there is something to be done!
France, listen to him who, ripe in years, bends down to you and speaks to you as a father.
Daughter of St Louis, listen to him! and tell him if you have now had enough of politics.
Listen to that voice of reason which comes to you, which explains and counsels,
That counsel like balm and that truth like gold!
A single blast on the trumpet does not bring the dead back to life!
It is present exigency and the poignant awareness of a duty to be done.
It is not because we are beautiful that we must live, but because we are indispensable!
Do you understand how remiss of you it is to be dead when you are needed?
Lift up your eyes and see something great and tricoloured in the heavens!

Something in the heavens for ever, which cannot but prevail.
Something which is, of itself, stronger than the darkness—the dawn!

December 1940

SELECTED BIBLIOGRAPHY

GENERAL

Incomparably the best book in English on modern French politics is Dennis Brogan's *Development of Modern France* (London, 1940). For Vichy, Robert Aron, *The Vichy Regime, 1940–44*, presents a balanced picture of an episode which still arouses partisan passions. For a view of Vichy as the revenge of the anti-Dreyfusards, see W. Herzog, *From Dreyfus to Pétain* (New York, 1947).

THE DREYFUS AFFAIR

The standard work in English is Guy Chapman, *The Dreyfus Case* (London, 1955). There are works without number in French on the affair. There is an excellent pamphlet on the affair in the Problems of European Civilization series, edited by Leslie Defler, which is probably the easiest access to the complex, politically directed historiography: *The Dreyfus Affair, Tragedy of Errors?* (Boston, 1963).

ACTION FRANÇAISE

Eugen Weber, *Action Française* (Stanford, 1962).

INDIVIDUAL AUTHORS

For de Maistre, Jack Lively's *The Works of Joseph de Maistre* (London, 1965), which has an extremely good introduction. There is no adequate book in English on Taine, though valuable remarks are to be found in P. Geyl, *Encounters in History* (London, 1963), and E. Wilson, *To the Finland Station* (London, 1963). For Sorel, E. Shils's edition of the *Reflections on Violence* (New York, 1961) contains an adequate introduction. Close students of Sorel should consult I. L. Horowitz, *Radicalism and the Revolt Against Reason* (London, 1961), which is excellent, though brief, on the relationship between Sorel and Nietzsche. Michael Curtis's *Three Against the Third Republic: Sorel, Barrès and Maurras* (Princeton, 1959) is rich and perceptive, though it goes only to 1914.

INDEX

70 71 72 73 10 9 8 7 6 5 4 3 2 1